uide to

g
and
ion

om Physical,
ullying

Cynthia Lowen

**ALPHA**

A member of Penguin Group (USA) Inc.

**ALPHABOOKS**

Published by Penguin Group (USA) Inc.

PenguinGroup (USA) Inc., 375 Hudson Street, New York, New York 10014, USA • Penguin Group (Canada), 90 Eglinton Avenue East, Suite 700, Toronto, Ontario M4P 2Y3, Canada (a division of Pearson Penguin Canada Inc.) • Penguin Books Ltd., 80 Strand, London WC2R 0RL, England • Penguin Ireland, 25 St. Stephen's Green, Dublin 2, Ireland (a division of Penguin Books Ltd.) • Penguin Group (Australia), 250 Camberwell Road, Camberwell, Victoria 3124, Australia (a division of Pearson Australia Group Pty. Ltd.) • Penguin Books India Pvt. Ltd., 11 Community Centre, Panchsheel Park, New Delhi—110 017, India • Penguin Group (NZ), 67 Apollo Drive, Rosedale, North Shore, Auckland 1311, New Zealand (a division of Pearson New Zealand Ltd.) • Penguin Books (South Africa) (Pty.) Ltd., 24 Sturdee Avenue, Rosebank, Johannesburg 2196, South Africa • Penguin Books Ltd., Registered Offices: 80 Strand, London WC2R 0RL, England

**Copyright © 2012 by Cindy Miller and Cynthia Lowen**

International Standard Book Number: 978-1-61564-206-9
Library of Congress Catalog Card Number: 2012933503

14   13   12      8   7   6   5   4   3   2   1

Interpretation of the printing code: The rightmost number of the first series of numbers is the year of the book's printing; the rightmost number of the second series of numbers is the number of the book's printing. For example, a printing code of 12-1 shows that the first printing occurred in 2012.

*Printed in the United States of America*

**Note:** This publication contains the opinions and ideas of its authors. It is intended to provide helpful and informative material on the subject matter covered. It is sold with the understanding that the authors and publisher are not engaged in rendering professional services in the book. If the reader requires personal assistance or advice, a competent professional should be consulted.

The authors and publisher specifically disclaim any responsibility for any liability, loss, or risk, personal or otherwise, which is incurred as a consequence, directly or indirectly, of the use and application of any of the contents of this book.

Most Alpha books are available at special quantity discounts for bulk purchases for sales promotions, premiums, fund-raising, or educational use. Special books, or book excerpts, can also be created to fit specific needs. For details, write: Special Markets, Alpha Books, 375 Hudson Street, New York, NY 10014.

**Publisher:** *Mike Sanders*
**Executive Managing Editor:** *Billy Fields*
**Executive Acquisitions Editor:** *Lori Cates Hand*
**Development Editor:** *Jennifer Moore*
**Senior Production Editor:** *Janette Lynn*
**Copy Editor:** *Amy Borelli/Lisanne V. Jensen*

**Cover Designer:** *Rebecca Batchelor*
**Book Designers:** *Rebecca Batchelor, William Thomas*
**Indexer:** *Angie Bess Martin*
**Layout:** *Ayanna Lacey*
**Proofreader:** *John Etchison*

# Dedication

*We dedicate this book to the courageous children, adolescents, and families everywhere whose lives have been interrupted by senseless and undeserved acts of cruelty, abuse, and violence. At long last, their voices are being heard. May they continue to grow louder as they lead us out of ignorance to join the movement to stop bullying and start respecting and taking good care of each other—a movement whose time is long overdue.*

# Contents

## Appendixes

# Foreword

"No problem can be solved from the same consciousness that created it."
These are the words of perhaps the greatest problem-solver of all time,
Albert Einstein. Einstein put his consciousness toward unraveling the laws
of our physical universe; the same can be said of our society's shifting attitudes, understanding, and response to bullying.

Until recently, bullying was considered to be an integral part of growing up.
At one time or another, most of us feared or felt resigned to being targeted
by a bully, and the bullies themselves acted with impunity, with little fear of
consequence. Bullies were taken for granted; they seemed inevitable; and it
was hard to imagine a world without them.

Today, we recognize the painful and damaging impact bullying has on our
children, our families, and our society. Bullying is corrosive and damaging and cannot be tolerated. Kids who bully or who are targeted are at risk
for depression, anxiety, substance abuse, low academic achievement, and
a host of other problems that, if left unaddressed, can follow our kids into
adulthood. As a society, we have seen far too many tragedies as a result
of bullying at school, online, and through text messages, social networks,
video games, and other places in our communities where kids should feel
safe. Bullying creates a chain of violent behavior that must be addressed
from a systemic point of view.

Responding to the challenges of our time calls for new and creative ways
of observing, planning, and collaborating to create healthy social and
emotional behavior. We must be able to envision a different kind of society where bullying behaviors are not accepted, where it is the norm to
intervene and stand up to bullying rather than to stand by, and to create
environments in our schools and communities where bullying simply cannot take root.

Combining the unique perspectives of co-author Cynthia Lowen, producer
and writer of the groundbreaking film *Bully*, and Cindy Miller, school
social worker and psychotherapist, *The Essential Guide to Bullying: Prevention and Intervention* offers parents, educators, therapists, and anyone who
cares about today's youth numerous prevention, identification, and intervention strategies. This book is a comprehensive guide that offers readers

an understanding of kids who are targeted, kids who engage in bullying behaviors, and the bystanders who often feel caught in the middle. This book also examines the reasons why bullying happens, how it has changed over the years, and the short- and long-term effects of being a bully, target, or bystander. While bullying may not be a new problem, we are beginning to view positive steps that we can take toward prevention, identification, and intervention.

The information contained in this book is an opportunity for readers to shift their own consciousness about bullying and profoundly change the lives of our children.

**Phylicia Rashād**
Award-winning actress and singer; mother

# Introduction

According to the U.S. Department of Education, 13 million American kids are bullied every year. This startling statistic represents a third of school-age youth, stretching across every community and state in our nation. Bullying transcends geographic, ethnic, faith, socio-economic, and gender lines and is an issue we're all touched by, whether we're kids, parents, educators, physicians, community leaders, advocates, or anyone who cares about school and community climate.

While the scope of this issue has been well publicized in the media, especially the numerous bullying-related suicides in recent years, we're just beginning to address how to implement comprehensive, long-term changes. Preventing bullying means taking a hard look at our attitudes and actions—online and offline—and working to transform behaviors and feelings that are often deeply entrenched.

To see long-lasting and community-wide change, bullying needs to be understood and addressed at home, online, at school, in our workplaces, and on the streets of our towns. Kids, parents, school staff, administrators, and community leaders all need tools to effectively address bullying and help each other tackle an issue that historically has been accepted as an intrinsic part of our human nature and society—or just "kids being kids."

We wrote this book with the conviction that our schools and communities *can* be transformed into places where all kids feel safe and supported; where teachers, principals, bus drivers, recess monitors, lunch aides, and all school staff have the tools to recognize, prevent, and intervene in bullying situations; where parents know how to foster kindness and empathy in their children; and where young people are empowered to stand up for those who are targeted, get help, and perhaps even save a life.

We hope you find this book a useful and engaging tool in exploring bullying prevention in your own home, school, and community.

## How to Use This Book

This book is divided into four parts to make it easy for everyone who cares about kids—from parents to educators, counselors, and community leaders—to learn to recognize, prevent, and intervene in bullying behaviors and institute long-term change in attitudes toward this insidious and destructive set of behaviors.

**Part 1, Twenty-First-Century Bullying,** begins with a look at today's bullying continuum, from the mild to the most severe forms of bullying behaviors. We explore some of the signs and symptoms that a child may exhibit, such as acting aggressively or being targeted by others, and take a look at the fluid nature of the bullying triangle.

**Part 2, Prevention,** examines ways that everyone who cares about kids can reduce the likelihood of their being targeted by or acting aggressively toward their peers. We share current trends in education, such as the implementation of social-emotional learning and character education as well as multiple strategies that everyone can use to foster a positive home and school climate.

**Part 3, Intervention,** covers everything from legislation designed to protect kids to how parents can get help from their child's school and talk to their kids about bullying. We talk about ways to help the targets of bullies, transform bystanders into "upstanders," and help bullies and aggressive kids make positive changes.

**Part 4, Moving Beyond the Triangle,** examines what parents, kids, teachers, counselors, and specialists have to say about bullying and explores situations where more help is needed. We also consider an entire-community approach to prevention and take a look at how grass-roots campaigns, celebrities, and everyday people are coming together to create a cultural shift moving toward a world without bullying.

## Essential Extras

As you read this book, you'll notice a number of sidebars that provide you with interesting, insightful, and helpful information.

Here we define terms that you may not be familiar with.

These sidebars present tips, facts, and thought-provoking ideas for parents to consider.

Look to these sidebars for warnings and precautions about a range of topics.

We provide ideas and strategies to bust through bullying behaviors in these sidebars.

You'll also see a name-changing sidebar that presents anecdotes, interesting facts, case histories, or other extended background information you should know.

## Acknowledgments

To Phylicia Rashād, you continue to be a pillar of kindness, compassion, and professionalism in America's national community, of which we are proud to belong. You are a role model and an inspiration to us all. Thank you so very much for your kind words and for taking an interest in this project.

To Rita Battat Silverman and Leap Over It, Inc., our literary agent. Thank you for your vision, infectious optimism, and relentless efforts to see this book move from a concept to a reality. You are the driving force behind this important project, and we will always be grateful for your encouragement, support, and faith in us.

To Randy Ladenheim-Gil, our fabulous and very talented editor, who embraced this project from the start. Thank you for your endless patience, encouragement, late-night phone consultations, and your wonderful work. This couldn't have been done without you.

To Lori Hand, Janette Lynn, Jennifer Moore, Lisanne V. Jensen, Amy Borelli, and everyone at Penguin Group (USA) Inc.—thank you for this opportunity, for working with us, and for your support, understanding, and expertise.

*Cynthia would also like to thank:*

All of the kids, families, and educators who shared their struggles and hopes with her.

Maya Libby, for her insights, smarts, and sisterhood—I couldn't have done it without you!

Abigail Brenner, for guiding the way.

Cindy, for your wisdom and commitment to making schools a positive, safe place for all.

*Cindy would also like to thank:*

Jim Burns, one of the most inspiring educators I've ever met. Thank you for sharing your knowledge and for all of your support.

My dear friends: Katherine, thank you for sharing this journey with me and for your amazing vision, support, and never-ending faith in me. Barbara, thank you for your eternal optimism, encouragement, and starting it all. Joyce, Maria, and Doreen, here's to our friendship and to a lifetime of so many shared ups and just a few downs.

My sister, Debora, whose insights, wisdom, and talents never cease to amaze and inspire me. To my sons, Michael and Casey, with all my love and gratitude every day. I'm so lucky to be your mom. It brings me unspeakable joy to know that you always believe in me, and I in you.

Paul, for your never-ending support, encouragement, and respect … and for the wireless printer!

Howard, thanks for everything.

Cynthia Lowen: it is with much gratitude and admiration that I say it has been a pleasure and a privilege to work with you on this project. Your work on the ground-breaking, no-holds-barred documentary *Bully* is a powerful call-to-action for everyone who cares about today's youth. I'm wishing you every success!

A very special thank you and acknowledgment to everyone in the Paramus School District. I'm proud to be a member of this caring school community where every child matters.

## Trademarks

All terms mentioned in this book that are known to be or are suspected of being trademarks or service marks have been appropriately capitalized. Alpha Books and Penguin Group (USA) Inc. cannot attest to the accuracy of this information. Use of a term in this book should not be regarded as affecting the validity of any trademark or service mark.

# Part 1

# Twenty-First-Century Bullying

This part focuses on the changing face of bullying today and its continuum, from teasing to more severe bullying behaviors to digital abuse and cyberbullying. We describe some of the societal changes and challenges families are facing today, and examine the characteristics of kids who act aggressively. This section also explores what motivates some individuals to use their power to bully, as well as the makeup of kids they're likely to target.

Bullying doesn't take place in a vacuum. We introduce you to the bystanders, the many people—kids and adults alike—who stand on the sidelines and witness bullying, and offer insights into the social hierarchy of bullying. We stress the importance of separating the behavior from the person, and we share some of the signs and symptoms to watch out for that may indicate that a child is either acting out aggressively or being bullied.

# chapter 1

# What Is Bullying?

Identifying types of bullying

Finding out where and how it's happening

Mapping the bullying triangle

Listening to what kids are saying about bullying

Making the connection between bullying and suicide

People often ask whether bullying is worse these days or if the proliferation of news stories about it indicates that the phenomenon has escalated into a social contagion. It's hard to say, but we do think that bullying has been around for as long as humans have used power to hurt, manipulate, and elicit fear in others. Anyone who went through high school 5 or 6 decades ago most likely has his or her own share of stories about bullying—either experienced or witnessed. However, it might not have been called *bullying* at that time.

Until recently, bullying was considered a "normal" part of growing up. Kids expected to be taunted by those who were older, stronger, or more popular; chased home from school by the neighborhood ruffians; or have their lunch money stolen by that grade's thug. Bullying was reflected in popular media, movies, and comic books throughout the twentieth century, from TV episodes of *Leave It to Beaver* to classic movies like *A Christmas Story* to contemporary fare like *Mean Girls*.

Bullying may not be worse today than it has been historically, but it *is* more visible. Behaviors that were once seen as rites of passage or normal pains of adolescence can no longer be dismissed as "kids-will-be-kids" events. That's because today, we recognize the consequences of peer abuse and the damage it does to our children, our schools, and our communities. And we're also faced with the many arenas in which bullying plays out—from home to school to the Internet, workplace, and beyond.

In this chapter, we explore bullying today—what it looks like, where it's happening, and how our kids talk about it.

# Types of Bullying

*Bullying* is the exploitation of an imbalance of power. It's a type of aggression that can be physical, emotional, or verbal, and can take place either in person or through electronic communication. Bullying behaviors exist on a continuum, from repeated teasing or name-calling to severe physical attacks with devastating—and sometimes deadly—consequences. When an individual or group intentionally targets another person to cause him or her physical or emotional harm, when there's a perceived or real imbalance of power, and when it continues over time, it's bullying.

## Verbal Bullying

Remember the old saying, "Sticks and stones may break my bones, but names will never harm me"? Well, anyone who has been verbally taunted day after day with words such as "fag" or "whore," or were told that he's worthless, that nobody likes him, or that everyone wishes he would disappear, can assure you that physical scars heal but the emotional ones that come with verbal bullying might last a lifetime. Verbal bullying can detrimentally affect a target's confidence, sense of self-worth, the ways he defines himself, the activities he participates in, and many other aspects of a target's identity. Verbal bullying can also include threats of physical violence and can take place in person, online, or through text messaging.

Although targets are often advised to "just ignore it," this attitude negates the seriousness of this kind of bullying and the fact that once a target has been bullied verbally, it has already had an impact. Verbal bullying may also constitute a civil rights violation if the content is bias-based (see Chapter 10 for details).

**What We Say Matters**

Words are powerful weapons when they're used to bully. There are many cases of young people who tragically took their own lives after experiencing ongoing verbal bullying, both online and offline. Tyler Long, a 17-year-old from Murray County, Georgia, was told to go hang himself by his classmates; he took his own life early the following morning. Likewise, Phoebe Prince was subjected to verbal abuse both in school and on her walk home from school; later that day she committed suicide. Teach your kids the power of words and to think about what the lasting impact might be before they use words to hurt.

## Physical Bullying

Physical bullying is designed to intimidate, threaten, or harm another person's body, property, family member, or friend.

Physical bullying behaviors include:

- Pushing, tripping, spitting, hitting or slapping (either with a hand, fist, or object), kicking, or hair pulling.

- Defacing or destroying property, such as making marks on clothing, books, or backpacks.

- Physical destruction of property, such as cutting up belongings or setting fire to a person or property.

- Stealing.

- Initiating fights or forcing someone to fight another person.

Although we historically picture boys when we think about physical bullying, plenty of girls also fight and threaten physical harm.

parent pointer

Sometimes parents and peers encourage their children or friends to fight back, and then those same parents become frustrated when the children are afraid to do so. But fighting back doesn't always work; in fact, it often can make things worse and lead to the target getting in trouble.

## Emotional Bullying

Emotional bullying has the intention of making someone feel bad about herself. It's often done by humiliating, taunting, and making fun of someone repeatedly in the presence of others. However, it isn't necessary that it be done in public or with spoken words. A bully can emotionally threaten a target when he is alone, passing in the hall, or online. Dirty looks; insults or threatening gestures; and embarrassing, criticizing, or making negative comments are all examples of emotional bullying. A lot of verbal bullying falls into this category.

> **parent pointer**
>
> The wounds of emotional bullying run deep and are hard to heal. Encourage your child to talk about what he's going through, and let your child know that it's not his fault. Share some of your own experiences, and give him opportunities to participate in activities that reaffirm his sense of self.

One of the most common things you'll hear when kids are bullying each other, particularly among boys, is calling someone gay—whether or not the target himself identifies as such. When a boy is being bullied, the term "gay" is often meant to embarrass or humiliate him and destroy his self-image. As we discuss in Chapter 10, this kind of bullying—whether a target is gay, perceived gay, or merely doesn't conform to gender stereotypes—violates his civil rights.

## Relational Bullying

Unlike physical aggression—which causes damage to the body, sense of safety, and threats to property—relational bullying is primarily aimed at destroying the target's friendships and peer acceptance. Relational bullying is closely linked with emotional bullying.

Relational aggression, as it is often called, is particularly problematic in middle school—a time when most young people are desperately seeking to fit in and are most vulnerable to peer rejection.

Relational bullying behaviors attack targets by spreading rumors, gossiping, or lying about the target; or isolating, ignoring, or excluding the child from a group. A relational bully may manipulate a target's friends to turn against him or participate in the bullying.

Relational bullying most frequently takes place among girls, who tend to be more sophisticated at understanding group social dynamics and are more likely to use indirect forms of bullying. Relational bullies often enlist the assistance of other girls in the group to isolate, shame, discredit, reject, and socially destroy the chosen target. Sometimes the bully will encourage one or more group members to pretend to befriend the target. By doing that, the "frenemy" is able to secure private information, including embarrassing or secret anecdotes and fears the target may share—unaware that she's being set up. Then, the frenemy discloses all the private and sensitive information to the group and other peers, either online or in person, and the target is devastated.

Students who have been the target of relational aggression, particularly in the middle school years, need to know that they aren't alone. This kind of bullying can be a wake-up call to a target about the kind of "friends" he seeks out and can lead to the development of more meaningful friendships with kids who make good choices. In time, targets often learn that many of the kids who were members of the mean group that targeted him were really afraid of being the bully's next victim. Unfortunately, it usually doesn't take long for the next target in the group to surface as the cycle repeats itself.

## The Bullying Triangle

Bullying obviously involves a perpetrator or group of perpetrators, who are doing the bullying, and the target, who is being hurt. But what about all the other kids who aren't directly involved? If you ask most kids, they know who the bully and the target are. So what do we call the kids who are neither bullied nor doing the bullying? This third group, whose members far outnumber either the bullies or the targets, are referred to as *bystanders*.

Bystanders are critical to the bullying equation. Their presence can make the situation worse if the target equates their silence with consent to what's happening. Bystanders very often feel incredibly conflicted and uncomfortable and are also negatively impacted by the bullying. They're also in a great position to challenge bullying and protect targets.

**The Snowball Effect of Bullying**

Studies show that the longer kids are bullied, the more likely bystanders are to believe that the target deserves it. Being chronically bullied can erode a child's confidence, take away the fun of doing things he used to enjoy, and lead to isolation and withdrawal. The more these feelings invade a child's evolving sense of self, the more it will be reflected in his posture, the way the child interacts with other kids, and the roles he plays in the social strata of school. It's important for children who have been targeted to know it doesn't have to define them. Labeling a target a "victim" may give bystanders the sense that the bullying is inevitable—part of who that child is—and that they're powerless to make a difference.

The dynamic of the bully-victim-bystander triangle is fluid. Kids who use bullying behaviors don't always remain bullies. Targets don't always remain targets, and bystanders aren't always in that position, either. Most of us can recall a time when we bullied someone, when we felt like the target of a bully, and when we knew about but weren't directly involved in a bullying situation.

Several distinct groups can be involved in bullying, including the following:

- The person bullying
- The person who is targeted
- The person who is a bully in some circumstances but targeted in others (called a bully-victim)
- Bystanders

We talk more about all of these categories in the following chapters.

## Where Is It Happening?

We know that bullying occurs with the greatest frequency and intensity during middle school years. But any situation in which kids are testing their dominance and influence can provide an opportunity for bullying. It can happen anywhere, from summer camp to soccer practice.

**Prevalence of Bullying**

According to the National Center for Education Statistics, 44 percent of public middle schools report that student bullying occurs at least once a week or daily. This statistic drops to 22 percent in the high schools surveyed, on par with elementary schools at 21 percent. The survey revealed that teachers also feel targeted by students: 10 percent of middle school teachers and 12 percent of high school teachers reported being verbally abused by students at least once a week.

The following sections map out some of the environments where bullying frequently occurs.

## At School

Aside from the relationships kids have with their siblings, most social interactions among kids are formed at school. It makes sense, then, that schools have traditionally been ground zero for bullying. Areas where there's minimal or no supervision can be hot spots for bullying, especially unsupervised places such as student bathrooms, hallways between classes, the playground, the locker room, and the school bus.

At school, kids mimic behaviors they've witnessed at home. If young children come to school using aggressive behaviors, it's probably time for a hard look at where those behaviors are coming from.

Bullying can also rear its ugly head in after-school activities, including sports. The stereotypical coach who harangues, berates, and belittles players to push them to play their hardest isn't entirely extinct. Schools that highly value athletics may have coaches who reinforce bullying behaviors or administrators who don't want to discipline star athletes because they're valuable assets.

In Chapter 7, we talk about steps that kid-friendly schools are taking to prevent bullying behaviors.

## Online

When people speculate that bullying is worse today than it ever has been, usually they're referring to the prevalence of cyberbullying, which has received a lot of notoriety. This is one way in which today's generation is living in a truly different world than the one in which their parents grew up. Kids today never experienced adolescence without social networking or text messaging. And while the Internet and technology have given us many more ways to connect and learn, it has also expanded the ways in which kids can bully.

Most twenty-first-century kids have access to cell phones and computers, which are platforms that can be used to harass, threaten, demean, spread gossip, impersonate others, or post private or embarrassing information.

*Cyberbullying* can consist of any of the following behaviors:

- Posting mean or hurtful comments to a social-networking group

- Posting hurtful pictures or videos online

- Spreading rumors or information meant to embarrass or alienate the target

- Using the Internet or cell phones to harass or convey physical threats of violence

- Creating a webpage intended to hurt a target and engage others in bullying

As the ways we use technology rapidly evolve, so do the ways these platforms are used to bully—and also provide support to targets. We talk a lot more about cyberbullying in Chapter 8.

## And Beyond

Bullying can happen at home between siblings or parents, in the highly charged social microcosms of camp, at a friend's house, at extracurricular activities, or through exclusion from parties, outings, or teams. Part of our job as parents is to help our kids recognize bullying when they witness or experience it, no matter where it happens.

# Speaking the Same Language?

Parents often miss the signs that their kids are being bullied—even though it's obvious to other kids. This disconnect is at least partly due to the fact that adults and youth use different language to describe the behaviors involved. Researchers Danah Boyd and Alice Marwick have found that teenagers often feel bullying is childish and don't want to associate their struggles with it, or to admit they're either a target or a bully. Many adolescents attempt to dismiss bullying and behaviors that actually really hurt and trouble them by referring to them as "drama."

However, if you break drama down into behaviors such as spreading rumors, gossip, and exclusion, you'll probably find it's indistinguishable from bullying. While kids may feel more in control of drama and the decision to take the high road and dismiss it, when it comes to bullying, ignoring it isn't likely to make it go away. While we want to empower our kids to handle bullying situations effectively on their own, contextualizing bullying as drama may prevent them from asking for help when they need it or intervening on behalf of others.

The language gap between kids and adults when describing bullying can have a major impact on the outcome of school climate surveys or attempts by adults to handle a bullying situation. When confronted with a question such as "Have you been bullied?", many adolescents who have been bullied answer "no" because they think of bullying as something that happens somewhere else to someone else—that it's something different from what they're going through, or that it only happens in elementary or middle school to younger children. Unless they have a lot of emotional support, kids don't want to identify as either a victim or a perpetrator. It is often more effective to ask more specific questions, such as, "Are other kids spreading rumors about you?" or "Has anyone at school stolen something from you?" Questions that identify the behaviors and remove the stigma kids associate with bullying may help both adults and kids bridge the gap.

# Teasing vs. Bullying

There's a big difference between playful, friendly teasing and teasing that's intended to dominate, hurt, shame, or embarrass someone. The former isn't bullying; the latter is. Playful, friendly teasing is intended to be light-hearted. There's no imbalance of power. It's not mean-spirited or meant to be hurtful.

Friends may tease each other about their physical attributes, abilities, or things that may seem kind of personal. If there's a mutual agreement about that kind of exchange and its limits, no one is going to get hurt. Friends usually know each other's soft spots and avoid them. Although playful teasing can become annoying, the purpose is never meant to embarrass or make anyone feel bad.

Teasing can be tricky, though, especially when two people don't know each other very well or when one of the parties lacks the knowledge and skills to engage in something that's friendly and harmless. However, attuned kids and adults can usually recognize the teaser's true intention. If a young person hurts another's feelings accidentally, he'll quickly acknowledge his mistake, apologize, and feel remorseful about any harm caused by his comments. The person he was teasing will most likely feel understood and not upset.

If the teasing isn't friendly or playful, and when the children aren't friends, the aggressive teaser won't acknowledge his mistake and feels no remorse, although he's likely to defend himself by saying, "I was just kidding." He's unlikely to make any effort at a real apology, and his target will feel bad or uncomfortable. That's when teasing becomes bullying.

parent
pointer

Sarcastic banter between friends who both enjoy the dynamic—and there is no harm intended—can be considered playful teasing. However, kids who have social disabilities such as autism may not recognize sarcasm and take it literally. If your child has a sarcastic wit, make sure he's attuned to the way it's being received and when he may need to follow up to clarify the intentions and desire not to harm.

## Conflict Is Normal

Conflict is a common part of our lives. It might be sibling rivalry; it can happen between married people negotiating who cooks dinner; it often happens between friends—say, if they're grappling over whether it's okay to date the other's ex—and it can happen internally, too: do we choose to have that hamburger we've been craving, or a salad instead? Conflict represents two opposing perspectives or needs. Whether conflicts are minor or serious, we must try to negotiate or solve them or learn to live with them.

Some kids are attuned to their internal conflicts and are able to control themselves; they possess problem-solving skills and have a healthy respect for themselves and others. Other kids don't have these skills. And some kids come from homes where aggression, violence, and disregard for the rights of others are the norm when dealing with conflict.

 parent pointer

Kids who bully generally don't have the ability to handle conflict well. They want immediate satisfaction, lack concern for others, and tend to be impulsive. In Chapter 13, we talk about ways to help your child learn to solve problems and make good decisions.

Bullying behavior isn't about normal conflict. When it's bullying, there's a perceived imbalance of power between the more aggressive and abusive child and the one he's assaulting. With normal conflict, some kind of resolution can be reached between the two parties because they're on equal footing. Resolving bullying situations is very different because the target and the perpetrator aren't equals; therefore, there's no position from which to negotiate a solution.

## Bullycide

In the last few years, there have been several cases of young people who were relentlessly and severely bullied and who took their own lives, eliciting public outcry across the country, from TV personalities to journalists and bloggers or everyday people commenting online. You've probably heard the expressions "bullied to death" or "bullycide" in connection with these tragedies.

Research has found that students who suffer from depression are both more likely to be bullied and also more likely to have suicidal thoughts. Targets of bullying consistently exhibit more symptoms of depression than nontargets. They have more suicidal thoughts and are more likely to attempt suicide than nontargets. A Yale University study of suicide and bullying in 13 countries found that targets of bullying are two to nine times more likely to report suicidal thoughts than those who aren't bullied.

Bullying and social rejection lead to distress. Being targeted, humiliated, abused, rejected, and bullied can be linked to anxiety, fear, sadness, hopelessness, depression, anger, rage, and pretty much any other emotional pain you can name. Most kids don't really want to end their lives—they just want the pain to stop.

For some kids, attempting suicide may be a way of trying to relieve themselves of the unbearable pain and suffering of being bullied. If they've been told that they're worthless or unwanted, or if peers have suggested they kill themselves, they may truly lack a sense of self-worth and not grasp the implications of their actions. Others may have asked for help but haven't received it, and they see suicide as a way to take matters into their own hands or to express to others the seriousness of what they've been experiencing.

These tragedies have been a call to action for communities nationwide and a wake-up call for those who downplay bullying as a normal rite of passage. These tragedies have sparked legislation around bullying and have been the catalyst for the launch of several grass-roots campaigns to raise awareness about bullying, all of which we talk about later in this book.

## Essential Takeaways

- Bullying may not be worse than it ever has been, but it's much more visible.
- Bullying can take place in any circumstance where kids misuse their power to establish influence and dominance.
- Bullying roles are fluid, but comprise three main groups: the perpetrator, the target, and bystanders.
- Kids often minimize bullying by calling it "drama." As a result, adults and kids themselves may fail to recognize bullying and adequately address it.
- There's a big difference between friendly teasing, normal conflict, and bullying.
- As a result of the numerous suicides in recent years, the term "bullycide" has come into the vernacular to refer to instances where severely and relentlessly bullied young people take their own lives. Several studies have linked bullying to depression and suicide.

# chapter 2

# What's Behind Bullying Today?

How bullying has changed over time

The role of changing family dynamics

The influence of the Internet, social media, and texting

The impact of changing values

We see bullying behavior portrayed on television and in the movies, we hear the term used to describe the activities of companies or the aggressive actions of nations, and of course, we experience bullying in our schools, workplaces, communities, and online. In the past few years, bullying has become part of our cultural consciousness; it has become integral to our understanding of our children's experiences, as well as our own. While 20 years ago the attitude about bullying was that it was a normal and inevitable rite of passage for adolescents, we now know it is neither normal, nor does it begin or end in adolescence.

People often ask if bullying is worse today than it has been in the past. Those of us who were in high school decades ago can attest to the fact that bullying isn't a new phenomenon. What *is* new is our ability to identify bullying, to recognize abusive behaviors that have been deeply entrenched in our communities, and to talk about the experience and its impact.

Although bullying has been around for as long as human beings have misused their power to intimidate, abuse, and hurt those who are weaker, bullying today has found new frontiers. While "traditional" bullying—including name-calling, physical assaults, ostracism, and rumors—is alive and well, bullying today has many new platforms, taking place through social networking sites, online videos, and text messaging. Not only have bullying behaviors found new expressions, but so have the consequences of those behaviors. Today we are acutely aware of the numerous tragedies caused by bullying, from kids taking their own lives, to those who have taken the lives of their peers.

According to the United States government, 13 million American kids will be bullied this year. We need to do our very best to gain as much understanding as we can about what's happening in the lives of our children and how we can help them to turn things around. Let's take a look at some of the factors that may be behind the kinds of bullying we see today.

## The Changing Family

The "traditional family" isn't so traditional anymore. Characteristics that used to define a "nontraditional" family are now increasingly common and shared by many American families. Here are some examples:

- **Single-parent households.** An increasing number of children are being raised in single-parent households. While the majority of children in single-parent households live with their mothers, the number in which the father is the primary caretaker is increasing.

- **Blended families.** More children are living in blended families, with stepparents and stepsiblings.

- **Interracial families.** More children are being born into and living in interracial and multicultural families.

- **Same-sex parents.** Increasing numbers of children are living with their parents and their same-sex partners.

- **Multigenerational households.** Many grandparents are responsible for the care of their grandchildren, with or without the assistance of the children's parents.

- **Non-English-speaking households**. Many kids today are being raised in homes where English isn't the first language, or where parents don't speak English fluently.

Any of these factors might increase the incidence of bullying, or make it harder for a parent to recognize a bullying situation. For example, children may find themselves being bullied for living with same-sex parents, or ostracized for not identifying with one particular ethnic group. In homes where the parents don't speak English fluently, it can be very challenging for a parent to advocate for her child, particularly in school districts that don't provide translators.

In addition to the emotional and economic challenges of parenting, the recent recession has created additional economic hardships for today's families:

- **High jobless rate.** Many parents have lost their jobs or are working multiple jobs, often without health care and other benefits.

- **Home foreclosures.** Millions of Americans have lost their homes to foreclosure, forcing families to relocate, or even into homelessness.

- **Increasing level of poverty.** In 2010, about 15 percent of our nation's children lived in poverty.

Many of these economic challenges have resulted in additional stress for parents, caretakers, and children. Parents who are juggling multiple jobs and financial insecurity may find it hard to take even part of a day off from work to meet with principals or guidance counselors if they suspect or know their child is being bullied.

Kids themselves are acutely aware of their parents' anxieties and hardships. If a parent is coping with unemployment, or the fear of losing her home, or not being able to provide for her family, kids may be exposed to tensions that might contribute to them bullying others or becoming targeted themselves. Additionally, kids who are sensitive to their parents' struggles may be hesitant to tell them if they're being bullied, for fear of adding to their parents' worries.

# The Social Networking Generation: How Bullies Use Technology

Perhaps the biggest change—both a gift *and* a challenge to today's families—is the prevalence of communication technology in our lives.

Do you know anyone who *isn't* on Facebook? While there may still be a few people who haven't become members of social networking sites and joined the Facebook revolution, the use of technology has become second nature to millions of us. More and more kids have cell phones today, too, and many of them have smart phones that enable them to get online at any time. Cell phones, the Internet, and social networking sites like Twitter and Facebook have completely changed the way we communicate.

The upside to all of these advances is that they enable us to communicate important information quickly and effectively. We are able to research topics of interest, locate ex-classmates and former colleagues, keep our world posted on day-to-day personal and professional events and activities, and post personal photos to share with the people we care most about, in real time.

But there's a dark side to the rise of cell phones and social media. Texting and the Internet offer new ways for bullies to victimize their targets 24/7. Bullies can abuse technology to harm their targets' friendships and destroy their reputations, reaching thousands, even millions, of people with the click of a button. Bullies can post comments on network walls and spread painful rumors about targets; they can humiliate their targets by uploading videos of them being physically attacked; they can distribute embarrassing pictures; or harass them with text messages. A nasty post on the Internet or via text message can quickly become contagious.

Because today's kids are often far more savvy with technology than their parents or even teachers, it can be very challenging for adults to become aware of what's going on or to intervene on behalf of kids.

## The Anonymity of the Internet

The Internet also offers an incredible opportunity for anonymity, and anonymity for many bullies is like adding oxygen to a fire. Anyone can establish a Facebook or MySpace account under an assumed name. Once they have their fake identify, they can tease, threaten, and otherwise bully without anyone knowing who they are.

Sometimes kids create social networking accounts under the names of classmates or peers, and use these accounts to bully others or create conflict among peer groups. The target may think she is accepting a friend into her social network, when that account has in fact been started by a bully, who is assuming the friend's identity to get access to information the target would only share with someone close to her, or to destroy a friendship.

And even when kids are online under their own identity, they may act with a kind of impunity that suggests merely being on the Internet offers a false sense of anonymity.

**Bully Buster**

If young people understand that nothing is really private in cyberspace, they will be less likely to use the Internet to bully others. They need to know that every stroke they enter on their computer, iPad, or mobile device can be traced back to them through their IP address or cell phone number. The police can be granted access to this information when investigating incidents of suspected bullying.

## Virtual Friendships

Most kids love to play outdoors, participate in sports, and spend time with their friends, but now they have additional alternatives for socializing. The Internet offers wonderful opportunities for kids to connect with other kids who share similar interests, even if they don't live close by. For kids who are shy or have interests that aren't shared by their classmates, the Internet has made it much easier for them to find others to communicate with.

Some kids have hundreds of online friendships. They spend much of their time checking their Facebook pages for messages or posts and waiting for their cell phones to vibrate with text messages or "tweets." While it's great for kids to be connected and find community, online friendships may have different standards of what "friendship" really means. The sands of adolescent friendships are often quickly shifting, and this can be especially true online, where kids don't have the benefit of face-to-face interaction or lack the self-discipline or good judgment to keep hurtful behavior in check. We've all probably had the experience of pressing "send" when we wished we'd just let our tempers cool, or when a misunderstanding of one's online tone led to a terse exchange. Adolescent brains, which are by nature impulsive, can be particularly prone to these kinds of online conflicts. When an online friendship becomes a bullying situation, and snowballs to involve several kids, the target can easily feel like the whole world is ganging up on them.

 **parent pointer** It's hard to know who your kids are "hanging out" with and being influenced by when they're online with virtual and anonymous friends. Many a child has been pressured into engaging in risky behaviors through online friendships.

## Social Isolation

One of the greatest needs of kids is to fit in. The desire to belong is so strong that many kids (and adults, too) will do almost anything to be part of the group, even if it means going along with something they don't really feel good about, or accepting being treated badly by their peers. No kid wants to be cut off from the pack. Kids who have trouble making friends or who have few friendships are especially vulnerable to bullying and the social isolation it brings.

Bullies separate their targets from their friends and peers. Much like the abuser in a domestic violence situation, who systematically destroys the relationships of his partner so she becomes completely dependent on him, the bully disrupts his target's connections to others, making her feel alone and vulnerable.

Here are some ways bullies isolate their targets:

- A group of girls invite everyone except the target to a party or other event, while letting their target know that she's not invited.

- Boys may keep a weaker or rejected child off the basketball court, make sure he doesn't get the opportunity to make a basket, or refuse to pick him for team play.

- Kids may make it known that they won't be friends with anyone who plays with, sits with, or is a friend of the targeted child.

- When the target comes to sit at the lunch table, everyone else turns their faces the other way, won't talk to her, or gets up and leaves the table.

- No one sits with the targeted child on the school bus or refuses to make room for her to sit down on a crowded bus.

- Peers may label the target with an undesirable tag, like *slut, whore,* or *loser,* and disassociate themselves from talking to so-called sluts, whores, or losers.

- Kids may progressively exclude the child from peers, either in person or online, until she feels she is totally alone.

# The Acceptance of Violence

Violence has become a part of everyday life in America. We're exposed to violent behavior and aggressive conversations, road-rage incidents, and blatant disrespect on a regular basis.

Music is filled with sexual and violent language and suggestions. Movies have become more violent, graphic, and sadistic in nature. Curse words are used in television with increasing regularity. And girls and women continue to be depicted as sexual objects in the media, including in video games.

Exposure to violence desensitizes people to the painful impact of acting with aggression toward others. Kids who are sensitive to violence, aggression, or bullying can be labeled weak, losers, or crybabies. When mistreatment becomes acceptable, it can make it even more difficult for caring bystanders to take action, for fear they will be labeled weak or even targeted themselves.

## Video Games: Kill for the Thrill

Many young people play video games for several hours a day, often online with others. A lot of kids say that playing violent games helps them relax. Although playing these games provides kids with an escape from dealing with stress, frustration, anxiety, family problems, learning differences, and depression, it doesn't solve any of their problems.

Many of the best-selling video games promote and reward violent behavior. In the game Bully, the player assumes the identity of the new kid at a high school, navigating the cliques and hierarchies with a plethora of weapons at his disposal, including baseball bats, sling-shots, firecrackers, and bottle rockets. This scenario creates a virtual world reminiscent of the tragic real world of the Columbine High School massacre in Colorado, in which two students, Eric Harris and Dylan Klebold, who had been bullied for years, killed 12 students and 1 teacher and then committed suicide.

In many online multiplayer games, groups of players band together virtually to destroy their enemies. Games with audio components enable them to speak with each other while they work toward successfully completing their missions, to simulate a military operation. Just as military training seeks to prepare soldiers for violent situations, repetitive acts of simulated violence may desensitize kids to aggression and the impact that these kinds of attitudes and behaviors have in the real world.

Recent research studies have found that playing violent video games can actually alter the chemistry of a child's brain. The physical and emotional responses triggered by game play mimic the responses to real-life threats or situations. Heart rates and blood pressure rise, and *adrenaline* and *dopamine* levels increase.

**Definition**

**Adrenaline** is the hormone that energizes the body to respond to perceived stress or excitement. It increases the breathing rate as well as heart rate and blood pressure. **Dopamine** is a neurotransmitter in the brain with multiple functions, including the regulation of emotion and reward-seeking activities.

Additional scientific evidence suggests that playing violent video games may increase aggressive behavior and moodiness, and desensitize users to violent language and actions while they're playing the game (and perhaps for a period of time afterward as well).

Video games are fast paced, stimulating, and highly interactive. Because there are constant opportunities built into the gaming program to encourage the player to experience greater and ongoing success in the form of achieving points, raising levels, and all kinds of sound and visual effects, playing video games is highly engaging, and many people—adults as well as kids—find it really hard to stop.

It's possible that excessive game play can be an early source of addiction for children and teens. You may have noticed that some kids become so preoccupied with them that they lose interest in other activities that are healthier, like playing outdoors, socializing, and taking part in other creative activities.

The trick is to help children find ways to balance the thrill and excitement of playing video games with the fun and satisfaction of spending time together, enjoying friendships, and experiencing the thrill of accomplishing new things, like learning to ride a bike, taking part in sports, learning to play a musical instrument, helping a friend, and solving problems. Learning what your child likes and helping her develop new interests and skills will increase her enthusiasm and develop her self-confidence. It's important to foster a sense of social cooperation and real achievement and to diminish the desire to dominate and humiliate others.

# Today's Media

The graphic, violent, and irresponsible nature of much of today's media and the effect it has on our kids is of grave concern to many. While the parents of the original TV generation may have been criticized for allowing their children to be "raised" by television, it's even more important these days to be aware of what your child is watching and listening to and the messages she's internalizing that are coming at her across 300-plus cable stations and via the Internet.

From mob boss Tony Soprano and the other idolized bullies of the hit television series *The Sopranos,* to reality show put-downs by *American Idol*'s Simon Cowell, bullying behavior continues to be celebrated in our culture. These shows often can set up a false idea of the effectiveness of bullying behavior and fail to depict the impact on the target and the long-term consequences for the bully.

## Role Models Gone Wild

Who are the role models of today? How are they impacting the ideas, values, goals, and self-concepts of our children? Many prominent voices in the media and public today use their voices to put down women, celebrate aggression, or engage in disrespectful political discourse.

**parent pointer**

It's important that children have good role models at home and in their community, not just on TV or in sports arenas. You are the most important role model your children will ever have. Even though they may not act as if they're listening or paying attention to you, they continue to need your love, support, and guidance. Stick with them; they hear you. The seeds you sow may take time to grow, but they often bear fruit when you least expect it.

Consider some of the things our children are routinely exposed to in the media:

- Brides who abuse everyone in their wedding parties, including their fiancés.

- Adults on talk shows who are aggressive and humiliate and embarrass each other.

- Toddlers who are dressed like mature, sexualized women for beauty pageants.

- Violence, brutality, and insensitivity in movies and music.

When these portrayals are accepted as the norm rather than the exception, our children's concepts of appropriate behavior and expectations are changed. It's important that children have good role models at home and in their community. That means immediate and extended families, schools, places of worship, extracurricular programs, and responsible media.

Kids need their parents and everyone who cares about them in their communities to model healthy family values and realistic expectations. Kids who feel they can't measure up to society's expectations or who believe that aggression and violence are acceptable between people who care about each other can feel very confused. They may become vulnerable to low self-esteem and succumb to peer pressure, and that may increase their chances of becoming bullies, targets, or bystanders.

## Lack of Accountability

How do we manage in a society where some people are held accountable for their actions while others aren't?

Does the child in your school whose parent is known to be a bully get treated differently than your child? Are certain adults in a school treated differently than others? Are bus drivers accorded the same measure of respect as teachers, or are they bullied by other staff members? Are there groups within our communities who are not treated equally? Is there a perception that the police are there to help, or are they distrusted by some members of our communities?

Kids see how some people get away with things when they know they're wrong. When kids witness bad behavior without consequences, they learn that bullying sometimes works. That's not the message you want your children to receive. You don't want them to be bullies, and you don't want them to become targets, either. Both come with a heavy price to pay for everyone involved.

## Essential Takeaways

- Because of the Internet and cell phones, kids have even more ways of going about it than they did in the past.
- Our changing society has added to the stresses families face, which in turn often makes it harder for parents to go to school to advocate for their kids and for kids to tell their parents they're being bullied.
- Technology can help kids develop new friendships and communities, but it can also make them vulnerable to being bullied online.
- Violent video games can normalize bullying and aggressive behaviors.
- Children need good role models to develop healthy self-concepts to know that bullying behaviors are not the norm.

# chapter 3

# Understanding Bullies

Bullies versus bullying behaviors

Status and the use of bullying behaviors

When bullying behaviors are learned, enabled, or encouraged

Bullying behaviors and coping skills

The age-old image of the schoolyard bully—a young person who terrorizes everyone around him, has no social skills, and displays an utter lack of regard for others—denies the complexity of bullying and fails to capture why it's so hard to effectively deal with. If it were just a matter of a few antisocial punks pushing other kids around, it would be easy to identify those young people and isolate them from the rest of us.

Instead, bullying is a complex set of behaviors that many children display. Bullying exists on a continuum. The child who is the target on the school bus may be the perpetrator in the cafeteria. Some kids may try out bullying once or twice, while others consistently use it to get their way. Some may do it because they want to maintain their status, while others do it to increase their status.

Bullying is deeply ingrained in our culture and the fabric of our schools and communities because it's not just a few intrinsically bad individuals, but rather the behaviors of many individuals navigating complex social dynamics who, in other situations, may be really good kids.

That said, bullying behaviors can be very severe, and the impact on targets, particularly when many young people are participating in the bullying, cannot be overestimated. While it's normal for growing children to test their power and influence over others, most don't turn into full-fledged bullies in the traditional sense of the word. However, those who continue to engage in bullying behaviors may be in for a lifetime of trouble.

## Who Uses Bullying Behaviors?

We can all probably think of a time when we've raised our voice or intimidated someone to get our way. Humans are social creatures, constantly navigating the power dynamics in our relationships whether we are at home, at parties, or at the PTA meeting. We can all probably think of a time when we've had to make that tough phone call to apologize for how we've behaved or treated someone else.

As we pointed out in Chapter 1, bullying behaviors can take many different forms. Some can seem quite harmless, like name-calling, and some are much more serious, such as in the case of Michael Brewer, a 15-year-old Florida boy who was lit on fire by several kids who were subsequently charged with attempted murder. Just as the types of bullying behaviors exist on a continuum, so does the frequency with which young people use them.

As young people develop physically, socially, and emotionally, they find themselves jockeying for position in their social spheres and figuring out how to exert and use their influence. This jockeying increases in the critical self-defining years of adolescence, from 12 to 18 years old, which is why bullying tends to peak in middle school, as kids are finding themselves yet still lack maturity. Some kids are naturally more outspoken "leader" types, and some are quiet observers, more likely to follow another child's lead or to assert themselves in different ways.

Bullies generally fall into three categories:

- Low-status kids who use bullying tactics as a means of jockeying for position on the social ladder

- High-status children who bully to maintain their dominance

- Socially marginalized kids who may exhibit sociopathic or anti-social behaviors, and who bully as a result of poor social, coping, and problem-solving skills, faulty thinking, learned negative behavior, mental illness, family stressors, or other factors

The following sections explore each of these types of bullies in more detail.

## Low-Status Bullies

Lower-status kids may seek out and befriend more popular kids who bully as a way to raise their own status. They may use bullying to impress their peers, to get approval from the group, or as a response to peer pressure to participate. They may also bully others to avoid becoming a target themselves and to gain power.

These kids are often referred to as bully-victims; in some scenarios, they're the aggressor, and in others, they're the target, depending on the makeup of the group. Bully-victims tend not to be perceived as "cool" or popular, either with teachers or kids. They do, however, worry deeply about peer relationships and are often motivated by those insecurities.

**Administrator Action**

When you pull a group of middle school kids into an administrator's office to unravel a bullying situation, the complexity of the group's relationships soon becomes apparent. You'll hear kids say, "He's my friend; I was just kidding around." And it may well be true. Perhaps when the target is alone with that other boy, they *are* good friends. However, when you put the group of boys together, the friend participates in calling the target names, or helps his peers stuff him into a gym locker. The bullying boy, who may be very decent to the target when they're by themselves, can turn on him in the presence of other more dominant boys in order to assert his place within the pecking order.

Although bully-victims aren't the most powerful aggressors, the harm they cause the target can be immense. Often, these are the kids who utilize the Internet to follow the target home.

## High-Status Bullies

Many kids who bully are often perceived by both peers and teachers as being popular and "cool." They're often well liked by everyone and can be charming, intuitive, charismatic, and intelligent; they are often seen as leaders. For these reasons, their bullying behavior often operates under the radar of teachers, administrators, and even their own parents.

Kids with a sophisticated understanding of social dynamics tend to be good manipulators and can talk a good game. They can be adept at evading accountability and responsibility, or feel that the rules don't apply to them.

High-status bullies are usually well aware of what the rules and behavioral expectations are at home, in public, and in school, but may feel that they're smart and charming enough to get around them.

When kids with high status use bullying behaviors, they often do it to enhance their power, dominance, and prestige, or to maintain their position by defending against kids they think might present a challenge. Because they're so intelligent, they're very adept at manipulating relationships among their peers and using nonconfrontational or indirect forms of aggression, such as gossip, rumors, and ostracism. Often these kids are very good at taking advantage of the social vulnerabilities of others, turning members of their peer group against other, weaker members of the group.

High-status kids who bully have found that socially aggressive bullying behavior works to achieve their goals. Such kids tend to associate with other popular kids, avoiding those who are socially marginalized, and often exhibit confidence in their peers' perception of their popularity.

Bully Buster

Adults may feel uncomfortable in the presence of a high-status, powerful bully for many reasons. Sometimes teachers have a hard time disciplining a bully because, like his peers, they don't want to become targets themselves. Some teachers want to be "popular" with their students, so they align themselves with the more powerful kids in the class.

## Socially Marginalized Bullies

Socially marginalized bullies often resemble the more traditional picture of a playground bully:

- They use violence, intimidation, and threats to get what they want; they frequently are involved in physical assaults or fights.

- They exhibit socially inappropriate behavior, such as a failure to follow rules, lack of empathy for others, frequent lying and cheating, and a lack of remorse for hurting or mistreating others.

- They surround themselves with other kids who don't fit into the social structure at school.

These young people often grow up to have various problems in adulthood, such as personality disorders, relationship problems, inability to hold a job, susceptibility to drug and substance abuse problems and, often, criminal records.

These kids may exhibit antisocial behaviors and may have backgrounds in which abuse and violence were the norm. Such children often haven't developed the tools to feel empathy. These kids may harm others for their own entertainment or in an effort to dominate, intimidate, hurt, and control them, without remorse, again and again.

# Characteristics That All Bullies Share

Whether a child is low status, high status, or marginalized, there are several characteristics that children who use bullying behavior often share:

- They use bullying as a way to navigate complex social hierarchies.

- They can be very socially intelligent and adept at recognizing and manipulating others' vulnerabilities.

- They like to be in control of others or situations and are accustomed to getting their own way.

- They may lack respect for authority or rules.

- They lack empathy and are more likely to interpret others' intentions as aggressive.

# How Gender Affects Bullying

Both boys and girls compete with their peers and siblings for status, friendship, recognition, possessions, and to get their own way. Kids in grade school are primarily concerned with befriending and gaining the approval of their same-sex peers. During the middle school years and beyond, their interests expand to opposite-sex relationships. Both boys and girls exclude peers from their group, but they typically use different tactics.

## Boys Use Direct Forms of Bullying

As boys mature, some of them establish dominance through physical power. Public displays of aggression may reinforce their bold and powerful reputation, minimize peer rivalry, and confirm their status over other males.

Research has found that boys are more likely than girls to engage in bullying behaviors, and also to be the targets of it. When boys bully, they tend to use more direct physical and verbal kinds of aggression than girls. Direct bullying can consist of any of the following behaviors:

- Kicking
- Hitting
- Spitting
- Shoving
- Beating up
- Damaging property
- Calling the target derogatory names
- Teasing and shaming
- Forcing a target into doing things he doesn't want to and threatening the target if he doesn't comply
- Lashing out in multiplayer online video games

**Bully Buster**

There is a strong correlation between boys who exhibit bullying behaviors and dating violence. Dating violence can include social aggression, such as spreading rumors or exerting control over their partner's peer relationships; verbal aggression, such as name-calling; or even physical aggression, such as slapping, punching, or choking. It can also mean spreading embarrassing pictures by cell phone or online. Studies have found this kind of bullying tends to occur among boys who have witnessed violence between their parents and, as a result, may view violence within the dating context as acceptable.

## Girls Employ Indirect Forms of Bullying

Although there are plenty of examples of girls physically bullying other girls—and boys—more often, girls engage in indirect forms of bullying behaviors, such as the following:

- Using their strong verbal and social smarts to manipulate social situations and dominate other girls in their group

- Using social exclusion and isolation against targets, such as rejecting them from a social networking group or not inviting them to parties or events

- Spreading rumors and gossip intended to damage a target's reputation or self-esteem, such as starting a negative email chain (see Chapter 8 for details on how girls use cyberbullying)

- Spreading pictures or other personal information online

- Using text messaging to harass their target

- Leaving nasty graffiti about their targets in the girls' bathroom

Bullying among girls often reflects the quickly shifting social dynamics among adolescents, and often girls vying for status within their clique may turn on each other, as a group or individually. Powerful girls can be very good at manipulating relationships and enlisting other girls to participate in bullying someone they have it in for.

Gracie

Often, the kinds of bullying girls participate in is more nuanced than boys' and flies under the radar of teachers and other adults. It can take a lot more investigative work and understanding of a group's dynamic to resolve. We talk more about creating kid-friendly schools in Chapter 7.

# Why They Do It

Often you'll see kids bullying each other on the very first day of kindergarten, for many their first foray into peer social dynamics. Although it may be their first opportunity to try out these behaviors, kids often learn about bullying behaviors long before they begin school. And often these behaviors persist long afterward because they're reinforced year after year. What are some of the root causes of bullying that lie beyond the school's front doors?

## When the Home Is Run by a Bully

When a parent is a bully, the world beyond the family's front door becomes their children's opportunity to model bullying behavior they've learned at home.

Here are some ways that bullying parents can encourage bullying behavior in their children:

- Neglecting or harming their children and creating bystanders to that abuse if siblings or others are present

- Creating a fearful environment in which siblings vie for their parents' affection or approval, and bully each other in the process

- Manipulating their spouse or their children, and playing their family members' behavior off each other in their own power struggles

- Modeling sadistic behavior or instilling a lack of respect for authority or rules

- Failing to acknowledge or recognize the pain they're causing the target, thereby passing on a lack of empathy and normalized reactions to violence to their children

**parent pointer** Studies have found that bullying among siblings is as frequent or more so than bullying at school, and that there's a strong correlation between kids who bully at home and kids who bully at school. A 2008 study found that 38 percent of kids experience more bullying and victimization at home than in school, perpetrated disproportionately by brothers—particularly older brothers.

Children may also learn bullying by watching their parents interact with other adults in the community. If you've ever attended a youth sporting event, you've probably witnessed aggressive adults screaming obscenities from the sidelines at referees, coaches, other parents, or even players. Their children might be embarrassed by their parents' behavior—or they might be learning how much they can get away with.

Unfortunately, a bullying parent is often very difficult to engage in preventing their child's own bullying behavior. Such parents are often defensive about their children's behavior to the extent it reflects upon their own or, alternately, they are dismissive of its seriousness. If a child has been picking up his bullying behaviors from his parents, the parents may not see anything wrong with it or feel proud to have raised a "tough" kid. Sometimes, bullying is a reflection of deeply entrenched family dynamics that will take much more than a meeting in an administrator or guidance counselor's office to unravel.

## When Bullying Gets You What You Want

As infants learn how to navigate the world, they also discover that they have strong feelings of their own. A natural part of our earliest human development is learning how to get what we need and want from our parents and others.

It's natural for babies and children to test their parents, their friends, and themselves. How else could they develop a sense of their own abilities and an understanding of the world around them? However, it's equally important that they learn boundaries, limitations, and expectations. Learning what's acceptable and expected provides children with a sense of security. Children who are given too much power and control in the family or at school may become anxious and angry. Parents and teachers are supposed to be in charge, and children know it—even as they're demanding their way.

Especially for children who have difficulty accepting rules and limitations and complying with authority, inconsistent or overly permissive parenting, as well as poor control in the classroom, will nurture and enable bullying behaviors.

> **parent pointer**
>
> Early experiences with other children provide great opportunities for a child to learn about himself and explore the limits of his emerging power. A child who takes a toy away from another child and hits him with it and suffers no repercussions has just learned that violence and aggression are great ways to get what you want. However, a child who isn't permitted to take a toy from someone else will learn communication skills and negotiation skills, and perhaps even make a friend.

When children are older, well-meaning parents can be taken in by a bullying child's evasion of accountability for his actions. Why wouldn't they want to believe the best of their child? However inadvertently, these parents will continue to reinforce their child's unacceptable behavior. Children are very unlikely to change either their attitude or their behavior as long as adults continue to reinforce it.

## When Bullying Is Okay

There's another reason bullying may be encouraged: adults themselves are often participants in a community's popularity contest, in which the behaviors among children can eerily mirror their parents' actions. Our standing in our community—the jobs we have, our economic status, where we worship, who our kids are friends with, which child was the lead in the school play—all affect our dynamics with other adults.

Parents who are very powerful in the community and use that power abusively often encourage their children to do the same. After all, it would reflect badly on such parents to have a "weak" child. They may not care if their child is bullying the son of another adult they don't like or who has less status than they do.

Parents who are insecure about their own accomplishments may push their children very hard to be the toughest, the most beautiful, the most popular, or the best. Often, these children are praised for being aggressive, dominant, or intimidating—or alternately may feel a lot of pressure to climb the social ladder. Kids who don't have the magic potion that leads to popularity may feel that bullying is the best way to gain status.

<table>
<tr><td>community watch</td><td>We know a family whose son had been brutally bullied by other children at his elite private school. His parents were unable to get the school to provide consequences for the bullies because the administrators were afraid that if they did so, they'd be sued. The children of these very powerful adults had been provided with their attorney's business cards, to give to any school official attempting to discipline them. In this case, the bullies acted with impunity because their parents encouraged such behavior and wouldn't accept the school's consequences.</td></tr>
</table>

# Underdeveloped Coping Skills

Every child's life involves people and situations that can lead to feelings of stress, frustration, or uncertainty. When threatened, we're biologically programmed to respond in one of three ways:

- Physically confront the situation

- Escape or avoid the situation

- Shut down or appear to freeze and become unable to respond

Children are constantly learning how to cope effectively with everyday stresses before they reach the fight-or-flight response, or get to the point where they can no longer deal with the stress of the situations they're confronted with.

The following sections consider some examples of difficulties children may encounter in coping with everyday situations.

## Low Tolerance for Frustration

Children who bully tend to have difficulty tolerating frustration. They're easily irritated and can find it difficult to work on challenging tasks, or feel their self-esteem is threatened when they can't quickly accomplish it. Feelings of frustration create stress. While it's natural to seek relief from uncomfortable feelings and situations, children who struggle with frustration may give up or act out impulsively toward themselves or others, or even damage property when agitated.

As young people, such behavior might involve disrupting a class. However, as kids get older, the stakes get higher. If they're frustrated by failing a driver's test or not having enough money from their after-school job to buy an iPhone, instead of retaking the driver's test or starting a savings program, they might steal money from a friend and bully someone into giving them rides.

## When Aggression Is Hard-Wired

Some degree of aggression is considered necessary to be able to compete for limited resources and to survive in nature. However, in organized societies it's important to learn how to cooperate with others and manage emotions and any aggressive impulses or behaviors.

Recent research has linked genetics and brain chemistry with *empathy,* aggression, and risk-taking behavior. Understanding a child's temperament can be extremely helpful to parents and educators when dealing with bullying behavior.

**Empathy** is the ability to understand how another might feel given a set of circumstances.

Definition

Scientists discovered a gene, which they dubbed the "warrior gene," that is believed to be associated with people who display higher levels of aggressive or impulsive behavior when provoked, and who also are more likely to engage in risk-taking behavior than those who don't possess this gene.

Scientists have also discovered the existence of "mirror neurons," which are believed to have a role in the ability to recognize and interpret the emotions and intentions of others. Scientists are studying this select set of brain cells, which appear to give clues as to how we communicate with each other non-verbally. There may be some correlation between a well-functioning mirror neuron system and healthy social interactions and a dysfunctional mirror neuron system and impaired social relationships. As we know, kids who exhibit bullying behaviors frequently misinterpret social cues, and children with social communication deficits are frequently the targets of aggression, so it will be interesting to learn more about the potential link between mirror neurons and social relationships, as brain-based research continues.

Studies have also found that some kids who participate in bullying behaviors have ADHD; this is especially true if the children also have trouble following rules, are impulsive, get frustrated easily, have dominant personalities, and find it difficult to build social relationships. Kids with ADHD may also be bullied and isolated by their peers for being different, so their bullying behaviors may be retaliatory.

Throughout this book we discuss multiple strategies to help kids increase their self-awareness, self-confidence, and self-control; improve their social relationships; reduce impulsivity and frustration; and learn to solve their problems more effectively.

## When Behaviors Don't Grow Up, but People Do

Bullying typically decreases in high school and beyond, but that isn't always the case. Studies show that one in every five boys who was a bully at the age of 14 continued to be a bully at age 32. A 2010 survey conducted by the Workplace Bullying Institute revealed that 35 percent of the U.S. workforce has been bullied at work. Bullies in the workplace can resemble schoolyard bullies in the following ways:

- They're verbally abusive

- They use threatening behavior

- They make it impossible for their peers to succeed through exclusion or sabotage, or by creating an environment of intimidation

The targets of workplace bullying may lose their jobs or end up on disability as a result of stress-related illnesses. Despite the real-world consequences of these behaviors, it's often difficult to get protection—especially when the boss is the bully.

Without understanding and intervention, young people who continue to use bullying behaviors as adults will continue to experience unhealthy and unsatisfying relationships throughout their lives. And they'll continue to make the lives of many people around them miserable, too.

## Essential Takeaways

- Bullying behaviors are often used to navigate social hierarchies: those who have a lower status may use bullying to gain a higher position or avoid being the targets themselves; those who have a high status bully to increase or maintain their popularity.
- Bullying behaviors can be inadvertently or intentionally learned, enabled, or encouraged by parents and the community.
- Often, kids use bullying because they haven't developed other coping skills for life challenges and frustration.
- Some kids are predisposed to aggression, frustration, impulsivity, and misperceptions of social interactions.
- Persistent bullying behaviors can lead to many problems in adulthood.

# chapter 4

# Understanding Targets

Types of kids who target others

Risk factors for becoming a target

Why targets don't tell

How targets deal with their stress, pain, and frustration

The lingering impact of bullying

Just as bullying exists on a continuum from mild to severe, the targets of aggression, social rejection, and bullying suffer a wide range of peer abuse. Kids may experience bullying for varying lengths of time, by any number of individuals, and to varying degrees of severity.

Targets can range from children who receive dirty looks to those who are subjected to unwelcome sexual jokes or racial or homophobic slurs to the kids who are assaulted with brutal acts of physical aggression and cruel social rejection by their peer group. No matter where targets fall on the continuum of bullying, the experience can leave lasting scars and, in some instances, result in devastating and irreversible consequences.

Kids may be targeted for many different reasons, at many different times, as social dynamics evolve, as they mature, or as the circumstances of their lives change. Some kids become targets simply because they're viewed as loners, unpopular, or odd. Many kids are targeted for their weight or physical appearance. Anyone who has ever been the "new kid" knows that simply moving to a new school can make a child a prime target. Kids on the *autism spectrum* tend to be targets far more often than their peers who aren't, and the same goes for LGBT youth or kids who are merely perceived to be gay. Some may be targeted because of their socioeconomic background or because their older sibling was a perennial target. Even popular kids can become targets, sometimes because others are jealous of them.

**Autism spectrum disorders** (ASD) are a group of developmental disorders that are believed to be linked to brain development. They are evidenced by impaired verbal and nonverbal communication deficits as well as impaired social interactions and a set of repetitive, restricted behaviors, interests, and activities. ASD includes Autistic Disorder, Asperger's Syndrome, Pervasive Developmental Disorder (PDD), Rett's Disorder, and Childhood Integrative Disorder.

In any given year approximately 13 million American children are targeted by bullies. Some estimates suggest that somewhere between half to 80 percent of all children feel they have been bullied at some point during their childhood.

## Who Are the Targets?

When we think about young people who are the targets of bullying, we generally picture those who have trouble fitting in with their peers, who get teased and pushed around, and are chosen last for team play. However, there are many different kinds of targets.

Targets aren't just the kids who are ostracized by their classmates, excluded from the lunch table, or overlooked when it comes to extending invitations to social events and parties. Anyone can be a potential target of bullying and aggressive behavior. Just about all of us have been on the receiving end of verbal, physical, or relational abuse at some point. In fact, it isn't uncommon to learn that a seemingly well-adjusted and successful student, who may even be in a position of power, is being dominated and overpowered by another, and that it has gone undetected by the majority of people with whom the target interacts.

The experience of having been bullied can have a lasting impact on a child or adolescent. Fortunately, for most kids these occurrences are brief, isolated, and mild. For others, though, the cruel taunting, humiliation, and assaults can be severe and may even go on for years. These kids are likely to suffer life-altering consequences. Their pervasive suffering outweighs any short-term pleasure they may experience. They feel powerless and come to believe that they have little control over what happens to them. The way they speak to themselves, referred to as *self-talk,* is often harsh, negative, and punishing.

Some targets of bullying begin to view themselves as stupid, ugly, worthless, and ineffective. Sometimes they think that they deserve the maltreatment and question their right to live. This negative self-perception leads to an inability to see themselves accurately. Targeted and socially rejected kids often fail to recognize their many strengths, positive attributes, and unique abilities.

These distortions in thinking can lead to a vicious circle for the target that can make the cycle of bullying hard to break. Negative self-image and a sense of powerlessness can often lead to depression. Studies have found that kids who are depressed are more likely to be targeted. Depression can also prevent kids from seeking help from adults, or taking proactive steps to establish new patterns of thinking, feeling, and acting. (We talk more about assertion and problem-solving in Chapter 6 and provide additional strategies for helping targets in Chapter 12.)

Experts on bullying have identified three categories of kids who find themselves on the receiving end of bullying much of the time: passive targets, provocative targets, and those referred to as being indirectly or vicariously affected. The following sections take a closer look at these types of targets.

## Passive Targets

Kids who are passive targets are regarded as being easy marks because they won't take action on their own behalf. Passive targets tend to have the following characteristics.

- They lack self-confidence and haven't developed the necessary skills to assert themselves in social situations

- They come across as being overly submissive and insecure, giving in quickly, crying, or not saying a word, rather than putting up reasonable resistance

- They display weak body language, such as failure to make appropriate eye contact, slouching, or using an inappropriate tone or voice or volume when speaking

- They lack the ability to resolve problems or to settle differences of opinion with their peers

Physical weakness is also a common trait for passive targets, particularly for boys. Boys who are physically underdeveloped compared to their peers or are otherwise unable to assert themselves physically are prone to bullying and targeting.

Kids who are passive targets often lack social interaction skills; they tend to have few friends and are regarded as having low status by their peers. Because they lack status, many other kids will resist befriending them for fear of becoming targets themselves or for fear of sliding down the social status ladder themselves. It's not uncommon to find that other kids are friendly with a targeted child outside of school but are too fearful to play or sit with them when peers are around. This is particularly painful and confusing to the child who is socially rejected.

## Provocative Targets

Provocative targets tend to overreact in social situations and don't know how to manage their emotions or behavior appropriately. They are seen as being annoying and may bother or even bully other kids. They provoke other kids and don't know when to stop arguing and walk away. They may actually engage bullies, drawing negative attention to themselves, thereby increasing their own vulnerability to the bullies' aggression.

## Indirect Targets

Indirect targets are bystanders to bullying abuse. These individuals witness bullies targeting other children, and they suffer because of it. They tend to be sensitive and empathic individuals but have difficulty taking action and feel bad about their inability to step up to defend targets or to make the bullying stop.

It's frightening for kids to be in the presence of violence and intimidation, knowing that it could happen to anyone next. We talk more about bystanders in Chapter 5 and about helping bystanders become upstanders in Chapter 14.

# How Kids Signal Their Distress

Some kids come home and tell Mom or Dad everything—the good things as well as the bad—that happened at school that day. More typically, though, and especially as they get older, kids keep what happened at school to themselves. Just as kids probably aren't going to tell you who they have a crush on at school, they aren't going to tell you that they are being bullied during gym. As a matter of fact, the older children get, the less they're usually willing to share with adults.

But even though kids might not tell you about a bullying problem directly, most young people send out distress signals, even if they aren't aware of doing so. Here are some of the signs to watch for that may indicate your child is experiencing social rejection, aggression, or bullying:

- Physical complaints, including stomachaches, headaches, or difficulty concentrating
- Changes in sleep patterns, appetite, or hygiene
- Lost or damaged clothing or property; bruises or scratches
- Lost enthusiasm for things the child usually enjoys; avoiding participating in activities or resisting attending events
- Changes in, or lack of, friends (early social isolation is a critical indicator of current and future difficulties)

- Decline in grades and classroom participation; avoiding going to school or making frequent visits to the school nurse

- Verbal or written expressions (including journal entries, poems, song lyrics, and drawings) indicating anger, sadness, loneliness, or other distress

- Bringing a weapon to school, either for protection or retaliation

**parent pointer** Teachers, caretakers, relatives, camp counselors, friends, and others who spend time with your child can be instrumental in identifying signs and symptoms that your child may be a target. Don't dismiss what they're trying to tell you, even if it's painful to hear.

# Nature vs. Nurture

Some children are born with characteristics that make them more vulnerable to becoming targets. A child's environment plays a big role, too. In this section, we explore both sides of the age-old nature vs. nurture debate.

## The Nature Part of the Emotional Equation

A baby's temperament can be evidenced as early as 2 months old. Research indicates that temperamental characteristics (such as general disposition, adaptability to change and novelty, physical regularity, and activity level) remain relatively stable throughout one's life. Some of these characteristics, as well as genetic, medical, or other conditions (such as ASD, cognitive impairment, sensory integration disorder, or any host of physical or neurological anomalies) can present challenges to children as they grow up, especially if their parents and caring adults don't recognize or understand their individual needs, personalities, or differences. Kids don't always have a lot of patience with other children who look or act differently, either. Numerous individual inclinations may make one naturally vulnerable to social challenges or targeting.

For example, children who are born with a high activity level, who are easily distracted, or who tend to be emotionally intense can be perceived negatively by both adults and peers alike, and thus be treated poorly. Similarly, kids who are very sensitive to stimulation such as bright lights, loud noises, and different textures may become overwhelmed or reactive in unfamiliar situations, like a loud, stimulating classroom or on the soccer field, where children are in close proximity. These sensitivities can cause them to overreact or to react differently than expected, leaving them misunderstood and vulnerable to maltreatment. Kids with any kind of disability or physical differences are also at risk for targeting and mistreatment. Kids who are LGBT, or perceived to be LGBT, are also frequently targeted.

## The Nurture Part of the Emotional Equation

It goes without saying that all parents want to raise happy, healthy, and successful children. It's at home where a child first begins to learn about herself. As she moves farther out in the world, to school and in the company of peers, her environment will begin to have a greater impact on her sense of self and the meaning of her life experiences. A child whose family is supportive, encouraging, and accepting of her unique personality, development, and needs, and who offer her healthy opportunities for socialization, is likely to be less vulnerable to having difficulties with peers.

But it doesn't always work out that way. Even the most well-intended parents can inadvertently contribute to the likelihood that their child will experience problematic relationships with other kids her age.

The following parental characteristics or behaviors can be contributing factors in their child's bullying:

**Overprotective parents.** A child whose parents are overprotective may interfere with her ability to experience challenges and face and conquer her fears. Parents who do everything for their child—make her bed, carry her backpack, don't require her to help out at home, often because it's easier and more efficient for them to do it themselves—unknowingly keep her from becoming independent and compromise her self-confidence. The child who is denied opportunities to explore and experiment with her peers doesn't learn to test her own limits and may become fearful and unsure of herself. A child who isn't challenged doesn't gain the assurance of knowing her own agency. Fear, insecurity, and lack of self-confidence make children highly vulnerable to social problems.

**Parents who have low self-confidence.** Parents who lack self-confidence, are anxious, or are easily dominated by others (including a spouse or an aggressive child at home) may unwittingly model those tendencies, which can make a child either uncomfortable and insecure, or dominant, demanding, and entitled.

**Aggressive parents.** Parents who are aggressive, argumentative, short-tempered, domineering, or critical may not realize they're bullying their own children. Some children in these kinds of families do just fine. But, as we saw in Chapter 3, some children harness their anger and implement the intimidation tactics employed by their parents to bully their peers or even adults. Others, though, have already begun to internalize feelings of powerlessness, shame, and unworthiness. These children are vulnerable to victimization and isolation.

**Parents outside the mainstream**. A child whose family's culture or religious values aren't in alignment with the families of the dominant peer culture in which the child lives are likely to encounter social challenges, particularly in elementary and middle school. (High school students often become more comfortable challenging social norms and seeking their own identities.) For example, a child who isn't permitted to have play dates or attend birthday parties, who enjoys different kinds of foods, or who dresses differently can be subjected to targeting. This child needs to learn early on how to embrace and celebrate the values and traditions of her family and also negotiate her social peer community successfully. In communities where diversity is welcomed and commonplace, different family situations are less challenging for kids.

**parent pointer**

Some parents (regardless of cultural background, values, and religious differences) are not attuned to the mores of their child's school, such as the ways most kids in school dress, the shows they watch, and the activities they enjoy. Learning how the children in your child's school dress, and being current with grade-level interests, can help reduce incidents of targeting and social rejection. When making choices with your child that may reflect different values than the dominant peer culture, help your child develop strategies to navigate possible reactions, and provide them with a community and places they know they are safe and supported.

# When a Child Is "Different"

As goes the old expression, "birds of a feather flock together." Kids who are perceived as being different by their peers are at risk for being challenged, rejected, and targeted.

Here are some differences kids tease each other about:

**Physical characteristics.** The most obvious and striking differences include height and weight, skin color, perceived degree of attractiveness, physical strength (especially for boys), and adolescent development (for both boys and girls).

**Social status.** As kids enter adolescence and begin the process of separating from their parents in the middle school years, the importance of peer relationships takes center stage. The need for social status (a student's rank, or social standing, among her peer group) peaks in importance in middle school. Everyone is looking for a place to belong, and many will do almost anything to fit in with the mainstream and to avoid targeting and rejection by peers. One's social status can be negatively impacted by any perceived differences in looks, intelligence, family background, race and ethnicity, gender identity, clothing, personality, friends, interests, level of wealth/privilege, or family standing within the community.

**MISC.**

**Bullying Has No Boundaries**

Keep in mind that although certain factors might make a child more vulnerable to bullying, victimization knows no boundaries and has no limitations.

**Social skills.** Kids with poor communication skills or who aren't social savvy are particularly vulnerable to bullying.

**Disabilities—physical, social, emotional, or behavioral.** If a child lacks social skills and has a disability, she's more susceptible to bullying. However, social skills trump learning differences when it comes to being teased or targeted by bullies. If a child has good social skills, her learning disadvantage often doesn't matter to other kids.

**Difficulties with nonverbal communication.** Because we take in so much information visually, kids who are unable to understand the subtle nonverbal cues of social communication struggle with understanding others. If they don't understand the meaning of facial expressions or body language, it's much more difficult for them to understand what others are feeling or thinking. Similarly, children with poor nonverbal communication skills may not be able to demonstrate the appropriate facial expression or body language that relates to their own thoughts, intentions, or feelings. Not only do they misinterpret signals from other children, they send out signals of their own that their peers perceive as confusing or weird. Children with nonverbal and social communication difficulties are particularly vulnerable to targeting and teasing. We talk more about body language and good verbal communication in Chapter 6.

Although certain factors can, theoretically, make kids vulnerable to bullying, not all kids who are different end up becoming targets. Some quirky kids who one would expect to have a high risk of being bullied are actually embraced and protected by their peers. Schools can help end the discrimination and rejection of children with differences by promoting inclusion opportunities for special needs children in the classroom.

Bullying isn't always about being different; it's about an abuse of power, dominance, aggression, cruelty, and injustice.

Some bullies try to pick on anybody; they're equal opportunity abusers who routinely test the waters to case out their next target. And it's not uncommon for bullies to target more than one person at a time.

## Why Targets Don't Tell

Children who are targeted usually try to find ways to solve the problem on their own. Even kids who have pretty good relationships with their parents and teachers may not tell them that they're being bullied.

Fear is probably the biggest reason why kids don't tell adults about being bullied. Many kids are afraid that telling will just make things worse. It's important to realize just how terrified of the bully they are. Even if it seems to you that the bully isn't bigger, stronger, more intelligent, or more popular than your child, the bully has the power to dominate, intimidate, humiliate, and socially weaken her.

Kids may also be afraid that their parents or teachers won't believe them or that their parents will tell them to hit back when they don't feel capable of doing it. Kids usually feel ashamed and embarrassed because they're unable to stand up to the bully and to make it stop. They don't want to disappoint their parents or cause them stress.

**parent pointer** Bullied kids frequently doubt that they will be protected or helped by adults. Targets often feel helpless, hopeless, confused, frustrated, and angry. Talking about the situation with a parent or other adult can make a target feel even worse, especially if they don't feel understood, or when they feel like they are being held responsible for something they can't control.

Many kids don't believe the adults in their lives will be able to stop the bullying. Sometimes they already know who the parents of the bully are and that they'll stick up for their kid, no matter what. Unfortunately, they're often right. Talking to parents who deny their child would do anything wrong or who actually support their child's aggression can make matters worse.

Kids also know that it's not cool to be a tattletale. Many middle school kids and teens are more likely these days to admit they're involved in "drama" than to say they're being bullied. It helps them to socially and psychologically minimize what's happening to them. Some kids in this age group associate bullying with being a "young" children's problem and feel embarrassed to be involved in such a juvenile dilemma. By minimizing bullying as being "drama" they feel more empowered in their attempt to deny it. However, when you talk about it and break it down to the behaviors involved, drama often amounts to bullying.

Kids have learned that, while many well-meaning adults are willing to intervene on their behalf, their efforts are often ineffective. The bully may say, "I was just playing," or "It's okay, we're friends," and in some instances that's pretty much the end of it because the target is likely to be too frightened to say anything to the contrary in front of the aggressor. Or a teacher may speak with the aggressive student about her behavior and mistakenly believe that their conversation has resolved the problem. Additionally, aggressive kids can be exceptionally good at hiding their behavior from adults, making teasing out the truth extremely difficult. Some schools use conflict resolution techniques to resolve problems between aggressive and targeted kids; however, such strategies are often ineffective and can be problematic; we talk more about conflict resolution in Chapter 6.

parent pointer

If you've ever had difficulty trying to get to the bottom of your own children's disagreements at home, you can certainly understand how difficult it can be for a school counselor or administrator to try to unravel the facts and figure out what may really be going on between kids at school.

## Where Does the Anger, Hurt, and Pain Go?

How do kids deal with the constant and overwhelming feelings of fear, hurt, anger, betrayal, anxiety, frustration, disappointment, shame, and loneliness of being targeted by aggressive and abusive bullies—and still manage to study for a biology exam?

A child who is bullied feels isolated and alone. She has been rejected by her peer group, which we know is the ultimate punishment any human being can inflict upon another. Not only does she have to endure this rejection, aggression, and isolation, but she must do so publicly. This makes her situation even more humiliating and intolerable.

All thoughts and feelings need a place to go; they don't just disappear by themselves. People of all ages employ a variety of conscious and unconscious psychological mechanisms in an attempt to make sense of and to deal with problems, feelings, and emotions. A victim of targeting or bullying might try to reconcile her feelings in the following ways:

**Deny, avoid, or minimize**. When something is too painful to think about, it's not uncommon to attempt to deny or avoid acknowledging or dealing with it. For example, minimizing what's happening, labeling it as "drama" instead of bullying, and focusing on other distractions and activities—such as hobbies, school work, or exercise—can help minimize and diminish negative feelings or allow one to avoid addressing and dealing with scary situations.

**Displacement.** Kids may act out their feelings of anger or frustration on others in an attempt to feel empowered or unleash their negative feelings. When an even-tempered and good-natured child is bullied, she may become irritable, moody, and aggressive at home. She may begin to transfer the hurt, rejection, and aggression she is receiving at school or online to friends or family members without realizing it.

**Cutting.** Some young people attempt to deal with stress and relieve their feelings of frustration, anger, and depression by cutting themselves. Such behavior should be taken very seriously and addressed immediately. Cutting oneself is a dysfunctional and self-destructive behavior and, while it may provide some temporary relief for extreme emotional pain, it is an ineffective and potentially increasingly dangerous and dysfunctional pattern of dealing with serious issues of anger, depression, anxiety, and self-loathing. Cutting in no way addresses or solves the real problems at hand.

**Suicide.** For a young person who is in an extreme amount of emotional pain, suicide might seem like a way to resolve the problem of unbearable depression, bullying, and victimization. Most victims of bullying and abuse don't want to end their lives; they just want the pain to stop. Young people who attempt suicide have been unable to find another way out.

community watch

Suicide is reported as being the third-leading cause of death among children and adolescents. Young people who have experienced bullying are increasingly attempting, and successfully committing, suicide. Children who are as young as 9 years old and who have been bullied have committed suicide.

**Retaliation and Revenge:** While the vast majority of victims of bullying and social rejection don't become bullies themselves, some do. Additionally, there is a high correlation between school shootings and students who were bullied. In April 1999, Eric Harris and Dylan Klebold, two high school students who had reportedly been bullied for years, committed suicide after killing 13 people and injuring over 20 students and faculty members at Columbine High School. In April 2007, Virginia Polytechnic Institute student Seung-Hui Cho, who was rumored to have been bullied in high school, shot and killed 32 people and wounded 15 others before killing himself.

Fortunately, the majority of kids who have experienced targeting don't act out aggressively toward others. Most kids take conscious and deliberate steps to solve their problems peacefully. Many seek to become more empowered and increase self-confidence and are open to employing multiple positive strategies, such as joining peer support groups, speaking with school counselors and specialists, seeking to explore their personal strengths, increasing self-awareness, developing skills of assertion, and increasing self-confidence. We explore ways kids can work on these skills in later chapters.

# When Targeted Kids Grow Up

Researchers have been looking into what happens to adults who were bullied as children. The results, as might be expected, are mixed.

Some targets of aggression and bullying struggle to get past it, though their lives are forever changed. They may struggle with depression, anxiety, and low self-esteem, and harbor revenge fantasies. Some get involved with crime, drugs, or alcohol to numb the pain, anger, and discomfort they continue to feel. Some act out in other ways. There is some correlation between adults who are bullied at work and those who were bullied as kids.

The best predictors of how a child who was bullied will fare as an adult have to do with the severity and the duration of the experience, how she comes to understand what happened to her, the meaning she attributes to the bullying, and her individual ability to bounce back from adversity.

## Essential Takeaways:

- Anyone can be a target of bullying behavior, although children who lack self-confidence and social skills, including difficulties with nonverbal communication, are particularly vulnerable.
- Adults can unknowingly increase a child's vulnerabilities to being bullied and socially rejected.
- Being targeted can elicit feelings of shame, anxiety, and fear; these kids may refer to their experience as "drama" instead of victimization, bullying, or targeting.

- Kids who experience targeting may fear that adults cannot help them or that they will make matters even worse.

- The meaning that someone makes of the experience of being targeted is impacted by the severity and duration of the experience, and impacts future success and life satisfaction.

# chapter 5

# Understanding Bystanders

Bystanders as witnesses to bullying

Why bystanders don't get involved

The role of adults as bystanders

How bystanders passively encourage bullying

You can probably think of a time when you've witnessed someone being bullied and have stood there not knowing what to do. Whether it was classmates teasing a friend, a supervisor putting down a colleague, or a customer harassing a storekeeper, you probably wondered, "Should I say something? Should I intervene? What should I do?" Even as adults we may think, "Everyone will think I'm a downer," or, "Surely it's none of my business," or, "If nobody likes the new secretary, *I'm* not putting my neck out to stand up for her."

Often, people who bully aren't seeking power over just one or two individuals, but over an entire group. Their behaviors also often feed off a crowd's response, or lack thereof. Because of this dynamic, most bullying takes place in the presence of the third critical element of what we refer to as the bullying triangle: the bystander.

Bystanders are a vital component of the bullying equation. For a target, the presence of bystanders can make it seem like everyone has turned against them. For a bully, the bystanders' silence implicitly supports his abuse. Fortunately, there are far more bystanders out there than either targets or kids who bully combined, and they have the opportunity to confront and challenge the bully's violence and abuse.

In this chapter, we take a look at who bystanders are, what keeps them from getting involved, and how they may unwittingly contribute to bullying behaviors.

# Who Are Bystanders?

Everybody has been a bystander at one time or another. A bystander is someone who witnesses bullying and victimization at school, online, in the community, or even at home. Bystanders may react to the bullying in a variety of ways, but unless they stand up and intervene, becoming *upstanders,* they not only enable, but often exacerbate, the bullying.

**Upstanders** are bystanders who intervene in a bullying situation. They might do so either directly, by standing up and saying or doing something to defuse the situation, or indirectly by getting help, supporting the target, or reporting it to an adult or person in a position of authority.

Like bullies and targets, bystanders exist on a continuum, which we detail in the following sections.

## The Silent Majority

Many bystanders remain silent when they witness bullying and don't intervene. They try to quickly slip by when they see a kid thrown into a locker or salt poured on a classmate's lunch. Or they may be part of a chat room, a multiuser video game, or a social networking group where bullying is taking place. Although they don't participate, they know it's going on and look the other way.

Often these bystanders avoid becoming involved because they fear becoming the next target. They avoid the places they know bullying occurs: they sit at the front of the school bus, stay away from the crowds of kids hanging out after school, and avoid joining social networking groups created to make fun of someone. Although they may empathize with the target, they remain silent out of fear of retaliation or embarrassment if they speak up, or they may simply feel they don't have the power or social status to challenge and change what they're witnessing.

Other silent bystanders may not fear becoming the bullies' target as much as they simply don't know what to do or don't want the distraction. Often kids who are well liked and successful don't intervene because they don't want to get involved in what they consider to be "drama." These kids may throw themselves into being successful students or great athletes or actors in the school play, and don't want to attract trouble. They may not feel equipped with the tools to help a target.

## Bystanders Who Enjoy the Show

Some bystanders are active supporters who appear to be amused by the bullying. These are the types of kids who might film a target being abused and humiliated and post it on YouTube. Since kids who bully are often seeking attention and prestige, such bystanders reinforce and reward bullying behaviors.

Although some of these bystanders may be uncomfortable with what they see a bully doing, by joking, spreading rumors, or laughing when they see a target react, they minimize and normalize the behaviors taking place. These responses often mask nervousness and uneasiness, and might be a way some bystanders cope with these feelings. However, by joking and making fun of abuse, they're rewarding the behavior and compounding the target's distress.

**parent pointer**

Teach your children that if they are witness to a bullying situation and laugh along with the crowd or add a hurtful comment, they are contributing to the problem. Even something that might seem like a minor taunt or act of bullying can have a snowball effect for the target when it's coming from multiple people throughout their day. You never know another person's breaking point, or all the other things someone might be going through. Help your children recognize the consequences of their actions and to not automatically join in just because everyone else is.

## Sidekicks and Wannabes

The most harmful bystanders are those who egg on a bully's behaviors and join in once he's gotten it started. These aren't high-status kids, and they align themselves with kids who bully as a way of increasing their own status. They aren't the leaders, but they follow pretty close behind and are quick to participate. Perhaps they'll throw in a shove or a kick themselves. Maybe they'll add to a chain of abusive comments on Facebook or gather a crowd to watch the target get beaten up after school.

These kids not only encourage the bully to act with impunity, escalate the bullying, and create a peer culture that rewards abusive behavior, but they also greatly aggregate the mental and physical scars for the target.

**MISC.**

**Team Bullying**

Bullying in the context of athletic teams can be especially brutal. Bystanders may worry that their coaches won't support them or, worse, will accuse an upstander of lacking team spirit or being in some way weak. Often coaches allow bullying by successful players against more vulnerable or younger ones as punishment for mistakes on the field, or out of the belief that it will make them stronger. Coaches are some of the most important role models in students' lives. They need to contribute to a positive school climate and teach kids that the truly powerful thing to do is to stand up to injustices.

# Why They Don't Get Involved

When kids and adults feel supported in standing up to bullies, they are more likely to do so. In environments where bullying is considered an unacceptable behavior, you'll find many bystanders transformed into upstanders. However, these environments aren't always so easy to find. The following factors may prevent people from intervening in bullying:

- They just don't know what to do or say, especially if they don't feel powerful or self-confident.

- They may be afraid the bully will turn on them and they'll become the next target.

- They may have been told to "mind your own business" in the past or fear getting a reputation as a tattletale.

- They may be afraid they'll make things even worse for the target.

- They may think the target deserves it, or they don't want to be associated with unpopular kids or kids who are weak and perceived as losers.

- They may not say anything if the peer culture says standing up is "uncool."

- They may believe the bullying behaviors will be supported by parents/adults and will continue regardless of what they do.

- They're stimulated or entertained by violence.

- They may feel that by not saying or doing anything about it, they're not involved and therefore are not doing harm.

The power dynamics around bullies, targets, and bystanders are deeply entrenched in a community's culture. Relationships among the kids often reflect the way the adults relate to one another. You can often get a pretty good sense of the culture of a school, household, or workplace from the feeling you get the moment you walk in the door. In an environment where the leaders are caring and supportive, that attitude is reflected in the relationship throughout the group. However, the opposite is also true. Kids pick up on tensions among parents or faculty members. In some environments, there are adults everyone fears, just as there are children no one wants to challenge.

## The Bystander Effect

You may have heard of Kitty Genovese, who was attacked outside her New York City apartment building in 1964. Although dozens of people supposedly heard her cries for help, nobody came to her aid, and only one person called the police. Perhaps everyone else assumed, in a busy city like New York, somebody else would intervene.

Although this story has come to be regarded more as parable than fact, researchers John Darley and Bibb Latane set out to test the hypothesis that the more bystanders there are to an emergency, the less likely, or the more slowly, any one bystander will intervene. They set up an experiment in which the subjects would believe they were witnessing an emergency and timed how long it took for them to respond, if they responded at all, based on how many others were also present. As expected, the more bystanders to the emergency (a person having a staged seizure), the longer it took for any one person to respond.

When the researchers asked those who failed to react why they were inactive, many admitted that they didn't know what to do. They reported feeling guilt and shame for not helping, but they also didn't want to embarrass themselves by blowing things out of proportion.

We need to recognize that bystanders to bullying situations experience the same emotions; they also are ashamed of standing by, but they don't know what to do and fear embarrassing themselves if they do something. If we can help kids understand the situational forces that prevent them from stepping up, we can help them overcome them.

## Diffusion of Responsibility

If you've ever seen someone collapse on the sidewalk, the first thing you'll often hear from the crowd is, "Is anyone here a doctor?"

It's natural when we witness trauma to want an "expert" to step in and relieve us of the responsibility we feel to help, especially if we don't know what to do. Often kids won't intervene in bullying because they don't feel anyone will join them, they don't know what to say, they're afraid of being embarrassed, and they don't feel they'll get support from adults. Or they may feel the entire community is powerless to change the situation, so they feel hopeless or even inured to the bullying.

The less kids are empowered to change a situation, especially ones they know are wrong, the more inclined they may be to shut down, turning off their empathy response. In schools where bystanders have stopped feeling empathy as a result of their own sense of helplessness, bullying behaviors will be normalized and targets will be ostracized and socially marginalized.

# Adults Are Bystanders, Too

Adults are often bystanders, too. They know who is perpetrating bullying behaviors, just as they recognize the targets: the kids nobody ever sits with, talks to, or invites to birthday parties. Teachers, principals, school bus drivers, and parents can all be bystanders. As a matter of fact, anyone who participates in the complex relationships in the community—and that's all of us—can be bystanders.

Parents often witness bullying when they pick their kids up from school, have a bunch of kids in their home, or see them hanging out at sports practice or at the mall. They have complex reasons for failing to intervene. For instance, they may be afraid of being excluded from their own social group if they step in, and taking action can be especially hard when a friend's child is doing the bullying. Like their children, parents may also fear being seen as overreactive or as tattletales. Aggressive people are difficult to challenge no matter how old we are. Many people would rather not take the risk.

Many people liken the growing awareness of and changing attitudes toward bullying to the raising of people's consciousness and shifts in attitudes toward child abuse, with the passage of the Child Abuse Prevention and Treatment Act (CAPTA) in 1974. Until that time, many things we'd today consider abuse were private family affairs. By bringing child abuse into the light, CAPTA challenged deeply ingrained behaviors and provided an opportunity to change our values. This legislation has expanded our collective responsibility to protect children from abuse, mandating that any professional who works with children and suspects that a child is being abused is legally required to step in and report it.

Teachers, bus drivers, lunch aides, and even principals who witness bullying also fail to intervene. Just like kids, these adults often don't know what to do or don't have the training or tools to feel confident stepping in. If they grew up in a family or community that had different attitudes about bullying, or just didn't recognize it, they might not be sure what kinds of behaviors constitute bullying, or may be inclined to minimize the behaviors they see taking place.

Many educators are overwhelmed with their work and might not believe they can effectively address the situation or that it's even their responsibility.

This is especially true for bus drivers, who have to keep an eye on the road, make sure they get in all their stops, and get the kids to their destination on time. Some teachers, bus drivers, or lunch aides with lesser authority may not feel that their administrators will back them up; should they attempt to intervene and fail, it may embarrass them and further undermine their authority. In addition, many high-status bullying kids are popular with teachers and administrators, who may be fond of them and align with them.

The community's social hierarchy and dynamics can also affect how bystanders behave. If the parents of the bullying child are very powerful and intimidate the faculty, they may well hesitate to intervene. Or the bullying child may be an important asset to the school, such as an all-star athlete whom no one wants to risk alienating. On the flip side, parents of targets who are not powerful in the community, or who have a "bad" reputation, may have a hard time getting adults to have empathy or act on behalf of their children.

When kids see adults witness bullying and do nothing about it, it normalizes the behavior and tells them that it doesn't need to be taken seriously. Although the attitude toward bullying is changing, until very recently it was accepted as kids being kids, a normal rite of passage. Indeed, in some communities, bullying behavior still isn't treated with the seriousness it requires.

## If You're Not Part of the Solution …

… you're part of the problem. First of all, bullies love the spotlight, and they've found it's a great way to get attention, achieve dominance, and increase prestige. Because bullies often have an *information-processing bias*, they'll perceive inaction from peers as support.

An **information-processing bias** is a phenomenon whereby people have a tendency to interpret social information in accordance with their own feelings and perceptions. Studies show that aggressive children are more likely than their non-aggressive peers to misinterpret the intentions of others as being hostile. This is due to their own faulty thinking and underdeveloped social-emotional, problem-solving, and executive functioning skills. When faced with an unclear social situation that requires problem-solving skills, they often react aggressively.

Provoking a target to react, gathering a crowd to cheer on a beating, or even getting a firm talking-to from the principal can provide a feast of attention to a bully who experiences little anxiety as a result of these actions. As we know, aggressive behavior can be an effective way for a child who seeks to establish or to maintain dominance to satisfy their desire for power and control.

If bystanders are complicit in a bully's behavior, they also risk becoming a target themselves. Researchers have found that those who witness repeated abuse can have psychological and physiological stress levels that, over time, mirror those of the victim's.

Research has also found the following with regard to bystanders:

- They often experience anger, helplessness, and guilt from not knowing what to do or by not taking action.

- They may have nightmares and anxiety about becoming the next target.

- They may become anxious about school and avoid certain activities and places in their town where they fear coming into contact with bullies.

- They may feel powerless in other areas of their lives and struggle with their own self-concept.

Most children are altruistic by nature and have a built-in desire to help others. That fact can present a serious dilemma for the bystander, who wants to avoid the hurtful behavior, but at the same time wants to stay socially connected to his peers. When someone is doing something he really feels badly about, as in the case of being a bystander or witness to something terrible, he needs to find a way to be able to reconcile it emotionally. If he can't stand up to the bully, he may be psychologically inclined to minimize the meaning of what's happening to the target so as not to become distressed or emotionally overwhelmed.

## Essential Takeaways

- Anyone can be a bystander, including kids, parents, teachers, adults, bus drivers, lunch aides, and principals.

- There are more bystanders than bullies and victims combined.

- The presence of bystanders increases the negative impact of the bullying for the target and can empower the bully.

- Bystanders may not intervene because they don't know what to do, fear being targeted themselves, or think bullying behaviors are funny.

- Being a bystander to bullying can lead to increased stress, fear, and feelings of hopelessness.

# Part 2

# Prevention

The good news about bullying is that parents, educators, and everyone who cares about kids have many tools at their disposal to prevent it, whether the aggressive behavior takes place at home, in school, online, or in the wider community.

In this part, we demonstrate how schools can take an active role in reducing the incidence of bullying by creating caring learning cultures where kids feel safe. We discuss the positive benefits of educating children not only in academic areas, but also in essential social and emotional skills and the development of positive character traits. These skills help kids develop into positive, productive, and empathetic members of their communities who get along with and support others. Everyone who cares about children can get involved in preventing acts of aggression and creating a community of happy, healthy, and well-adjusted children and adolescents.

# chapter 6

# Target Proofing Our Kids

Helping kids understand the difference between assertion and aggression

Teaching conflict resolution and problem-solving skills

The importance of relationships

Giving children the tools to conquer their fears

Developing confidence through competence

How your child sees, feels, and thinks about herself determines the way she treats herself. These impressions also guide her in establishing standards for how she expects to be treated by others. Kids who view themselves as being competent, worthy, and lovable develop self-confidence and a positive self-image; they're likely to treat themselves with respect and expect others to do the same.

It makes sense, then, that kids who possess a negative self-image become insecure and are more vulnerable to becoming the targets of a bully. Lack of self-confidence and social acceptance can result in anxiety, loneliness, and depression. A child might try to ease that pain by succumbing to peer pressure, injuring herself, or even committing suicide.

In this chapter, we take a look at some of the ways adults can help kids learn to assert themselves, solve problems, and confront their fears. We also talk about the importance of belonging and building confidence and competence—all skills which lead to greater self-confidence and target proofing.

## Assertion Is Not Aggression

How do kids go about getting their needs met? Before they acquire the ability to express themselves well with words, it's not uncommon for very young kids to bite, kick, push, or hit in an attempt to get their way, to reduce frustration, or to release stress.

 **parent pointer** A child's most important relationship is ultimately the one she has with herself. Fostering your children's sense of self-worth, while also emphasizing the worth of every other child, can balance love and respect of oneself with respect for others.

By the time most kids enter kindergarten, however, they have learned to assert themselves by using their words to ask for what they need or want.

Asserting oneself is the way an individual states, or affirms, how she feels, what she wants, or what she's willing to do. Done correctly, it comes as a statement or request that doesn't humiliate or violate the rights or needs of anyone else. Learning to be assertive is an important skill to develop in order to be successful in the world, to be able to get along well with others, and to meet one's needs. Kids need to become comfortable advocating for themselves as well as for others.

Aggression, on the other hand, is an immature and inappropriate way of solving a problem, meeting a need, and relating to others. Kids who push and shove other kids on the playground at school are using aggressive behavior, rather than assertive behavior, to get their way. Aggressive people tend to be demanding, dominating, and selfish and create conflict and distress in others.

 **Bully Buster** Kids who are subjected to aggression are at greater risk to become bullies or targets themselves. Is there anyone in your child's life who could be modeling aggressive or disrespectful behavior? If so, you may want to take an opportunity to initiate some positive changes at home. Try using some of the strategies we share in this section.

# "Just Right" Responses in Social Situations

Remember *Goldilocks and the Three Bears?* When Goldilocks tasted the porridge of each of the three bears, she found that the first one was too hot, the second was too cold, and the third just right. It's important for kids to learn how to use a "just right" response in social situations. That's because kids who are overly reactive or fail to respond at all can be prime targets for bullies.

Here's a rundown of the three basic types of responses children typically exhibit in social situations:

**Overreactive responses.** Overreactive kids have a hard time discriminating between what's important or meaningful in social situations and what isn't. It can take very little effort on the part of an aggressive or sarcastic kid to elicit a strong, exaggerated, and upset reaction in an overly reactive child. That child may respond with anger, yelling, crying, or other inappropriate behavior. Children (including those with social-communication disabilities) who lack these social skills and overreact are especially vulnerable to targeting and bullying.

**Under-responsive behaviors.** Some children are under-responsive, meaning that they don't respond or make an attempt to communicate or assert themselves in the way that would be expected by most children. When kids don't stand up for themselves, they make other children feel uncomfortable and are especially vulnerable to targeting and social rejection.

**Responsive behaviors.** Responsive behavior involves calm and deliberate responses to social interaction and signifies a sense of self-confidence and self-control. It isn't emotional or highly energized, so it doesn't give bullies anything to latch on to. These "just right" responses don't feed into bullies' need to feel powerful and in control. You'll find examples of how kids can express themselves calmly, assertively, and appropriately as we move along this chapter.

# Using Body Language and "I" Statements

Understanding how to use verbal and nonverbal communication effectively can really help reduce incidents of targeting as well as to increase self-confidence, improve one's reputation, and improve social relationships.

## Body Language

We've all heard the expression, "It isn't what you say, it's how you say it that counts." The words we use to convey information to others is only one aspect of the message we are sending.

Understanding body language and being able to use it appropriately is a social-emotional communication skill that can help kids communicate with others as well as to understand what the body language of the other person is saying about them. Developing assertive and appropriate body language can improve self-confidence and relationships, as well as decrease anxiety and reduce the likelihood of being targeted.

community watch

Students with nonverbal learning disabilities often have a lot of trouble with body language, making them particularly vulnerable to bullying. Kids with social-communication differences need lots of support, direct instruction, and many opportunities to practice these skills, which very often can be learned. Speech-language therapists and behaviorists, as well as teachers who work with special needs children, have excellent training in helping kids learn to understand body language and to improve their own.

Here are some important body language elements that can impact a child's likelihood of being targeted:

**Making appropriate eye contact.** Children need to be aware of the importance of appropriate eye contact when speaking with others. Maintaining eye contact shows interest, respect, and self-confidence. (Of course, we also need to teach kids that too much eye contact and staring can make people uncomfortable.) If a child is uncomfortable looking someone in the eye, she can practice looking at others between the eyebrows, just above their eyes, or at the tip of their nose.

**Recognizing facial expressions and using them appropriately.** Facial expressions that don't match the words being spoken confuse the listener.

For example, a person who claims to be happy but who doesn't look happy makes others wonder how they are really feeling inside. Similarly, smiling when someone is talking about a sad situation is seen as highly inappropriate.

**Having good posture.** Standing up straight with shoulders back, head up, and hands at sides projects an air of self-confidence. Kids (and adults) who hunch over or slouch appear less assertive and sure of themselves.

**Maintaining good hygiene.** Children need to be taught that keeping their body, hair, breath, and clothing clean and smelling fresh is not only important for good health but to establish a good reputation and maintain good relationships. Good hygiene also involves washing hands after using the bathroom, not spitting while speaking, and not slobbering while eating. Kids with poor hygiene are often rejected by their peers and can be easy targets.

**Respecting other's personal space.** It's important for children to know how to maintain an appropriate physical distance between themselves and the person they're speaking with to avoid being a "space invader" or "close talker."

**Using appropriate body gestures and movement.** The way we move sends strong communication signals. Someone shaking their leg, turning their head away, or looking down may be indicating impatience, anxiety, or disinterest; arms folded tightly across the chest can indicate disagreement, resistance, anger, or discomfort. Help your children be aware of how quickly they walk; moving at the general pace of other kids can help them look and feel like part of the group.

**Speaking appropriately.** Help your child understand that the rate, volume, and tone of his voice can send strong signals. How quickly or slowly they speak and the loudness and the tone of their voice also affect their interactions with others. Have your child listen to how others speak for additional clues.

## "I" Statements

Confident and assertive verbal communication is just as important as confident body language. If a child keeps the focus on her own feelings when she makes requests of others, she'll not only become more comfortable and confident in her ability to assert herself, she'll make others feel better about themselves, too. People don't like being blamed or criticized. When you think about it, criticism is really a request disguised as a judgmental and negative complaint. It puts the blame on the other person and makes them feel wrong; nobody likes to be made wrong or to feel put down.

"I" statements are a great way for your child to express how she feels, and why she feels that way, in response to the action of another child or adult. They enable her to share her feelings and make a request without being aggressive, argumentative, accusatory, or shaming. "I" statements can be successfully employed in many situations: when one child takes a toy away from another, if a teen spreads a rumor about a peer, if a parent doesn't fulfill a promise, if a student misunderstands a teacher's homework requirements, if a boyfriend and girlfriend have a misunderstanding.

You name it, "I" statements are very useful tools for communicating and fostering greater understanding and problem solving. Not only do they help with interactive situations, they also help individuals reduce impulsivity and gain greater self-awareness.

Consider the following statement:

> I hate you for calling me a liar. You're a stupid liar. I
> hate you, and I'm not your friend anymore.

Now look at how such an accusatory statement can be turned into an "I" statement:

> I felt angry and embarrassed when you called me a
> liar because I didn't lie. I thought we were friends,
> but friends shouldn't treat each other that way. I want
> you to tell the others I didn't lie.

## Teaching Conflict Resolution Skills

Conflict resolution is the process of problem solving between two or more people. It requires communication, negotiation, and, often, compromise. The ability to resolve conflicts peacefully and amicably is a critical skill for success in interpersonal relationships. In fact, kids routinely resolve their own conflicts successfully.

Conflict resolution can be very effective when used between cooperative equals who both seek to resolve an issue. However, it's important to point out that bullying isn't a conflict in the true sense of the word. A child who is using bullying behavior against another, less powerful child isn't in conflict. The person doing the bullying doesn't have a problem, unless an adult has made it a problem for her. It's the target who has the problem; the bully is doing exactly what she wants and is the one with the power, so she has nothing to resolve and no vested interest in negotiation. In fact, having the target sit in the same room with someone she's actually fearful of and engaging in the steps of conflict resolution is not only highly unlikely to resolve her problem, it's more likely to leave the target feeling frightened and re-victimized.

The primary exception to this imbalance in bullying situations is with very young children. Younger children can be assisted through conflict resolution techniques if they haven't fully forged their identity as either an aggressive, dominant child or a submissive, fearful target. Before that shift takes place, where there is still no significant imbalance of power, there's a good chance that conflict resolution techniques may be successful. However, they should take place under the close supervision of an astute adult.

Here are the general steps to conflict resolution (specific techniques can vary):

1.  Each person shares her perspective of the problem.

2.  They share how they feel and what they would like to have happen as a result of the process.

3.  Each confirms and expresses their understanding of each person's perspective, feelings, and desired outcome.

4.  The parties jointly generate possible solutions and consider possible outcomes of each.

5.  They agree upon the best choice/plan of action.

6.  They implement their agreed-upon choice/plan of action.

7. They jointly evaluate how it worked out. If it was successful, great, nothing more needs to be done. If not, they go back to the drawing board to generate more ideas.

# Teaching Problem-Solving Skills

We problem solve all the time, and it's a good idea to help kids learn the steps to effective problem solving early in life.

Here's how it works:

1. **Identify what the problem is.**

   *Someone is using the toy I want to play with.*

2. **Decide what you want to happen.**

   *I want to play with the toy.*

3. **Generate a list of ideas that could resolve the problem, feeling free to ask for help in brainstorming ideas, and think about what might happen in each case**

   *If you snatch the toy away from the other child, she might start crying and you might get in trouble.*

4. **Make a choice.**

5. **Give it a try.**

6. **If you solved your problem without causing a problem for anyone else, great! If your problem didn't get resolved, go back to your list of ideas and try something different.**

Using the example of a child who wants to play with a toy being used by another child, here's how it would work:

1. Someone is using the toy I want to play with.

2. I want to play with the toy.

3. If I snatch the toy away from the other child, she might start crying and I might get in trouble. But if I ask the other child if we can share the toy, I might get to play with it and we might have fun together.

4. I'm going to ask the child to share the toy with me.

5. "Can we play together and share the toy?"

Kids can be great problem solvers when given the chance. Having a stake in the problem-solving process makes them feel good about themselves and increases their self-confidence. It also develops their leadership skills and ability to plan, generate ideas, consider their own needs, respect the needs of others, make good decisions, and evaluate outcomes. The problem-solving process remains the same no matter how old you are.

## Teaching Kids to Advocate for Themselves

Although kids should be taught problem-solving skills from an early age, it's important to let them know that some problems are too big for them to handle by themselves. Bullying is usually one of those "too big" problems.

When a problem is too big for a child to handle on his own, he needs to be able to advocate for himself. He needs to know how important it is to tell someone if he, or someone he knows, is being bullied. A child also needs to feel comfortable talking to trusted adults about bullying, and to learn how to better identify and understand it.

**Knowledge Is Power**

Many schools experience a dramatic uptick in reports of bullying when they begin to implement prevention programs, not because bullying is increasing but because students are better-equipped to recognize it when they see it and discuss it with trusted adults.

## Building Relationships

Children who feel liked, accepted, and valued by their families, peers, and caring adults usually feel good about themselves.

## The Need to Belong

What's the ultimate punishment in a prison (aside from the death penalty)? Time spent in solitary confinement.

What's the ultimate negative sanction imposed on a member by a church or spiritual community? Ex-communication.

What's the most painful and damaging thing a parent can do to a child or adolescent? Reject her.

What are the most emotionally damaging and painful things an individual or group can do to another? Ostracize and isolate her.

As these examples illustrate, a sense of belonging and acceptance are critical to our physical survival and social and emotional well-being. Humans are social beings who have an innate drive to belong and be accepted. In an emotionally healthy family, children feel loved, safe, and accepted for who they are. Infant and early childhood experiences provide the foundation for successful social-emotional relationships and healthy self-esteem. Challenges and opportunities for social interaction and the development of social competence continue throughout our lives.

## Connecting Comes Naturally

Babies come hard-wired for connection and are born with the biological, neurological, and emotional elements that foster attraction and communication with others. It's because of these abilities that we're able to think, connect, communicate, problem solve, and work collaboratively to form highly organized and functional societies.

Social interactions help children to learn about themselves. Beginning with parent-child and family relationships, extending outward toward friendships, teacher-student-classmate relationships, and other social affiliations, children begin to discover who they are as a part of another and as individuals. It's natural for kids to want to have friends. Even a very young child who has had limited exposure to peers is still likely to be socially curious. It's important to offer your child the opportunity to spend time with others her own age. Doing so will help her to develop social self-confidence. She will begin to learn to get along well with others, and develop the skills of negotiation, compromise, cooperation, self-assertion, and healthy competition. She'll learn to have fun with others of her own age while she's learning about herself at the same time. Kids who get along well with other kids are far less likely to be targeted or socially rejected by their peers.

| parent pointer | Children with developmental disabilities such as Autism Spectrum Disorders may need varying degrees of support, encouragement, instruction, and assistance when it comes to forming relationships. These youngsters are vulnerable to misunderstanding and discrimination by peers and adults. Children with disabilities can benefit immensely from comprehensive early intervention services, as well as by having opportunities for inclusion with nondisabled (often referred to as "typical") peers in a variety of settings (school, martial arts, yoga, scouting, clubs, and so on) with adequate supports and positive, welcoming attitudes. |
|---|---|

## Kids Want to Contribute

It's natural for children to want to help and to get involved. Kids who contribute learn how to work with others, become part of a group, and are accepted by their peers. Kids who are perceived as being a group member, who are active socially and express themselves through participation, are less likely to be ostracized or targeted by peers and by adults, too. Everyone gets along with kids who chip in.

Just think about how many kids enjoy helping out in the kitchen and want to stir the batter, put in the chocolate chips, or sprinkle the cupcakes. Ever watch kids on the playground negotiate the rules of a game? Everyone has something to say about what's fair and how the game should be played.

Most kids like being the line leader in school, helping an adult figure out how to look up something on the computer, or sharing their point of view. It's rewarding to parents to see their child extending herself by offering to tutor a friend in math, teach her little brother to play basketball, drive her sister to the mall, or stand up to an aggressive kid who is picking on another child or teen.

**You Can Make a Difference**

Some of most important contributions we can make come in the form of challenging ideas, behaviors, and the status quo. Just think of Rosa Parks and Mohandas Ghandi. John Lennon joined the social action call for peace and challenged the status quo through his music. Songs like "Imagine" continue to be popular and inspirational, even decades after they were written.

It's empowering and affirming to experience our ability to initiate action and to be able to reflect upon how that action is received. Was it accepted? Did it stir up controversy? Was it rejected? Was it ignored? The impact gives us information about the effect and significance of our actions (or inactions) upon others and how we're being received by our peers.

When kids make a contribution, they have the opportunity to make an impact, which increases their self-confidence and motivation to be an active participant in life. Kids who don't get opportunities to make positive contributions may choose to make negative ones, or give up and contribute nothing at all.

# Encouraging Courage

We've all been afraid or unsure of ourselves at some—or many!—points in our lives. It's important for parents to help their kids learn to distinguish the difference between fears of something potentially dangerous and fears that should be confronted.

Fear isn't only necessary for survival; it's a gift that can be utilized to develop courage as well as self-confidence and competence. Learning to harness, face, and conquer fears will enable your child to have a more exciting, enjoyable, and rewarding life.

Children need opportunities to confront their fears in ways that won't overwhelm them. Begin working with your child to face her fears at an early age. As she confronts them, with your support and encouragement, she'll develop self-confidence, courage, and a willingness to take calculated risks. She'll begin to trust her own judgment and become more comfortable initiating and participating in activities, rather than sitting on the sidelines and isolating herself.

Kids who are fearful and won't take action on their own behalf are particularly prone to being targeted. They have a hard time fitting in and knowing how to play, either verbally or physically, and are often overly dependent upon adults for assistance.

It can help to let your kids know that aggression is natural, but too much aggression is not socially acceptable. You might want to drive this message home by taking your child to a local playground and having them observe the behavior of young children. Together, watch while two kids get into a disagreement and observe how it gets settled. Watch multiple interactions, and you'll both see the varying ways young children resolve problems. Some respond to aggression by physically holding their ground, others return the aggression, some move away, others cry, and some run to their parents. All of these reactions are natural. Talk with your child about it and ask her what she learned from the observation. Talk about how various responses could work in her own life and with her own personality. This experience could be a real eye-opener for both of you!

We talk about some of the steps you can take to help your child deal with bullies and aggressive kids in Chapter 12.

> **parent pointer**
>
> "Helicopter parents" hover over their children, overprotecting them and doing things for them that they need to learn to do for themselves. While they mean well and think they're helping, they don't realize they're actually creating feelings of inadequacy and discouraging their children's willingness to experiment with acting courageously.

Fearful children require extra patience and energy. Begin working with your child with baby steps. Your gentle, calm, and positive approach will go a long way to help her face her fears and become more self-confident. Many children are fearful about attending a new school. You can help your child confront this fear by creating familiarity through drive-bys, a visit to the school to meet her teacher beforehand, becoming familiar with the school routine, and helping her realize what to expect and to whom she can turn if she needs help there.

# Building Academic Competence

Children spend several hours a day in school and attending after-school activities, and when we add in homework, studying, test prep, and projects, school becomes our children's focus for most of each year. The kids who possess the ability to achieve academic competence with limited frustration are fortunate.

When students experience difficulties in school, they can become so stressed that they have trouble dealing with other aspects of their lives. Many factors can impact a student's ability to be successful in the classroom. Here are just a few:

- Inadequate sleep or nutrition
- Poor teacher-student relationship or classroom management
- Parents who don't understand the language spoken at school
- Changing schools when families relocate
- Developmental or learning disabilities or delays
- Social concerns or issues
- Bullying

It's very difficult for a child—or an adult, for that matter—to tolerate repeated frustration or failure. Children who are having difficulties in school may suffer from low self-esteem and diminished self-confidence. At some point they'll recognize that they aren't keeping up with their peers, which can lead to feelings of inadequacy, anxiety, embarrassment, shame, and sadness.

parent pointer

Be mindful of how you feel about your child's challenges and how you express those feelings verbally as well as with your attitudes and actions. Children want to please their parents and teachers. If they have difficulty in school, they're already feeling unsure of themselves. By letting your child know that you think she's great and by making yourself available to work with her to make things better, you're expressing your confidence in her and showing her that you aren't worried yourself. Your faith in her can help move mountains.

It's important that academic difficulties be identified as early as possible so that appropriate strategies and interventions can be implemented to address areas of need. If you have a concern about your child's performance at school, don't hesitate to contact her teachers; they're there to help. And if you're contacted by your child's school, keep an open mind. When you work together, things can get much better for your child, and her academic successes will spill over into other areas of her life.

Kids who feel good about their success as learners are able to participate in school with confidence. Kids experience increased self-esteem, resiliency, perseverance, and pride when they feel competent, supported, and encouraged. Kids who feel successful are resistant to peer rejection or targeting.

## Interests, Talents, and Self-Confidence

There's more to life than ABCs and 123s; because kids are constantly judged by their academic success, it can be easy to forget that grades aren't everything. Every child has strengths, even if they aren't the things they're graded on in school.

What does your child love to do? What does she want to become when she grows up? What makes her feel good? What is she really good at? And what would she choose to do if she could just do what she wanted all day long?

There are many ways to learn about oneself and to discover new avenues of interest. Help your child discover more about herself by offering her a range of opportunities to try new things. Sometimes parents become frustrated when their children sign up for and drop out of activities as they find their way, but your patience and understanding will help her feel more comfortable with herself. (It is a good idea to encourage your child to give a new activity a reasonable chance before making changes; some kids take a little extra time to warm up to novel situations or tend to lack persistence when they experience challenge.) Developing her interests and talents will lead to competence and self-confidence in multiple aspects of her life. Having interests and building confidence inside and outside the classroom make children less vulnerable to being targeted.

Let your child know that she is more than just a pretty face. Reject media stereotypes that misrepresent the value of girls and boys, too. Challenge the status quo and help your children to develop a healthy respect for their unique talents, characteristics, and personalities. We have more to say about ways you can help your children develop positive social-emotional skills and enhance their character development in Chapter 9.

Children have so much to learn about themselves and the world. They're doing their best to figure it all out. Sensitive children, in particular, tend to be attuned to their parents' feelings and stress levels. Your patience, encouragement, and positive attitude will go a long way to help your child become happy, self-confident, capable, and successful. And that, in turn, makes your child much less likely to struggle with social difficulties or targeting.

## Essential Takeaways

- Self-assertion skills are a powerful and effective way to build self-confidence.
- Conflict resolution techniques aren't effective with most age groups when there's an imbalance of power. In fact, they can result in increased distress, discouragement, and frustration for targets.
- Peer acceptance is one of the most important experiences a child needs to feel good about herself.
- Children need patience and support while confronting their fears; overprotection and shaming increase vulnerability to targeting and bullying.
- Identify and address social and academic needs early to keep your child feeling capable, confident, and excited about learning.

# chapter 7

# Creating Kid-Friendly Schools

Meeting the requirements of the Safe Schools Improvement Act

Taking a comprehensive approach to bullying prevention

Drawing on the guidance of counselors

Undertaking responsible reporting

Creating welcoming, respectful classrooms

The start of the school year is an exciting time for children and parents. It's a time filled with anticipation, wonder, and hope. School is a child's home away from home. If your child had a good teacher last year, you're hoping for another one just as good this year. And if he didn't, you have your fingers crossed for a better experience this time around. It can be scary to return a child to school if he had negative experiences the year before. You want him to be as happy and comfortable at school as he is at home, or as close to that as possible. You hope he'll be a successful student and that he gets along well with other boys and girls. You want him to enjoy school and feel good about himself.

Teachers anticipate the new school year with excitement and enthusiasm, too, preparing themselves and their classrooms for their new students. They're wondering what their students will be like and asking themselves a number of questions: How can I make the curriculum more interesting and meaningful? How can I set the tone for a positive school year? How can I make a difference in the lives of my students this year?

The best schools put the needs and interests of students first. They understand and respect the needs and opinions of all members of the school community—students, faculty, administrators, and parents—in service of its children. It's important that school administrators, teachers, and other professionals working with students have a good understanding of children's developmental, academic, social, and emotional needs. Schools need to be a safe place where children feel welcomed and where their opinions matter.

## What Schools *Must* Do

School-based bullying is one of the greatest concerns for today's youth. Among students who are or have been targets of bullying, there is a high correlation between academic failure, anxiety, and depression, and school shootings and suicide. In the aftermath of tragedy, it's not uncommon for others to recall those individuals as having exhibited signs of distress while they were in school.

On March 10, 2011, President and Mrs. Barack Obama welcomed students, parents, and teachers, along with representatives from the Department of Education, the Department of Health and Human Services, advocates, nonprofit leaders, and policymakers to the White House for a first-ever Conference on Bullying Prevention. That same week, a bipartisan group of legislators introduced antibullying legislation that would require schools to develop and implement bullying prevention programs (called the Safe Schools Improvement Act).

Most states have now initiated legislation mandating that schools develop policies and procedures to prevent, address, and intervene in suspected incidents of harassment, intimidation, and bullying (HIB). Responsible and caring school districts take this legislation very seriously. In the following sections, we take a look at some things kid-friendly schools can do to address this very important issue and to work toward creating safe and caring schools for everyone.

# A Comprehensive, School-Wide Approach

Many school districts have adopted a comprehensive, school-wide approach to creating a safe, caring, and supportive school community, which includes the prevention of bullying behaviors and intervention when it occurs. Research indicates that schools that utilize comprehensive, systematic, evidence-based anti-bullying prevention programs can significantly reduce bullying and aggression and improve school climate. The Olweus Bullying Prevention Program is probably the best known and most extensively researched program of its kind. However, schools use a variety of prevention and intervention programs, with reported reductions in bullying and aggressive behaviors that vary anywhere from between 20 to 70 percent.

Bully Buster

In order to maximize a program's effectiveness, there must be a school-wide commitment to instituting positive changes and make bullying behavior socially unacceptable to students and faculty alike.

It's the responsibility of district administrators—superintendents, principals, vice/assistant principals, and their designees—to establish, implement, and facilitate antibullying and violence-prevention policies, procedures, programs, and curriculum.

Leadership at the top impacts the entire school community. Wise and respectful administrators collaborate with teachers, counselors, staff members, students, and parents in the creation of a positive, caring, and responsible school climate. Research indicates that positive changes can be made and bullying can be significantly reduced when everyone is invested and committed to sticking with a good program for as long as it takes for real changes to take hold.

## Acknowledging That There's a Problem

Any good problem-solving strategy begins with identifying the problem. With that in mind, administrators must acknowledge that bullying behaviors exist and present a serious problem that must be addressed.

## Gathering Information

Before attempting to solve the problem, it's a good idea to get more information. Through surveys and meetings, members of the school community can provide valuable information and insights about bullying, including where it takes place and how it might be prevented. Administrators can then use this information to select, design, and implement a school-wide anti-bullying initiative.

## Putting Policies and Programs in Place

Every school should have a discipline policy in place, with rules, consequences, and procedures for addressing a variety of disciplinary issues, including bullying. This information must be made available to parents, students, and faculty members. The policy should also include information about how students, parents, and faculty members can seek assistance. Many schools provide this kind of information on their websites, in school handbooks, in student agenda books, and through mailings and handouts.

## Kick-offs and Other Events

Once a prevention program has been selected and staff has been trained, many schools hold a kick-off event to launch the initiative. Examples of kick-off events include pep rallies, assemblies, or a series of events held during anti-bullying, respect, or violence prevention weeks.

A wide variety of other programs and workshops are available to help schools build caring communities and decrease bullying. Challenge Day (challengeday.org) is one such program designed for students in grades 7 through 12 that focuses on building connections and increasing empathy, breaking through stereotypes, and helping kids understand each other— and themselves—at a whole new level.

Many schools are fortunate enough to have outstanding faculty members and specialists who are willing and able to create and implement excellent programs and presentations, along with the ability to follow through beyond the kick-off celebrations.

## Educating Students

Students must be educated about bullying and abuse, including understanding and supporting the needs of potentially vulnerable groups. They also need to be informed, at age-appropriate levels, about sexual harassment and aggressive behaviors. Teachers need to know how to secure assistance, either for themselves or for someone for whom they have concerns, and how to become resistant to targeting and bullying behaviors, including such skills as self-assertion, conflict resolution, and problem-solving.

## Keeping Parents Involved

Parents are vital members of the school community. Kid-friendly schools try their best to include and invite parents to join in bullying prevention efforts in a number of ways, such as by inviting parents to join the school safety or bullying prevention and intervention committee, welcoming and valuing parent input, as well as reaching out to parents to involve and inform them of what's going on at their child's school. Welcoming schools also encourage parent attendance at open school meetings, assemblies, and special events. They make an effort to publicize such events on the school website, through direct mailings, announcements in the local newspaper, and so on.

# Maintaining a Safe Environment

Kid-friendly schools provide students with the physical and emotional security and academic supports they need in order to maximize their ability to learn. That safety and security must apply to all students, including those who may be particularly vulnerable to targeting and social rejection, such as LGBT youth, kids with social communication skills deficits, disabled students, and students with learning differences. Parents, teachers, and counselors know that a student's ability to learn and to make good decisions is compromised when under stress.

## Physical Safety

Your child can't concentrate on mastering mathematical equations if he's worried about walking through the school hallways without being teased, having to sit alone at lunchtime, getting assaulted in the locker room, or being beaten up on his way home.

Some things kid-friendly schools do to help ensure the safety of their students include:

**Provide adequate adult supervision,** particularly in the "hot spot" areas of school, such as hallways between classes, on the playground at recess, in the lunchroom, and in the bathrooms and locker rooms. Classrooms, school libraries, and gymnasiums need to be adequately staffed so that teachers can ensure the safety of their students in those settings, too. And don't forget about the dreaded school bus!

community watch

Kids need extra supervision on the school bus, a potentially dangerous place for any child who is vulnerable to bullying. It's unrealistic to believe that a bus driver can safely keep his eyes on the road and, at the same time, on the child who is picking on another student in the back of the bus. Schools might consider assigned bus seating, having bus monitors, introducing bus drivers to students off the bus to set guidelines, and giving bus drivers authority to discipline students.

**Provide a safe place for students** to go during unstructured times, such as lunch and recess, and on school trips.

**Organize structured activities during recess** in elementary and middle schools.

**Include opportunities for kids to release physical energy during the day,** including physical education classes, sports teams, dance, and so on.

**Offer high-energy kids more opportunities to move,** like running errands, helping a teacher, or coaching other kids.

**Adopt a clearly defined, appropriate, and enforceable policy for physical aggression and bullying.** Communicate school expectations and consequences to students, faculty, and families, and impose sanctions that are age- and developmentally appropriate with consistency and neutrality.

**Follow state and district policies and procedures** in any cases of suspected bullying and intimidation. We provide information about mandated reporting in Chapter 10.

## Social-Emotional Safety

The strategies we've discussed for dealing with physical safety also have application for social and emotional safety. Additional strategies include:

**Monitor school computer equipment** and have clearly defined, appropriate, and enforceable policies for the use of personal cell phones during the school day.

**Connect students with faculty resources** (teachers and counselors) with whom they can meet to discuss their concerns.

**Provide students with a safe place to go and a professional to talk to** should they become upset, anxious, or distressed, as well as a peaceful place to work out problems with other students, under adult supervision.

## What School Counselors Can Do

Schools employ many helping professionals to assist students and their families. Counselors, social workers, psychologists, nurses, behaviorists, learning/educational consultants, student assistance counselors, and substance abuse counselors have specialized training to help students, faculty, and families. Some schools also have school resource or safety officers who are linked with law enforcement and can be extremely helpful in dealing with bullying.

While these helping professionals wear many hats, this team of specialists work to assist students in successfully managing the following kinds of issues:

- Social, emotional, behavioral, academic, and interpersonal challenges, including dealing with aggression and bullying
- Advocating for oneself and others
- Problem solving, conflict management, friendship and peer relationships, and sexual responsibility

- Fostering positive self-esteem, increasing self-control (which includes dealing with emotions such as anxiety, depression, and frustration)

- Accepting personal responsibility

- Dealing with learning difficulties, academic motivation, and promotion of acceptance and celebration of diversity

Given their unique training and skill set, these specialists are often called upon to respond to crisis situations and to assess students for risk for self-harm or threat to others. This group contributes in the creation and implementation of school-wide or more specific programs, and works with general education students as well as those with special needs.

Specialists routinely provide a safe haven for kids when they are upset, need to talk something through, are in need of assistance for themselves, or are concerned about a friend or fellow student. In many schools they provide small group and individual counseling, classroom presentations and assemblies, and staff development presentations; they also can act as a home-school liaison and link children and families to community agencies and needed services. We share some perspectives of school counselors in Chapter 17.

## What Teachers Can Do

Teachers make all the difference in the lives of their students. Students whose teachers know how to create a safe, accepting, and positive learning environment feel welcomed and comfortable in the classroom. They also feel comfortable going to their teachers for help if they're being bullied, and know they'll be taken seriously. Teachers who are educated and knowledgeable about their students' academic and social-emotional strengths and weaknesses are better equipped to have a positive impact on reducing incidents of bullying.

Teachers are on the front lines. They may catch things out of the corner of their eye that go on between students while they travel between classes, or may even see kids getting roughed up in the parking lot on their way into and out of school. As more and more cases related to bullying reach our courts, we're learning that it's not only the teacher's ethical responsibility to take action, in some states it's a legal mandate.

**Bully Buster**

Kids often spend more time with their teachers and coaches than they do with their parents. These adults are vital role models in children's lives, and parents expect them to exemplify the behaviors they hope to see in their kids. Some coaches have an incredible ability to rally a team around all its members, even when they lose the game. Many teachers are great at bringing an entire class around to help a struggling student solve a problem.

Teachers must get the facts about bullying and talk with their students about suspected instances of bullying within their school community.

While administrators establish policy and procedures and create the basis of school climate, a child's classroom is an entity unto itself. His teachers are responsible for setting the tone for the classroom and determining what will or won't be tolerated there.

Parents should demand that their children's teachers set their classroom expectations high and maintain a positive and professional attitude. Teachers (and often counselors, too) have the responsibility to provide education about bullying, and to let them know that bullying behavior is an abuse of power that will not be tolerated. Your child's teacher should work diligently to create a classroom culture that makes it uncool to be a bully.

## In the Classroom

In addition to everything we've shared so far in this chapter, there are some additional ways teachers can help support their students, help them feel safe, and reduce incidents of bullying and aggression in their classrooms.

Teachers can involve their students in the creation of a code of conduct for their classrooms. When students are part of the development of the rules, they're more likely to take ownership of them. The code should include positive consequences for good behaviors, as well as negative sanctions for infractions, along with a clear procedure to help students reflect on and learn from their mistakes or poor choices.

In lower grades, kids really enjoy posters, stickers, and visual reminders about the code. As they grow, the focus of class rules should change to cover more mature themes. For example, you might see a friendship tree in an elementary classroom, with the leaves bearing the names of children who have exhibited acts of kindness toward others; you might find middle schoolers exploring the qualities of friendship and navigating sticky social situations through discussion, readings, personal reflections, and efforts to create a more friendly and welcoming school climate; at the high school level, kids are likely to explore topics such as social injustice, healthy dating relationships, sexuality, and the influence media has on shaping male/female stereotypes, integrity, substance abuse, and responsible decision making.

Some teachers or schools have their students create an anti-bullying pledge, which is an agreement that outlines a set of behaviors and expectations of what kids will do, and refrain from doing, with regard to bullying. We provide sample pledges for students in elementary, middle, and high school in Appendix A of this book.

The word *discipline* means "to teach." Teachers should make use of every appropriate opportunity to help kids learn how to get along well with others, solve problems, manage difficult emotions, make good choices, and consider the consequences of their actions. We take a look at some of the ways schools can teach social and emotional skills and character development in Chapter 9.

## Consistent Consequences

Using the code of conduct and anti-bullying pledge as a guide, teachers need to consistently reinforce consequences for both positive and negative behaviors. Things work best when teachers take the position that the purpose of consequences is to reinforce and teach students to make good decisions and to accept personal responsibility, rather than to punish.

Consequences should be implemented in a neutral, non-shaming, and non-agitated tone of voice, immediately following an infraction. When kids know what's expected of them and realize that their teacher enforces the rules, they rarely put up much of a fight and accept the consequences.

Having these kinds of procedures in place greatly reduces incidents of bullying, helps kids feel safe, and lets everyone know what to do and what will happen when rules are broken.

Teachers must intervene immediately if they witness or suspect bullying or if they receive a report that someone has been bullied. (For more information on assessing and reporting mandates, check out Chapter 10; for suggestions on securing assistance from your child's school, head over to Chapter 11.)

**Teacher Tip**

misc.   If consequences are inconsistently applied, negative behaviors will be more difficult to extinguish. When teachers discipline their kids while they're angry, their delivery can result in a negative emotional reaction from their students, which can create additional problems. As hard as it can be, it's best to try to keep a neutral tone when trying to make a correction.

## Effective Classroom Management

Teachers are the facilitators of student success. In order for things to run smoothly and efficiently, it's important that they be skilled in managing multiple aspects of the classroom environment.

Anyone who visits the classroom of a good teacher will sense a pleasant and positive environment and see productive and comfortable students. However, when a teacher lacks good management skills, the classroom may take on chaotic or negative energy, with the students behaving impulsively or aggressively. In such environments, learning and emotional safety are diminished, and students are more prone to bullying.

As a good classroom manager, a teacher should understand, anticipate, and respond appropriately to the academic, behavioral, social, and emotional needs of students. Teachers should also create and support respectful and positive relationships with students and between fellow classmates.

Good teachers take the personalities and interpersonal relationships of their students into account when it comes to arranging seating and group work. A kind, empathic, socially confident child can do wonders to support or befriend a less secure or shy child. An aggressive student needs to be both closely monitored and carefully placed, preferably in the company of others who model appropriate student and social behaviors and who are able to assert themselves with a potential bully. Good teachers help their students to help each other in all kinds of ways—academically, socially, and emotionally.

## Encouraging Children to Report Concerns

It's crucial that children learn the importance of telling an adult if they think a child (including themselves) may be hurt, frightened, very upset, or is being bullied.

Most kids don't want the reputation of being a tattletale; it's important that they learn the difference between tattling and reporting, and to whom they should report concerns.

Ratting, or tattling, is done to get somebody else in trouble or deflect attention from their own negative behavior. It's also done so the tattler will gain attention. A tattler might tell his teacher, "Johnny's making a mess" when it's really the tattler who hasn't cleaned up his things, or "Judy's being mean" when she's not doing anything of the kind.

Unlike tattling, responsible reporting shares potentially important information about another person who is physically or emotionally hurt, in potential danger, having a serious problem, or seems like they may need help.

In grade school, a responsible student might tell the teacher when a classmate has thrown another student's lunch in the garbage, or that someone is crying in the hallway or school bathroom. As young people move on to middle school and high school, the reports might increase in urgency: "Billy's afraid to go home because his dad's been drinking a lot lately," or "Molly's been eating lunch in the bathroom every day because Lisa told her she's an ugly loser that nobody likes," or "Sean is worried because David's been hitting his girlfriend," or "Janet says if I won't cut school with her she'll go on Facebook and tell everyone I'm a slut."

Kids need to know whom to go to with their concerns: parents or adult family members, teachers, guidance counselors, school social workers, psychologists, administrators, the school nurse, after-school caregivers, clergy, or school resource officers are all good resources. They need to know that if there's a potential for danger, they shouldn't take the responsibility on their own shoulders. Even teenagers should speak with an adult.

In cases of suspected bullying or violence, kids should be encouraged to report the information immediately and directly to an adult. Schools must do their best to protect the confidentiality of student reporters whenever possible.

There are a number of ways that students can communicate with their teachers or other school professionals, either directly or indirectly.

**Concerns box.** Some schools invite students to write a note to their teacher or to another adult in the building to express a concern or to request a conversation. These notes can be signed or submitted anonymously. Schools have had success placing these boxes in classrooms, corridors, or outside the counselor's or main offices. The boxes should be checked on a daily basis. Some teachers and counselors post clipboards, which can be used by students to make a report, express a concern, or request a conversation.

**Secret signals.** In some schools students let their teachers or counselors know they're uncomfortable or need attention by having a secret signal set up between them that won't be obvious to other students.

**Journal entries and written assignments.** Whether students realize it or not, their writing often reflects challenges and concerns they're dealing with. Class assignments can be very useful in letting adults know when a child needs help.

Of course, the fastest way for a student to get assistance is to speak with an adult directly and immediately.

# The Student-Teacher Relationship

When teachers establish a safe and caring classroom in which children feel connected, accepted, respected, and appreciated, a trusting relationship of mutual respect and appreciation is fostered.

Students who have teachers who take the time to get to know them and genuinely care about them, who create a positive learning environment, and who possess good classroom management skills feel better about themselves. They are apt to be willing to take greater academic and social risks, and will be more likely to enjoy coming to school. Students are willing to work harder when they feel their teachers like and care about them.

Parents can help teachers learn more about their children in a variety of ways. With younger children, some teachers send a letter home at the beginning of the school year, asking parents to provide any information they want to share about their child. If your child's teacher doesn't do that, you may wish to contact the teacher directly, either by letter or by email, in order to learn the best way to provide important information about your child.

It generally takes a little time for teachers to get to know their students, so unless you have a pressing concern, it's usually best to give your child and his teacher some time to get to know each other before stepping in. As kids get older and more comfortable at school, teachers will be less likely to contact you for information about your child.

While most teachers welcome parents in for one-on-one conferences, with the busy schedules of so many working parents, some people prefer to participate in telephone conferences, which can be conducted either during the day or after school hours, or through email or other written communication, which many find to be efficient and effective. Once you determine the best way for you and your child's teachers to interact, be sure to keep them posted on any important information and new developments or concerns as the year progresses.

**parent pointer**

Some of the things you might want to share with your child's teachers are his academic strengths and weaknesses, medical or pertinent family information, and any particular fears or social concerns he may have. Be sure to let the teacher know if he has ever been bullied or acted as a bully toward other kids and whether or not the situation was successfully resolved. In fact, if he needs to be separated from another student because of a bullying situation, let the school principal know this before the school year begins. Don't hesitate to contact your child's school principal, teacher, or antibullying specialist if you suspect he's involved in a bullying situation.

Sometimes kids misinterpret the meaning of a teacher's actions. A child may come home and tell Mom or Dad that his teacher is mean because she never lets them do what they want and is always telling them to stop talking. Or he may feel his teacher doesn't like him because she told him he had to redo his homework. Most of the time the teacher isn't being mean, just enforcing classroom rules or providing valuable feedback.

You might be surprised, though, to know how accurate kids can be when it comes to knowing how their teachers feel about them. They're often right on the mark when it comes to recognizing their teachers' feelings toward them and their classmates. What can parents do when a child's teacher really doesn't like him?

Sometimes the teacher-student relationship really isn't an ideal one. However, it's the teacher's responsibility to make it work by being professional, treating the student with respect, and doing everything within her power to create a physically and emotionally safe and positive learning experience for every student in her class. It's also her responsibility to examine and address any issues of her own that might be negatively impacting their working relationship.

## When Teachers Are Bullies

Unfortunately, teachers can be bullies, too. They may use their position of power to humiliate, disregard, or abuse their students (even sexually). They may yell, insult, berate, or be physically aggressive toward the kids in their class in general, or just toward one or two students. That's a serious problem that must be addressed immediately with school administrators. If your child exhibits signs of being targeted or complains about how his teacher makes him feel, what she says, or how she behaves toward him, don't hesitate to contact his school.

## Essential Takeaways

- Kid-friendly schools put the needs and interests of their students first.
- Schools must develop policies and procedures to prevent, address, and intervene in suspected or reported incidents of bullying.
- School counselors and specialists possess a unique set of skills that enable them to provide students, faculty, and families with prevention, identification, and intervention education and strategies with regard to bullying and other serious problems at school.
- Responsible reporting isn't the same as tattling. Kids should be encouraged to learn when and how to share their concerns with adults.
- Teachers can be bullies, too, so it's important to carefully listen to what your child has to say and take the time to check it out.

# chapter 8

# Making Kids Cyberwise

Bullying with the click of a button

Locating cyberbullying hot spots

Identifying cyberbullies and their targets

Reporting on and protecting against cyberabuse

Although technology and the Internet have made our lives better in a multitude of ways and have brought our global community closer, these developments also provide new opportunities for abusive or criminal behavior.

When so many of our transactions and communications take place over the Internet, it can make us feel especially vulnerable when we're threatened online. Internet scams are very attractive to the perpetrators because they involve little risk or discomfort. The perpetrators don't have to physically rob us or be faced with their conscience when we resist, and they have a good chance of getting away with it.

Similarly, those who cyberbully see the opportunity for a big impact at little personal cost. They don't have to be faced with their targets, they can often bully behind a veil of anonymity, they know they have a pretty good shot at getting under their target's skin, and they can be hard to catch.

While it's important that we teach our kids responsible digital behavior and how to be safe online, the Internet is a portal to a big world we can't always control. As parents who are also contending with the new ways the Internet can jeopardize our safety, we must also give our kids the tools to effectively respond to the challenges we encounter in the digital age.

# The Cybergeneration and Bullying

In many ways, using the Internet is like learning how to drive. It requires foresight, an understanding of consequences, caution, and respect for road signs. Unfortunately, these things can be antithetical to the rapidly changing and impulsive teenage brain, which is why kids are not permitted to drive until late in adolescence. These days, however, most kids are getting online long before they get behind the wheel, as computers and the Internet have become important tools in education and an integral part of family life.

Bully Buster

A study from the Pew Internet and American Life Project found that 39 percent of the teenagers in the study revealed that they'd tried to play a trick on someone or pretended to be someone else using instant messaging.

## Where Is It Happening?

For young people who are socially awkward or have social anxiety, texting might be a great way to reach out to peers. Likewise, the Internet can be a great opportunity to overcome inhibitions. Kids who are shy may have a totally different identity among their online friends. The Internet gives many kids the opportunity to have a voice and feel heard.

On the flip side, kids who might be hesitant to bully someone to their face may feel perfectly free to do so online. The inhibitions and restraint they might show in person can often dissolve with the anonymity of the Internet, or merely with the distance Facebook provides, regardless of whether or not the user is anonymous.

In the remainder of this section, we detail the channels of communication where kids might be susceptible to cyberbullying.

**Cell phones.** Over a quarter of American teens have been bullied or harassed through their cell phones, more often girls (30 percent) than boys (23 percent). Almost half of kids with cell phones report having sent a text message they regret, with kids with unlimited texting plans and those who text the most being most likely to report regretting a sent text.

Sexting with cell phones is also a common phenomenon of cyberbullying, where young people are convinced to send a peer an explicit photograph of themselves via text message. Those pictures are then used to embarrass the target and spread to others throughout the school community.

**Social networking sites.** There are hundreds of social networking sites out there, where users can create profiles for themselves with photographs, statements, songs, and any information they'd like to share with the world. These sites allow users to connect with others, see the new activity on each other's profiles, read what other users are saying, privately communicate with members, or publicly join a conversation.

Facebook is by far the world's most popular social networking site. It only takes minutes to create a profile for yourself or a group. As such, it can be a great way to get people to quickly rally around a cause. Alternately, it can easily extend the trajectory of bullying at school. There are hundreds, if not thousands, of groups created for the sole purpose of bullying. If you go on Facebook and enter into the search bar "I hate ___" (fill in the blank with any name you like), you'll probably pull up dozens of groups dedicated to bashing someone.

Formspring, popular with teens, offers users the opportunity to ask each other questions and provide answers, while being able to keep their identity anonymous. Often these questions and answers are great conversation-starters that can be intriguing, or funny, or even philosophical, but can often veer into cruel personal attacks, particularly when the users are anonymous. No matter what social networking site your teen might be using, talk to them about how to be safe, respectful members of their online communities.

### Avoiding Anonymity

The effect to which anonymity contributes to cyberbullying can't be underestimated: a 2006 study indicated that approximately half of middle school children who are bullied online don't know who is doing it.

**YouTube.** Who doesn't want to be a star? These days that often means going viral on YouTube. Lots of kids post videos of themselves dancing or singing or showing off their best talents in the hopes they'll score millions of views.

However, stardom often comes at a price. YouTube is rampant with roaming "haters" who anonymously post bullying and abusive comments under other users' videos. It's common to see hundreds of such comments under anything that's gone viral. YouTube is also used to humiliate those who have been targeted in face-to-face bullying. There are hundreds of postings on the site depicting teens being physically bullied and brutalized, which bystanders or participants film with their cell phone cameras and then upload.

While it's great to support your daughter's ambitions, if she's posting videos of herself on YouTube singing that song she wrote, be sure to monitor the comments and remove and report those that are inappropriate. Remind her that the negative feedback is probably coming from someone who lives thousands of miles away, doesn't know her, may well be three times her age, and would rather spend his time harassing people online than doing something productive.

**Interactive video games**. Many kids who have social anxiety or are ostracized at school delve into video games for the escape and opportunity they provide to take on another identity or to be an actor in a world in which they have more control over their circumstances. However, in games such as *World of Warcraft,* bullying can take place when players gang up against a target to kill him or prevent him from playing the game.

**Instant messaging.** Lots of kids use instant messaging or the chat functions of social networking sites to communicate. As any adult knows who has ever been in a rush and sent an email that inadvertently sounded a bit brusque, conflict over IMing can often arise out of a misunderstanding of tone or a badly translated attempt at sarcasm. Often, these conflicts can escalate and result in bullying.

**Chat rooms and email.** There are lots of additional ways and lots of places that kids are cyberbullied, including chat rooms such as 4Chan, generally for people who share a particular special interest, or over email, though young people use IMing and social networking sites far more than they do email to communicate.

### Bully Mom

Misc.

As shocking and inappropriate as it is, parents have become involved in cyberbullying others' children, as in the case of Megan Meier. The mother of one of Megan's friends created a fake profile on MySpace for a non-existent boy named Josh, with the intent of finding out what Megan might be saying about her own daughter. Following Megan's suicide, her parents discovered Megan had received a barrage of abuse from Josh. Although Lori Drew, the mother of Megan's friend, was found to have created the profile, she was acquitted of all charges. If you suspect an adult is communicating with your child, listen to your instincts, and either cut off the communication or monitor it very closely.

## Who's Doing It?

Today, 20 to 35 percent of kids and adolescents have been involved with cyberbullying, either as a target, a bully, or both. The more time kids spend communicating online, the more likely they are to participate in cyberbullying.

Research finds that the roles of bullies and targets in the real world stay fairly consistent online. Most kids who bully online also bully at school or in person, and often the same targets.

However, cyberbullying also opens up a new class of bullies: kids who wouldn't do it in person but feel uninhibited to do so online. These may be kids who are smaller than their peers and don't bully in person because they're physically outmatched; online bullying offers them a much greater degree of power than face-to-face bullying would. Others, who tend to follow the rules and seek social approval, may use the anonymity afforded by the Internet to do things they know they'd be punished for. Some kids may take what starts as teasing far over the line when they fail to realize that things are getting out of hand.

**parent pointer** In 2009, a group of sixth-graders posted a video on YouTube that they had animated and set to music called *The Top Six Ways to Kill Piper,* about one of their classmates. The methods included with a gun, by pushing her off a cliff, and suicide. While the video is shocking, the technical skill it took these 11- and 12-year-olds to create it is notable. If your child is interested in technology, help foster her skills by giving her positive challenges and ways to channel that knowledge and curiosity.

The Internet also gives rise to those bully targets who see it as an opportunity to level the playing field. These kids often have low social status in their community and most likely would be unsuccessful at striking back in person. They may see their cyberbullying as a just effort to overcome their bigger, more popular, more powerful bullies. With skilled use of technology, the Internet can be a way for a target to turn the tables on a bully. One study found that 64 percent of those who were both victims and aggressors of cyberbullying were targets of offline bullying.

There are numerous reasons kids cyberbully. Here are just a few:

- To act out aggressive or violent fantasies

- Because they're bored

- Jealousy over shifting friendships, particularly among girls

- To gain power, prestige, and social status

- Revenge over something someone said, or after a romantic rejection or breakup

- An attempt at asserting dominance, humiliating a target, airing personal problems, or getting attention

- They didn't realize that responding to a negative chain or joining a negative bullying group on a social network constitutes cyber-bullying

parent
pointer If your child has been a target of face-to-face bullying, talk to her about the temptation of retaliating online. Although it may seem justified, it never helps solve the problem and usually only makes things harder to resolve. If your child acts out against her bully online, that other child may use it to cloud the power dynamics between bully and target. Although the imbalance of power is probably obvious, the bully's parents, administrators, counselors, and even the police may see the bullying as a two-way conflict, and your daughter may be punished for bullying behaviors herself.

## Who Are the Targets?

The kids who are targets of face-to-face bullying are often the same ones who are cyberbullied, which means they're not only harassed at school but at home and anywhere else where text messages or the Internet can reach them. Because they suffer from increased levels of social anxiety and decreased self-esteem, they often seek out social connections online, where, as we've seen, bullying can continue. This can lead to a vicious circle: the more social anxiety a child feels, the more she will look to the Internet as a social outlet. The more time she spends online in these venues, the more likely she is to be cyberbullied.

## Who Are the Bystanders?

Online bystanders are often members of a public forum (such as a chat room or a Facebook group) where bullying erupts between one or more members. With the distance the Internet affords, these bystanders often participate by adding to the chain of abusive comments. However, when a bully creates a group on a social networking site with the express purpose of bullying someone, those who join the group align with the bully and become active bystanders just by joining, whether or not they participate in the dialogue.

Just as online disinhibition and anonymity can lead to cyberbullying, it can also give bystanders the courage to stand up for the target. Often you'll see young people sticking up for the targets of online bullying, even when the target is a stranger. In Chapter 14 we talk more about how to be an upstander in an online environment.

# Understanding the Effects of Cyberbullying

Kids who are cyberbullied often feel there's nowhere to go. If your son is being bullied online, there's also a good chance he's being bullied at school. It's understandable why many kids develop extreme depression, low self-esteem, worry, anger, insecurity, anxiety, and perhaps even self-harming and suicidal thoughts and behaviors as a result of cyberbullying.

For the many kids who don't know the identity of the abuser, it can feel like the whole world has turned against them. How many kids know about the rumors that are going around? How many kids will join that Facebook rant? Who can they trust? When the bullying is taking place in the solitude of a child's bedroom, and no one is there to counter the negative things coming at her, she can feel totally alone.

**parent pointer**

Many of the parents who find themselves coping with a child's suicide later discover the barrage of hatred their child was contending with online. They speak of their shock at the brief amount of time it took for their seemingly happy daughter—who just a few minutes ago was doing her homework or washing the dishes—to disappear into her bedroom, read something hateful online, and take her own life. Be sure to set rules about Internet use that will ensure that you're close by whenever your child is online so you can support her and remind her that she's not alone if something upsetting comes her way.

# What Parents Can Do

If your daughter seems upset after she receives a text, or if you find her online and in distress, she may be getting cyberbullied. This is especially the case if you're aware she's being bullied at school, because there's a good chance it's following her home.

Just as with bullying in person, kids often don't tell their parents they're being cyberbullied; here are some of the reasons why:

- They don't think their parents can help
- They're afraid their parents will make them go offline or take away their cell phones

- They may fear getting in trouble if the bullying is happening on a site they weren't allowed to be on

- They may be embarrassed if the bullying is a result of sending explicit photos of themselves

 **parent pointer** Breaking the rules is a normal part of being an adolescent. Remind your kids that you'd much rather they ask for help if they ever get in over their heads for doing something that they shouldn't have than to try to handle it themselves. A daughter or son who has disobeyed the rules but who can come to you for help is much better than a child who is secretly in danger.

Effectively handling cyberbullying can often take time, some detective work, and the combined efforts of school administrators, police, and, ideally, other parents. In the meantime, there are several things you can do immediately if your child is being bullied online or through their cell phone:

**Document, document, document!** Print out all web pages, chat windows, instant messages, emails, or pictures, and take screen shots of any videos. Be sure to preserve all text messages. This is your evidence, and you'll need it later!

**Block messages from that sender.** Go to the settings on the website or email, or remove that person from your daughter's "friend" list.

**Block the sender's phone number** if the bullying is coming via cell phone, and suspend the text messaging function on your child's phone by calling your provider.

**Contact the hosting site/your Internet provider.** Most websites and Internet service providers have terms of use that make bullying a violation. You can ask that the perpetrator's account be suspended and that the damaging material be removed by contacting the site, and sending the messages or a link to the abusive content.

**File a complaint.** If someone has set up a fake profile or a group dedicated to bullying your child on a social networking site, file a complaint and ask that it be removed.

Many sites now make it easy to file a complaint or report inappropriate content or bullying. Facebook allows you to directly report or block a user from the settings bar on your profile. For sites that don't have a built-in reporting function, find "Contact Us" on the home page and send an email reporting the complaint along with the supporting links and documents. If you can't find contact information on a site, go to www.whois.net to find the site's owner and host company. You can then send the complaint via the "Contact Us" option of the host site.

## Engage Other Parents

If you know the identity of the child or group of children involved in the cyberbullying, you may consider approaching their parents for help. In the event they are unreceptive or unresponsive and the behavior continues, don't hesitate to take it to school and perhaps the police.

Check out Chapter 11 for advice about how to engage the parents of a bully, and how to respond with an open mind if you're contacted with a report that your child has been bullying.

## Report It to the School

If you're able to determine that the cyberbullying is being perpetrated by an individual or group of individuals at your child's school, you should report it to the principal to find out what kind of support he or she is able to provide. Even if the bullying doesn't take place on school grounds or with school computers, many state laws allow schools to get involved with off-campus bullying if it creates a hostile school environment. Chapter 10 focuses on state and federal laws around cyberbullying; however, even if your school can't provide consequences, counselors and administrators can be very helpful in facilitating dialogue with other parents and educating all students about appropriate online behavior.

If your child's school has a school resources officer (SRO) from the local police department, he or she can provide a valuable link between behavior at school and behavior in the community. The SRO can also give the school legal assistance in contending with the issue. Report the cyberbullying to the SRO and ask that he or she engage administrators and counselors in an intervention that might also include charges of harassment.

## Take It to the Police

Contact the police immediately if the content of cyberbullying amounts to any of the following:

- Physical threats

- Stalking or harassment

- Bias or hate crime

- Defamation of character

- Bribery

- Sexual exploitation

- Pornography

These days more and more police departments have units dedicated to cybercrime. Once they've established that criminal behavior has taken place, they can track down the perpetrator through advanced website security, Internet service, or email providers and take action to press charges.

Although the Internet and cell phones can offer the illusion of anonymity, cybercrime units have many tools at their disposal to determine the location of a computer or the owner of a cell phone, and root out a bully.

# Prevention = Knowledge + Boundaries

The Internet is an exciting place, and kids should feel enthusiastic about the opportunities it provides to learn, connect, and discover new things. It's not realistic to try to protect our kids from bullying by unplugging the computer. That said, there are many tools we can give our kids to ensure that they get the most out of being online, and do so safely.

## For Parents

Here are some simple, valuable tips for parents to follow:

**Keep the family computer in a place that is public in the home and set curfews for Internet and cell phone use.** Don't let your child slink off to her room with her laptop or cell phone so she can use it alone all night.

**Consider getting a limited texting plan for your child's phone.** You might want to consider a device that doesn't have camera/video capabilities as well.

**Consider using filtering or blocking sites** that will protect your kids from viewing sexually explicit, violent, or otherwise inappropriate websites.

**Make sure you know all of your child's passwords, profiles, and screen names.** Help her set up her social networking profiles to make sure the privacy settings don't leave her vulnerable.

**Give your child positive challenges and learning opportunities with the computer and Internet.** Not all usage should be about playing games or social networking.

**Talk to your kids about what kinds of negative comments they feel able to handle, and when it's time for you to step in.** Develop a strategy and show them you trust and support them.

**Encourage your kids to be online upstanders,** and teach them positive online skills. It's good practice for intervening face-to-face.

**Google your child.** More and more of our lives are being catalogued online, and it's important that you be aware of what's being posted about your children. A simple Google search can clue you in to what's being said about your child online. Whether your child just won the state championship soccer cup or is being bullied online, there's a good chance these things may come up on Google.

**Check out your child's browser history and friends lists.** Let your child know that if she doesn't respect your guidelines, you may investigate further.

**If you know your child is cyberbullying,** immediately restrict her Internet usage to school purposes, and strongly consider installing parental control software. And make sure she knows that cyberbullying can carry major consequences, such as arrest and criminal charges, and that she isn't as invisible online as she may think.

**Taking Cyber-Control**

Parent control software enables you to limit the websites your children can access and monitor all computer activity, among other features. Some recommended products include Bsecure Online, Safe Eyes, Norton Online Family, and Net Nanny.

**Keep an eye out for online use that seems secretive,** such as quickly switching screens when you come in the room or clearing the browser history.

**Encourage your child to talk to you if she reads a peer's post online that worries her** or makes her think a peer may be thinking of harming herself.

## For Kids

As children go online to learn new things, explore the world, and find community, they need to be aware of what to do should they encounter bullying on the Internet. When you talk with your children about staying safe online, share these tips with them:

**Don't respond in anger to offensive or bullying messages.** That can often escalate the situation. If the best thing to do is respond, do so calmly and assertively. Otherwise, ignore or block it.

**If you're in a group that's bullying someone,** don't participate or add to the negative comments. At the least, report it. Stand up to it if you feel you can do so safely.

**Never give out personal information, such as phone numbers, address, age, and so on,** on the Internet, and don't accept friend requests from people you don't know.

**Never give out the passwords** to your email, social networking sites, screen names, and so on.

**On sites that allow you to choose whether or not you accept anonymous comments,** such as Formspring, accept only comments from people whose identities aren't hidden.

**Save the content of any text message or online bullying.** If you're worried you may lose it, print it out.

The good news is, with all the attention cyberbullying has been getting in the media, several leaders in the online and social networking sphere and youth culture are taking a vocal stand against it. In Chapter 14 we talk more about the ways upstanders are turning the Internet around.

## Essential Takeaways

- The roles of targets and kids who use bullying behaviors stay fairly consistent offline and online. If your child is being bullied at school, she may well be experiencing cyberbullying as well.
- Limit your child's exposure to sites where people can easily behave anonymously.
- Many kids who may not bully in person for a variety of reasons will use the Internet to do it. Sometimes, these are kids who are targets of traditional bullying using the Internet to retaliate.
- If your child is being cyberbullied, take action immediately.

# chapter 9

# Social-Emotional Learning and Character Development

Encouraging empathy

Instilling the importance of good sportsmanship

Fostering trust and truth

Children first learn their core values at home. This includes what it means to be a good person, and the difference between right and wrong. As parents, you convey your values and beliefs to your children through your attitudes, words, and behaviors.

Character can be measured by how we treat ourselves and others, whether they're your best friend or a stranger, and whether or not anyone is watching. Developing positive character traits will help your child make good decisions throughout his lifetime and will provide him with an anchor of self-confidence and the conviction to do what he believes is right. Having this foundation will help him successfully navigate his way through most any storm.

In order to thrive in today's society, children need to develop the ability to understand, get along with, and demonstrate empathy for others. They also need to understand their own feelings, manage their behavior, and be able to deal with conflict effectively and appropriately. Kids need to develop a good sense of themselves, including their strengths, weaknesses, and abilities. These abilities are often referred to as *social-emotional skills.* The seeds of healthy social and emotional development begin to take root in the home.

Developing positive character traits and increasing social-emotional skills leads to decreased incidents of aggression, violence, and bullying. Kids who possess these skills enjoy good relationships with others and feel good about themselves. They are more likely to stand up for themselves and others in bullying situations, including stepping up for more vulnerable kids, such as those with Autism Spectrum or other disabilities or who may be LGBT, or are perceived as being different.

## Acceptance vs. Tolerance and Appreciation of Others

When we accept someone into our group, we're saying that he's welcome to join us, despite any differences we may have. Acceptance reflects an appreciation and respect of similarities and differences, whether they're related to race, ethnicity, culture, disability, sexuality, gender, religious, socioeconomic, or other status.

Tolerance, on the other hand, reflects a willingness to deal with, or put up with, a condition, an individual, or a difference that's considered undesirable. Tolerance implies that the person being "tolerated" is in some way displaying negative traits. Kids should be encouraged to not merely "tolerate" others, but to celebrate their different perspectives or backgrounds.

parent pointer

Acceptance and appreciation begins at home. Children are naturally curious about similarities and differences among themselves and their peers. Are you aware of your own prejudices and where they came from? Are you open to reexamining their validity?

When children have the opportunity to play and interact with kids from differing backgrounds, their world expands. They grow socially and intellectually, developing a respect and understanding of the equality of all people and enjoying friendships and connections with others from all walks of life.

Here are some ways to help your child develop acceptance and appreciation:

- Encourage your child to develop friendships with children whose background is different from your own.

- Watch movies, visit museums, and read books about kids who live in different places, speak different languages, or have differing lifestyles; discuss the strengths, challenges, and values of other cultures.

- Challenge prejudice when you encounter it.

- Volunteer at your child's school cultural festival.

- Eat new foods, listen to music from other cultures, or try learning a new language as a family.

- Host a foreign exchange student.

# Caring, Forgiveness, and Generosity

Caring reflects a genuine interest in and respect for others. Caring kids enjoy positive relationships, have good reputations, and are ready and willing to step in and help make things better for themselves and others.

The compassionate child is sensitive to the feelings, needs, and suffering of others. Compassionate kids experience a sense of self-satisfaction and achievement by acting on behalf of others who may be subjected to targeting by bullies by providing them with a sense of safety, support, and encouragement.

Someone who is kind is respectful and courteous. He enjoys doing things for others to make them happy and is willing to help them when in need. Children who are kind to others are usually treated with kindness and respect in return.

The child who can forgive is able to let go of anger, resentment, and other negative feelings associated with the actions of others. The child who can forgive responsibly—that is, not excusing aggressive and abusive people, but able to let go of relatively unimportant and unintentional slights or mistakes by others—is also willing to do the same for himself. Forgiveness doesn't mean thinking that someone who acted badly was correct; it simply means that the child who forgives releases himself from bad feelings and chooses to live a peaceful existence instead.

A generous and humble child is one who is neither selfish nor a braggart; he enjoys sharing his time and possessions and makes an effort to befriend and help others. A child with a generous spirit is cheerful and pleasant to be around.

community watch

Everyone loves being around someone with a sunny disposition. Model and encourage an optimistic attitude and help kids around you avoid getting trapped in negative thinking.

Here are some things you can do to help your child develop the qualities of a caring, forgiving, and generous person:

- Be a good role model; demonstrate concern for the needs of others and take positive action on their behalf.

- Encourage generosity and sharing.

- Provide opportunities to volunteer, donate, and help others. Your son might like to tutor another child, raise money for a worthy cause, or do Grandma's food shopping.

- Model the Golden Rule: Treat others the way you wish to be treated yourself.

- Recognize acts of kindness and caring. Kids love stickers, leaves on a kindness tree, acknowledgment, and appreciation. As they get older, these rewards will be replaced by internal motivations.

- Use kind words and behavior. Treat everyone with respect. Don't insult, shame, abuse, or mistreat others, either verbally or physically.

- Teach your child the value and importance of responsible forgiveness by being a forgiving person yourself.

# Be a Good Citizen

To be a good citizen is to be a valuable member of the community—someone who respects the values and abides by the rules of his home, his school, his town, his country, and the world. A good citizen enjoys the benefits of the positive culture of a group and takes action to address problems. Good citizens stand up for other members of their community and maintain good relationships with others. They're loyal to their group members and act with integrity, staying true to their beliefs and values.

Good citizens are resistant to targeting because they're self-confident; they have no need to bully others because they know what's expected of them and place importance on treating themselves and others with respect and care.

Here are some ways to help children become good citizens:

- Invite your child to participate in the formulation of family rules, encouraging him to make age-appropriate decisions.

- Read, watch TV programs, and discuss issues affecting your family, your community, the nation, and the world with your child.

- Practice democratic values in your home, demonstrating respect for each other's viewpoints.

- Participate in community service projects or grass-roots movements as a family.

- Bring your child with you when you vote.

- Visit museums, historical recreations, and your state and the nation's capital. Discuss with your kids the history of their country, personal freedoms, and civil rights.

- Reach out to offer a helping hand to others in need, or who may have a physical or other difference, in your community.

# Empathy and Social Awareness

Empathy is the ability to understand how someone else might feel in any given situation; in other words, it involves being able to put yourself in their shoes. As most kids mature, their ability to empathize develops from an understanding of how they might feel in a situation, to acceptance that another person may feel differently.

Aggressive children and bullies lack empathy. While some don't recognize or understand the feelings of their targets, others are willing to put their own desire for power, control, and dominance above the rights of their victims, even though they know what they're doing is wrong. More disturbed and pathological bullies derive pleasure from intentionally causing pain, humiliation, and suffering.

Developing empathy is crucial to preventing bullying. Empathic kids are less likely to act out aggressively or be targeted, and are more likely to come to the defense of a child who's having problems.

 Bully Buster

When kids make the connection between feelings and behaviors, and when they feel understood and accepted by their families, peers, school, and other adults, an empathic and caring community begins to form. Acts of violence decrease and a sense of belonging and safety increases.

Here are some ways you can help your child develop empathy:

- Talk about the different ways people express their feelings, including through body language.

- Read stories or watch a television program and talk about how the characters may be feeling based upon their body language, statements, and actions, and how they were being treated by the other characters.

- Encourage your child to seek clarification of others' behavior if he is feeling confused. In fact, checking things out leads to greater understanding and improved relationships.

- Help him to understand that people from different cultures may have different ways of expressing themselves.

- Role-play situations in which your child takes on the persona of someone who may be perceived as being different; act it out and see how he felt. Help him reflect on what it felt like to be treated differently.

# Everyone Needs Friends

The earliest predictor of future targeting is social isolation and rejection. It's very important to help your child develop good social skills. Not only does having friends create a decreased likelihood of being targeted by other children, it also means having someone to sit with at lunch, to talk with and listen to, and someone who will help who cares about you, too. The benefits of friendship are, as they say, priceless!

Here are some things to keep in mind when your child is starting and maintaining friendships:

- Encourage play dates and new experiences that put him in the company of children his age.

- Help him find other kids who have similar interests or dispositions; teachers and others can help with that, too.

- Make sure he has basic social skills, such as using body language appropriately and knowing how to join in a game or activity, give and accept compliments, and not be possessive with friends.

- Encourage your child to maintain good hygiene; kids with poor hygiene (body odor, greasy hair, unbrushed teeth, and so on), or who pick their noses are vulnerable to targeting and social isolation.

- Try not to hover; kids need to learn to negotiate their relationships and work through their own problems.

- Explain what being a good friend is about: caring, consideration, wanting good things for each other, and so on.

- Share your social experiences in middle and high school with your teen, and encourage him to talk about how kids in his middle and high school treat each other and what he thinks about it.

# Be a Good Sport!

Participation in sports offers children numerous opportunities to develop physical, social, and emotional skills; positive character traits; and life skills. Kids who participate in sports enjoy the benefits of physical health and fitness, friendship, and fun. In addition, they develop leadership skills and learn about themselves through competition and cooperation. Playing sports helps kids develop self-discipline and self-confidence and can enhance respect for authority, persistence, and an understanding of the importance of playing fair, following the rules, and accepting consequences.

Sports provide a safe outlet for physical energy and offer the opportunity to channel aggression in healthy ways. Children who participate in sports, as well as other individual or team activities such as dance, debate, or chess, benefit from the opportunity to learn how to be both good winners and good losers and to have respect for others.

Here are some things you can do to help your child enjoy participating in sports and other creative activities:

- Be aware of your own attitudes about competition and your desire to win. Your child's participation should be safe and fun, and make him feel good about himself.

- Make sure that your child's coaches are positive role models; similarly, encourage parents on the sidelines to control any negative comments or aggressive behaviors.

- Encourage your child to do his best, enjoy the process, and treat others with respect. Winning isn't everything and losing doesn't equate to being a failure.

- Encourage your child to be kind and respectful toward members of his own as well as the opposing team.

- Measure your child's success in terms of his personal improvement, positive relationships with teammates and coaches, willingness to cooperate with others, and persistence.

# Respect for Self and Others

Self-respect—regarding yourself as being important, valuable, and worthy—leads to healthy self-esteem and the establishment of friendships with people who treat you well. A person who respects himself is resilient against being targeted or accepting mistreatment from anyone else, including himself. Learning to respect others is equally important, leading to maintaining positive relationships and exchanging mutual support, cooperation, understanding, and the ability to help others in need.

Parents can help their children be more respectful by ...

- Being authoritative; the children of authoritative parents tend to feel safe, loved, worthy, and cooperative.

- Developing a parenting style that reflects high expectations and reasonable boundaries.

- Respecting children's opinions by offering age-appropriate choices.

- Getting off your cell phone and listening attentively when your child has something to say.

- Leading by example; hold yourself and others in high regard and act accordingly.

- Speaking to your child with kindness and care.

# Self-Assertion

Kids who are able to assert themselves don't need to be aggressive to get their needs met. They're able to stand up for themselves and are respected not only by their peers but by adults as well. Kids who are able to assert themselves are far less likely to be the targets of bullies because they're able to stand up for themselves and others.

Here are some ways to help your child assert himself:

- Let him know that he has the right to be treated with respect by others, which includes the right to not be bullied or intimidated by anyone, including in dating relationships.

- Encourage him to express his feelings, opinions, ideas, and needs to others in an appropriate and respectful manner.

- Explain the use of "I" statements and problem-solving techniques (see Chapter 6).

# Self-Awareness

A person who is self-aware has the ability to recognize and understand his own feelings. He has a sense of his interests, talents, and what he thinks is important, along with an understanding of his strengths and weaknesses. He's aware of what motivates and inspires him, how he learns best, and how he relates to others. Because he's attuned to his own feelings, he's less likely to join in negative behavior.

**parent pointer**

Ask your child, "How can you tell when someone is angry? How can someone else tell if *you're* angry?" Not only will these kinds of questions help him think about how others express their feelings, they'll help him understand his own behavior.

Here are some ways you can help your child increase his self-awareness:

- Ask for and respect his opinion, even if you don't necessarily agree with it.

- Take opportunities to discuss his feelings: what makes him happy, sad, scared, frustrated, excited, and so on. Talk about what happened in school that day and ask him how he felt about it.

- Talk about what he's good at and what he might need help with. Focus on his strengths, but support any areas of relative weakness.

- Point out to him some of his own behaviors and help him increase his ability to reflect on how his behavior is linked to his thoughts and feelings.

# Self-Control

Self-awareness greatly influences self-control. Everyone has their own way of dealing with their feelings. Lots of kids act out impulsively, without thinking, and suffer the consequences later. Others are calm and think things through before acting. Having self-control means being able to know how you feel and using good judgment before taking action.

 Impulsivity is a common challenge for kids who have attention deficit hyperactivity disorder because they have issues with planning, sustaining attention, and staying on task. Children with ADHD may require extra support, understanding, and assistance to learn how to slow down, get along well with others, and make good decisions.

Here are some things you can do to help your child develop self-control:

- Model emotional and behavioral control yourself; stop and think before you speak or take action.

- Make sure he understands that all feelings are okay; what's important is expressing them appropriately.

- Help him recognize the signs that he's getting angry, afraid, or frustrated, so that he stops and thinks before he acts in that emotional state of mind.

- Teach him relaxation strategies, such as breathing techniques, progressive muscle relaxation, and meditation.

- Work with him to use positive self-talk and affirming statements: "I can handle this," "I can stay calm," or "I can figure this out."

# Trustworthiness, Honesty, and Responsibility

A trustworthy person can be depended upon to keep his word and accept responsibility. He tells the truth and doesn't spread rumors or divulge secrets. Of course, responsibility and trustworthiness increase with maturity, so you're well advised to try to avoid overreacting or becoming distressed should your young child falter or fail to follow through on a promise. A 7-year-old who desperately wants a puppy will promise to walk it, feed it, play with it every day, and take good care of it. While he probably really means it when he makes that promise, he can't be expected to follow through on it with complete consistency.

How many people do you know whose marriages ended in divorce despite their best intentions to love, honor, and cherish until death do they part? Your child is working very hard to earn your trust and to keep his word; should he not follow through, it's important to use the experience as an opportunity to help him develop a greater sense of himself without shaming or blaming.

Kids who are regarded as being trustworthy, responsible, and honest should enjoy the benefits of respect, recognition, and special privileges in appreciation for doing the right thing.

Here are some things you can do to help your child develop trustworthiness, honesty, and responsibility:

- Expect the best; kids will try to rise to the expectations set by their parents, teachers, coaches, and friends.

- Give him chores he can handle successfully.

- Offer age-appropriate choices and opportunities: "You can sit at the table and color with us, or you can play with your Legos" or "If you'd like to use the car this weekend, you'll need to complete all your homework before you go." By helping your child make responsible choices you're helping him feel empowered, respected, and accountable.

- Keep your promises, and if you can't, don't be defensive or dismissive about it. The promises you make to your children may seem like little things to you, but kids see them as a really big deal. Acknowledge their feelings, apologize, and try to make things right.

- Set rules and consequences; it's best when everyone knows what's expected. If your child doesn't fulfill his responsibility, talk things through. Try to make it a good learning experience, deliver the consequence in a neutral tone, and move on.

- Recognize and appreciate responsibility and honesty when you see it: "Nice job. Your room looks great!" or "Thanks for helping Sophia with her homework; I think your help is really making a difference" or "I'm glad you shared this test with me. Wow, it looks tough. What do you think you could do to get a better handle on the math for the next time?"

# School Programs

Many schools incorporate education in character development and social-emotional skills into their curriculum. Research indicates that students who receive instruction in social-emotional skills and character development (SECD) at school benefit in a variety of ways. Schools that offer these kinds of programs are viewed by students, parents, and faculty alike as being caring, which leads to greater student connectedness to school and concern for peers. There's also evidence of increased academic success and graduation rates, reduced absenteeism, decreased fighting, and fewer incidents of violence and bullying in schools that offer these kinds of programs.

Antibullying education can either be handled as part of SECD or in its own unit. Any antibullying education program should, at minimum, provide instruction in the following core ideas:

- Identifying what constitutes bullying
- Understanding the bully triangle
- Recognizing aggressive language and behavior
- Distinguishing between normal conflict and bullying
- Resolving conflicts and solving problems
- Distinguishing between tattling and telling (reporting)
- Identifying ways that students can get help for targets of bullying
- Practicing cybersafety

Many SECD programs include opportunities for parent involvement and education as well. SECD programs have been proven to be highly successful in increasing empathy, understanding and managing one's feelings and behavior, improving interpersonal relationships and problem-solving skills, and reducing violence and absenteeism. Their effectiveness is optimized when they are used with all grade levels, from pre-K through 12, and when the tenets of the SECD are incorporated into lesson plans, field trips, extracurricular activities, and all aspects of a child's life.

## Essential Takeaways

- Character education and social–emotional learning begin at home and form the foundation of self-esteem, self-confidence, and positive social relationships.

- Parents and caring adults can help to reduce a child's vulnerability to targeting and bullying behaviors and positively enhance self-confidence and social competence by modeling good character and positive, respectful relationships.

- Positive character traits and social and emotional skills can be learned; schools that provide education in these skills report increased student success and decreased incidents of bullying and victimization.

- Many schools offer SECD as part of their K-12 curriculum. Topics help kids develop strong moral character, self-reflection and control, and interpersonal and problem-solving skills.

# Part 3

# Intervention

In response to highly publicized bullying incidents around the country in the last decade, many states have enacted antibullying legislation. Targets of bullies are also often protected under Title IX education amendments to the Civil Rights Act, which prohibits discrimination on the basis of race, color, national origin, sex, disability, and age. Additionally, many schools have their own antibullying policies in place. In the following chapters, we take a look at these laws and describe how you can use them to protect yourself or your child from aggressive behavior.

We also discuss ways parents and other adults can talk to kids about bullying, how to seek help from schools, and what further actions can be taken if necessary. We introduce a variety of intervention strategies that everyone who cares about kids can use to help children who are targeted as well as the kids who engage in bullying behaviors. We also talk about how the silent majority, the bystander, can be transformed into an upstander.

# chapter 10

# Assessing and Reporting

Knowing when bullying violates civil rights

Sorting out variations among states' bullying laws

Tracing online bullying to school

Transforming tragedy into legislation

Following the 2010 suicide of Phoebe Prince, a South Hadley, Massachusetts, high school student who was called names like *slut* and *whore*, was threatened with physical attacks, had things thrown at her, and was taunted on Facebook, five of her peers were charged with crimes ranging from criminal harassment to civil rights violations.

These charges represented a watershed moment in restorative justice around bullying cases. Five of the teens were sentenced to probation and community service, and the family reached a $225,000 settlement with the district for the school's failure to stop the harassment. As a result of Phoebe's suicide, as well as the 2009 suicide of Carl Walker Hoover, an 11-year-old boy from nearby Springfield, Massachusetts, in May 2010, the commonwealth passed a series of comprehensive bullying laws that also address cyberbullying and require every school district to follow a Model Bullying and Intervention Plan.

At the time of this writing, the only state yet to pass some form of anti-bullying law is Montana. That being said, laws vary widely from state to state. Some states define bullying with great specificity, mandate comprehensive reporting requirements, and require that all districts adopt prevention programs and professional development. Other states merely require that each school board include within the student code of conduct a clause prohibiting bullying and harassment, yet they don't even define what constitutes bullying behavior.

Bullying legislation is a rapidly shifting terrain; refer to the resources at the back of the book for additional ways to find out more about your district's policies and your state's current laws. In the meantime, let's take a look at where federal and state bullying policies stand today.

# Federal Laws: The Office for Civil Rights

When bullying violates the protections guaranteed by Title IX of the Education Amendments to the Civil Rights Act, the federal government has the authority to intervene. Title IX prohibits discrimination on the basis of race, color, national origin, sex, disability, and age at any educational institution that receives funding from the U.S. Department of Education.

In 2010, following the bullying-related suicides of five kids in the span of just a few months, the Office for Civil Rights (OCR) published an open letter to school districts nationwide, clarifying how bullying is related to their Title IX obligations. It also outlined schools' responsibilities to investigate and respond to bullying and signaled the extent to which the federal government is taking this issue very seriously.

## Bullying Prohibited by Title IX

If a hostile school environment is created through peer harassment and bullying based on disability, race, color, national origin, or sex, and school staff haven't appropriately responded or addressed the behavior, that school may be in violation of Title IX. These laws also protect young people from harassment on the basis of their LGBT status, as well as kids who don't identify as LGBT but are bullied on the basis of their perceived sexual identification or gender stereotype.

These guidelines include bullying behavior across the spectrum, from name-calling and verbal attacks to cyberbullying or bullying via cell phones to behavior intended to physically threaten, harm, or humiliate. The OCR letter goes on to say that harassment doesn't have to include threats of harm, but can create a hostile environment severe enough to limit a student's opportunity to participate in school and related activities.

**Bully Buster**

A child doesn't have to identify as gay, lesbian, bisexual, or transsexual to be the target of gender-based discrimination that qualifies as harassment prohibited under Title IX. For example, if a boy is of slight build and has effeminate mannerisms and is constantly taunted with homophobic slurs online and at school, and the school has refused to intervene because he isn't gay, that's an example of a Title IX violation.

## Who Is Responsible for Upholding Title IX

Under the OCR's guidelines, all school personnel are legally required to address bullying as part of their responsibility to uphold civil rights laws. School officials are expected to address all incidents of harassment they're aware of or, notably, that they *should have been* aware of, including bullying that's apparent and takes place during school, on school grounds, on a school bus, or at extracurricular activities, as well as misconduct the school becomes aware of that happens *off school grounds* but which creates a hostile environment *at school.*

Schools risk being in violation of Title IX when harassment is encouraged, not adequately addressed, or ignored by school officials, to the extent that it creates a hostile environment for any group protected by civil rights laws.

For many parents who have attempted to get protection for their children but have gotten no response from other parents or the police and no action from their school district, Title IX may be an opportunity for recourse. If a school fails to uphold its Title IX responsibilities, it could lose federal funding and provide the basis for a lawsuit.

If your educational institution receives federal funding and has failed to effectively respond to bullying your child has been the target of on the basis of race, color, national origin, sex, disability, or age discrimination, you can file a complaint with the Office for Civil Rights. Complaints must be filed within 180 days of the event, and can be filed through the OCR's online system, by email or fax, or by mail. For more information, visit www2. ed.gov/about/offices/list/ocr/docs/howto.html.

# All State Laws Aren't Made Equal

While the overwhelming majority of U.S. states currently have laws that mandate school districts adopt policies regarding bullying, these laws vary widely in their depth, detail, and effectiveness, and even the ways they define bullying. A 2011 report from the Department of Education found that three states don't even define the behavior that constitutes bullying, leaving their policies open to interpretation. Some state laws go a long way in defining procedures districts must take to address bullying, while others just say districts must enact some kind of policy. Some states inform districts to clearly post and familiarize staff and students with their bullying guidelines; others don't. And many states use terms such as "bullying" and "harassment" interchangeably, though the two can have very different legal implications if the harassment is based on the target's characteristics, and therefore subject to civil rights protections.

Many state laws define bullying as the repeated use by one or more students of a written, verbal, or electronic expression or a physical act or gesture or any combination thereof, directed at a victim that:

- Causes general harm, physical harm, psychological harm, or threats or fear of harm,

- Results in property damage,

- Constitutes a reprisal for reporting bullying, harassment, or intimidation,

- Creates a hostile environment at school for the target; infringes on the rights of the target at school; or materially and substantially disrupts the education process or the orderly operation of a school.

Many states prohibit bullying in the following places:

- On school grounds

- On property immediately adjacent to school grounds

- At a school-sponsored or school-related activity, functions, or programs, whether on or off school grounds

- At a school bus stop, or on a school bus or other vehicle owned, leased, or used by a school district or school

- Through the use of technology or an electronic device owned, leased, or used by a school district or school

Bullying doesn't have to happen at school for a school to have the authority to take action. For example, Massachusetts legislation mandates that schools must take action, regardless of where or through what device the bullying occurs, as long as it "materially and substantially disrupts the education process or the orderly operation of a school."

Some states go further than others in specifying the kinds of behaviors that constitute bullying. For instance, Utah's laws include "forced or unwilling consumption of any food, liquor, drug, or other substance by a school employee or student; any forced or coerced act or activity of a sexual nature or with sexual connotations such as asking prospective or active team members to remove articles of clothing or expose or touch private areas of the body." Utah also includes forced exposure to cold or the elements as bullying behavior.

Some states, such as Texas, also mandate schools to provide counseling for bullies and targets, and require parental notification of incidents and action regarding dating violence.

## Professional Development Requirements and Curriculum

Over half of the states with bullying policies mandate that districts create professional development and training for school staff to educate them on their district's policies and how to effectively handle bullying. Some legislation goes much further in outlining the kinds of professional development districts are required to provide than others. New York State's Dignity Act, for example, mandates that one staff member at each campus receive special training in handling conflicts arising through discrimination related to race, color, weight, national origin, ethnic group, religion, religious practice, disability, sexual orientation, gender, and sex.

Massachusetts requires all schools to implement a bullying prevention curriculum for all grades and to provide professional development on how to identify, prevent, and respond to bullying for all staff—including teachers, administrators, school nurses, cafeteria workers, custodians, bus drivers, athletic coaches, advisers to extracurricular activities, and paraprofessionals—to prevent, identify, and respond to bullying.

## Enforcement from State to State

Several states now have laws that include criminal consequences for bullying, although the requirements and sanctions vary significantly. Some require schools to report any bullying acts that may constitute unlawful behavior to law enforcement; others outline ways to determine when bullying acts should be reported to law enforcement. Missouri laws stipulate legal repercussions for school staff who don't comply with that state's reporting requirements if bullying behavior constitutes criminal activity.

In Texas, disruption of class is a class C misdemeanor; in Delaware, the bullying law states "harassment, which is any attempt to harass, annoy, or alarm another person, is a class B misdemeanor offense." When states have their own antidiscrimination laws (separate from federal laws), such as in New Jersey, school districts can be held accountable for failing to uphold those laws and allowing discrimination-based bullying to take place in school.

## State Laws and Youth with IEPs

Under the Individuals with Disabilities Education Act, any child who has been determined to be eligible to receive special education and/or related services due to having a disability is eligible to receive a free and appropriate education in the least restrictive environment. The student is to be provided with an Individualized Education Program (IEP), a legal document that includes detailed information about a child's disability, and how that impacts progress and performance in school; the student's unique set of educational needs, including strengths and weaknesses and interests; and details of her educational program and placement.

Statistics show that a child with special needs or a learning disability is disproportionately more likely to be the target of bullying, so an IEP can be a vital part of those families' bullying prevention plan. Parents can work with their child's case manager and IEP team to identify and meet her individual needs and to:

- Identify an adult in the building she can go to for help or to report bullying.

- Develop a plan for how school staff will report and document all bullying incidents.

- Develop a plan for how she'll navigate safely through hallways between classes.

- Create a plan to build awareness and understanding among her peers about special needs and learning disabilities.

- Ensure staff members are aware of her disability and that they have been instructed to shadow or keep an eye out for her, especially in areas of low supervision, such as at lunch or recess.

Some state bullying laws, such as those in Massachusetts, specifically mandate that if a child with an IEP has a disability that limits social development, or if it's determined that her disability affects social skill development or that she's vulnerable to harassment as a result of her disability, her IEP must include provisions for how school staff will respond and protect her from bullying. Although Massachusetts has some of the most progressive antibullying laws in the country, parents in other states can contact their department of education to learn whether there are mandates for youth with IEPs and bullying in their districts.

**parent pointer**

Keep in mind that regardless of whether your state's laws carry specific guidelines for incorporating bullying prevention into IEPs, federal law entitles every child receiving special education to free, appropriate public education; if they're being bullied, that can be an impediment to receiving that education.

# Cyberbullying Laws Have Teeth

More and more states are enacting laws that mandate that school districts adopt policies related to cyberbullying and the use of electronic communication to harass, intimidate, or bully. As with traditional bullying, every state's cyberbullying clause is different; however, most share the following basic guidelines, prohibiting ...

- Bullying and harassment (as defined under each state's definition of bullying) of any student or staff through electronic communication.

- Using a school district's computers, software, or network to bully or harass.

- Bullying and harassment via electronic communication that interferes with a student's educational performance, opportunities, or benefits, or substantially disrupts the orderly operation of a school.

Many state laws lack detail on what constitutes cyberbullying, while others go to great length to outline the kinds of behaviors, including the following:

- Creating a web page or blog in which the creator assumes the identity of another person

- The knowing impersonation of another person as the author of posted content or messages

- Spreading or posting of material on an electronic medium that may be accessed by one or more persons

Some states also mandate that each district's bullying prevention plan include professional development for staff that addresses the nature and incidence of cyberbullying and Internet safety issues. Certain states also require every public school providing computer access to students to have a policy regarding Internet safety.

The Department of Education's 2011 report found 13 states included provisions in their cyberbullying laws that give schools jurisdiction over electronic bullying that takes place off campus if it creates a hostile school environment. In Tennessee, "threatening by electronic communication to take action known to be unlawful by any person," not specific to a school environment, is a class A misdemeanor. North Carolina recently passed a law that criminalizes cyberbullying, making it an offense punishable as a misdemeanor for youths under 18, and Kentucky passed the Golden Rule Act, in which harassing behavior and communications fall under statutes in the state's criminal code. And a few states, including Texas and Rhode Island, include specific "sexting" stipulations in their cyberbullying clauses.

MISC.

### Administrator Action

Although more states are taking on cyberbullying that takes place outside school, after school hours, and without the use of school property, initiating penalties for off-campus behaviors poses a challenge to school districts. Many districts imposing in-school consequences for out-of-school behaviors may be confronted with lawsuits alleging First Amendment violations, which guarantee a student's right to freedom of speech and expression. Several states, therefore, expressly limit the school's jurisdiction to cyberbullying taking place on school property, committed with school-owned or -leased computers or networks, or other electronics.

# Bullying in the News and New Laws

In the fall of 2010, in New Jersey, a Rutgers University freshman, Dharun Ravi, set up a webcam to spy on his roommate, 18-year-old Tyler Clementi. Dharun captured an encounter between Tyler and another man, which Dharun streamed online and tweeted about to classmates. Several days after Tyler discovered the encounter had been broadcast, he posted a final message on his own Facebook page, "Jumping off the gw bridge sorry." On September 21, 2010, he leapt to his death from the George Washington Bridge. Ravi was indicted on 15 charges of bias intimidation and using a webcam to spy, and Tyler's story has created a national outpouring of outrage. In the wake of this tragedy, New Jersey passed what many antibullying experts consider the most comprehensive bullying legislation in the country. (In March 2012, Ravi was convicted of invasion of privacy, bias intimidation, witness tampering, and hindering arrest.)

And in 2011, Texas passed Asher's Law, named after Asher Brown, a 13-year-old who committed suicide after enduring years of relentless bullying. This bill includes stipulations for dealing with bullying and state reporting requirements for each of its campuses, and requires all public schools to adopt suicide prevention programs, in addition to anti-bullying policies.

## School Reporting Requirements

Many state laws establish two kinds of reporting requirements: one for all school personnel to report incidents to school authorities, and the second for districts to report data on bullying incidents to the local school board or state department of education. Several states also mandate that districts establish procedures for anonymous reporting by students, and the state of Colorado has enacted specific legislation to establish the Safe-To-Tell electronic hotline, which provides students, teachers, and other school employees with the means to relay information anonymously regarding threats in the school setting.

Many state laws also require districts to adopt policies to provide for an assessment of the prevalence of bullying at each campus within the school district. As with other elements of bullying laws, different states have different ways of assessing school climate and focus on different elements of the problem, such as determining locations where students are unsafe, the prevalence of certain kinds of discriminating behaviors or name-calling, and how safe kids feel at school.

For the most up-to-date policies in your state, visit http://www. violencepreventionworks.org/public/bullying_laws.page.

## The Bullying Specialist

By law, many states now require school districts to designate one person in each building who is the recipient of all bullying, harassment, and intimidation complaints. This person is responsible for upholding the district's policies, procedures, and responsibilities under the state's law, as well as for working with kids and families to help them know their rights and implement bullying prevention plans.

**Parent pointer**

If your district has a designated bullying specialist, he or she can be a great resource in providing support if your child is being bullied, and can also help you navigate your district's policies and responsibilities and determine if your child's bullying constitutes harassment that violates her civil rights. Your district should list your bullying coordinator on its website, or you can call your school to find out how to reach that person.

Different states mandate different school staff be the district's bullying specialist. Massachusetts law designates that each school's principal is the person responsible for implementing the district's bullying plan. In New Jersey, with some of the newest and most progressive laws, principals are required to appoint one of their staff members as the school's antibullying specialist, specifying that the position must be filled by the currently employed guidance counselor, school psychologist, or another similarly trained individual to fill this role. In addition, New Jersey law stipulates that there must also be a district-level antibullying coordinator, appointed by the superintendent, who works with each school's coordinator, implements districtwide bullying prevention programs, and creates reports for the state's department of education.

As state laws regarding bullying and cyberbullying become more comprehensive, and as schools increasingly find themselves navigating tricky territory between bullying, harassment, and offenses that violate civil rights and the law, both parents and schools are being given a quickly increasing array of resources to protect children from bullying.

## The Safe Schools Improvement Act

Introduced by Representative Sanchez and Senator Casey, the Safe Schools Improvement Act (H.R.1648/s.506), currently in both the House of Representatives and the Senate, would for the first time establish a federal definition of bullying and protect all students nationwide from bullying. The SSIA would mandate that all schools and districts receiving federal funds adopt antibullying policies that prohibit bullying and harassment on the basis of disability, race, color, religion, national origin, sex, sexual orientation, and perceived or actual gender identity. SSIA would also create stricter policies for how schools prevent and effectively handle bullying, and would include reporting and data collection requirements to the Department of Education. Stay tuned as these bills gain support in Congress!

## Essential Takeaways

- The federal government has taken the lead in providing guidelines and requirements for school districts to fulfill their obligations to uphold all students' civil rights. Where bullying violates civil rights, schools must take action.

- The majority of U.S. states currently have laws on the books regarding bullying, though these vary greatly in their breadth and depth and the kinds of behaviors they restrict.

- More and more states are adopting laws that prohibit cyberbullying, both inside and outside school if it creates a hostile school environment.

- As a way of making schools accountable, many states have reporting requirements in their laws at both the local and district levels, as well as the designation of bullying specialists to ensure that state policies are being followed.

# chapter 11

# Getting Help from Your Child's School

Talking to your kids about telling

Taking advantage of the many ways to report bullying

Meeting with your child's school staff

Recent studies have revealed that a third of middle school students and a quarter of high school students feel school staff aren't doing enough to prevent bullying. Many students feel that when staff intervene, they often make the situation worse, and most kids say they're far more likely to go to a friend than talk to an adult if they're being bullied.

When researchers compared students' and staff members' perceptions about school bullying, they found huge discrepancies between how prevalent staff felt bullying is at school versus the opinions of young people themselves. Kids report witnessing far more bullying, and identify far more targets of bullying, than do adults. Studies have also found that school staff had an easier time identifying bullying among elementary school students, where bullying behaviors tend to be overt, than among middle and high school levels, when bullying behaviors become much more nuanced.

If our kids can't talk to their own parents about bullying, they're probably not talking to school staff, either. Starting the conversation can be an important part of helping them recognize the problem, develop the skills to resolve and report it, and, when necessary, to get help.

## How to Talk to Kids About Telling

If your son is being bullied, there are numerous reasons he might not want to tell you about it. While he may have reported even the slightest injustice to you as a young child, as an adolescent—when bullying peaks—he's in the process of separating and becoming more independent from you. Maybe he feels he can handle the situation on his own. Maybe he's embarrassed and doesn't want to admit it's happening. Maybe he's seen how busy you are and doesn't want to add stress to your life. Perhaps he thinks you won't be able to help, or fears you'll only make it worse. Or maybe he's afraid that you'll just tell him to "man up." Here are the some of the top reasons kids don't tell:

- They fear retaliation, or developing a reputation as a tattler.
- They don't want their friends to think they're lame or to lose status in their group.
- They don't recognize certain behaviors, such as exclusion or social manipulation, as bullying.
- They feel like they deserve it.
- They think adults will intervene in such a way as to make the situation worse.

Like other forms of trauma in which targets experience a sense of shame, silence often surrounds bullying. If your child is willing to talk with you about it, believe him. It's important for you to consider that there is a good chance the situation may be much worse than he's letting on.

One mom we know visited her son's school to sit with him during lunch after he shared with her the extent to which he was being bullied: routinely locked inside lockers, thrown into garbage cans, and his head held in the toilet while other students flushed it. Despite this mother's best intentions, her son was embarrassed by her actions, and warned her if she ever came to school again, he'd stop talking to her about bullying. Shortly after the lunch they spent together, the 13-year-old took his own life. Although our kids, while in the moment, may resent our intervention, if you suspect your child is experiencing bullying beyond what he can handle, it's important that you persist in asking for help and following up: you may be his only advocate.

## Kicking Off the Conversation

When kids are in elementary school, they want to tell their parents every detail of their day and often are anxious to disclose anything bad that's happened. At that point in their development, their connection with their parents is their primary relationship, and they expect their mom and dad to protect them.

If your child comes home from school upset about something that's happened, or doesn't want to go to school, there are several questions you can ask that might help you identify if he's being bullied:

- Did somebody hurt you? What happened? Was it physical? What did they say? Did they call you names?

- Did they know they were hurting you? Did they do it on purpose?

- Did anybody else do or say anything?

- Has it happened before, or does it keep on happening?

- Have you been feeling left out? Why? At what point in the day?

- Was the child who hurt you bigger or older than you, or do you feel like he's more powerful?

- How did it make you feel? How did you respond?

Of course, as kids enter their teens, getting them to talk to their parents can seem like pulling teeth. Their peers are quickly replacing Mom and Dad as their primary relationships. Sometimes the best way to talk about bullying might be to start by talking about things tangentially related.

Here are some questions that might spark a conversation about bullying:

- Where have you been sitting on the bus? With whom?
- Who did you sit with at lunch?
- Which classes/teachers do you like and why—and vice versa?
- Where's your locker? Who else's locker is yours near?
- Are there a lot of cliques inside and outside of school? Do they have titles, like "jocks," "band kids," or "nerds"? Where do you feel like you fit in?
- Which teachers do kids feel like they can talk to?
- Do you see administrators and teachers in the halls between classes?

## Listen Before You Act

If your son tells you he's being bullied, try to remain calm and give him an opportunity to talk. Our children don't always want us to spring into action; often they come to us to help them define the problem. Perhaps your son needs your advice to help him untangle what can feel like a complicated social web. If he's being taunted or pushed around on the bus, his first reaction might be to try to shrug it off and minimize it. Even as adults, we can relate to trying to laugh off a comment or action that has deeply stung us.

Talking to you about bullying might be your child's first chance to grapple with his peer's behavior and realize what's taking place isn't just "drama" or horseplay, it's serious and it isn't funny. Your reaction to the kinds of behavior your child is experiencing can help him see that bullying isn't okay, and he doesn't deserve it.

Try to remain calm, hear your child out, and try not to respond in anger. Let him know that you won't take any action until you discuss it with him, and that you'll work with him to figure out the next steps. Let your child be part of the solution; doing so will help him develop skills he'll use for the rest of his life.

## The Who, When, and How of Telling

Most adolescents are more likely to tell their friends they're being bullied than anyone else. However, if your child is being bullied, it's important to let him know there are lots of people he can go to for support, inside and outside of school, including the following individuals:

- Parents, siblings, grandparents, and other family members or friends' parents

- Teachers, school counselors, school nurses, coaches, bus drivers, peer mentors, school resources officers, IEP aides, the district bullying advocate (if there is one), or afterschool program staff

- Clergy and doctors

- Camp counselors, tutors, and extracurricular activity instructors

- Website administrators and reporting mechanisms on social networking sites or multiplayer gaming sites

Targets can't be the only ones expected to report bullying. If your child is a bystander, whether or not he intervenes in the moment, it's important that he also know to report bullying he witnesses. Often bullying takes place outside of the sight or awareness of adults, in places like bathrooms, hallways between classes, at recess, and online—beyond adults' eyes and ears. If adults don't know bullying is taking place, there's no way for them to intervene.

parent pointer

Most states with bullying policies prohibit retaliation against reporting bullying. If your child is hesitant to file a report, either as a target or a bystander, reassure him that the law is on his side, and that there are major consequences for retaliating against reporting.

## When to Tell: Problem Solving Together

An important part of parenting is teaching kids strong problem-solving skills. Although parents who hover over their kids may have the best intentions, they won't always be there to protect their kids. One of the greatest tools kids can have is how to advocate for themselves and others.

As we covered in Chapter 6, on target proofing kids against bullying, there are lots of ways our kids can respond directly to bullying situations and feel empowered to intervene. Have a conversation with your child about when it's time to tell. Here are some conversation starters:

**What kinds of situations they think they can handle:** name-calling or gossip sometimes can be dealt with on the spot with an assertive response.

**What situations require that they tell an adult**: when bullying consists of physical threats, if it's placing a target in danger, or if it's still going on after bystanders have tried to intervene, it's time to act.

**When it's time for a parent to come to school:** if your child has been a target or a bystander to bullying and has reported it to school staff and no action has been taken to resolve the bullying behavior, it's time for parents or guardians to get involved.

## How to Tell

The distance and anonymity afforded by the Internet makes it easier for some kids to talk about bullying. If you search "bullying" on YouTube, you'll find dozens of testimonial videos from kids sharing with the world their experiences of being bullied and their feelings of frustration and helplessness. Unfortunately, the same is true for the many Facebook memorial pages for young people who have committed suicide due to bullying.

Schools are beginning to recognize that kids are more likely to report bullying if they can do so anonymously, or at least don't have to do it in person. Many schools now have ways for students to anonymously file reports if they've been a target or a witness to bullying. Some districts have boxes throughout school where reports can be submitted; others use online services where a child can file a report that's sent to the school principal.

These days most school websites provide parents and students with ways to email staff and the superintendent's office. Email is a great way for kids (and parents) to report bullying because it enables them to make a note of the date and time the report was sent. With email, you or your child can also attach documentation such as pictures or links to online sites where the bullying might be taking place.

You can also write a letter to your school's principal to report bullying behaviors. As with email, attach as much documentation as possible, such as printouts of any material online, or pictures, and be as specific as possible as to what the behaviors were, who was involved, and whether you have made previous reports. Be sure to date your letter and keep a photocopy for your own records, and send it certified mail, so that you have a record that the letter was received.

Your child can also report bullying the old-fashioned way, by verbally telling an adult. If your child reports bullying to a school faculty member, make sure he makes a note of who he spoke to, what he said, and the date and time. If your child doesn't receive help from school staff, you want to be sure you can document his attempts to get protection before, or in addition to, your getting involved.

## When It's Time for Parents to Get Involved

Although it's important to give your child strategies that will empower him to respond appropriately to bullying and to tell adults, it's time for you to get involved if any of the following situations apply:

- If the bullying persists or escalates
- If it isn't handled appropriately by school staff
- If it contains violent or threatening behavior
- If it's making school toxic for him
- If he's asking for your help
- If the behavior is outside of the parameters you and he have determined he can handle

## How to Make a Report

As we mentioned earlier, there are several ways for you to make a report: through a school's online reporting mechanism, via email, by sending a letter to the school via certified mail with receipt of delivery, over the phone, or in person. Before you pick up the phone or get in your car, you should submit your report in writing so you can document having made the report, including as much information as possible:

- The date, time, and location of the incident(s)

- Details about the behavior that occurred

- The names of all known perpetrators and witnesses

- Any actions your child has previously taken to report the bullying, including who was told and the date

- Any documentation you may have if the bullying is taking place online or through cell phones

**parent pointer**   Be sure to make copies of all correspondence and reports. You should also consider including several people on the correspondence if it's by email, such as the principal and assistant principal, the school's bullying advocate (if applicable), any staff members to whom the bullying was previously reported or who witnessed it, and your child's school counselor.

Once you have the report in writing, follow up with a phone call or a personal visit to your child's school to request a meeting.

## Preparing for the Meeting

When you request a meeting about bullying, ask that the principal, a counselor, and any teachers who may have witnessed the bullying be present. If your child has an IEP, ask that the leader of the IEP team be present.

It's always a good idea to talk to other parents who have had bullying meetings so you know what to expect: Is the principal inclined to be helpful? Was he or she empathetic? Did the school take action or, alternately, were administrators defensive and dismissive? Did other parents have a sense that the problem is pervasive and being swept under the rug, or that administrators are proactive?

These meetings can be very intimidating, especially in schools that don't take bullying seriously, so the more you know ahead of time, the better prepared you'll be. Here are some things to do in advance of the meeting:

- Plan to bring your spouse or a family member or friend for support.
- Familiarize yourself with all state laws, your school's bullying policy, and the district's responsibilities.
- If your child's bullying consists of bias or discrimination, familiarize yourself with your school's obligations to uphold their Title IX obligations (see Chapter 10).
- Bring all documentation of reports you or your child has made, and any documentation of the bullying.
- Bring a notebook and pen so you can take notes and follow up later.

Come prepared with any questions you may have, such as:

- Have there been other incidents of bullying in this class, school bus, bathroom, etc.?
- If so, what steps have been taken to resolve it?
- Is there any other information the teacher or witness may have?
- Has the counselor or other adults noticed a change in your child's behavior or academic performance?
- What are the school's policies for resolution?

## What Will Happen

It's natural that if you're going into a meeting because your child is being bullied, you feel frustrated and perhaps even outraged if it's been ongoing. It's also natural to feel like you may have somehow failed, especially if you're just finding out about a situation that has been happening for weeks or months. If your child has been chronically bullied for years, you may also feel helpless and marginalized.

**parent pointer**

Whether it's your first or fifth time meeting with the principal, you have every right to expect that your school's staff will help you resolve the situation and provide a safe learning environment for your child. Be direct and assertive in outlining your concerns and expectations.

The meeting should give you the opportunity to fully present the context of the bullying, to explain the actions you've taken to report it, and to ask questions of the staff. If your child has an IEP that includes stipulations for a social disability, you should also make sure the principal understands the disability and the IEP plan. You may also want to ask the school for a letter to bring to your employer, if you risk losing pay or are forced to take a day off work in order to attend the meeting.

By the end of the meeting, you and the school staff should have a plan of action you feel good about. This may include the following actions by the school:

- Launch an investigation
- Call the parents of the bullying child to engage them in the resolution
- Provide consequences for the bullying child
- Remove the bully, *not the target,* from a class, the cafeteria, a school bus, a sports team, or, in extreme cases, from the school's campus altogether
- Provide counseling for the bully and the target
- Address the failure with that staff member if the bullying has been witnessed by faculty who failed to respond

- Educate all students about that disability if the bullying is the result of a disability discrimination

- Give your child strategies to deal with the situation, such as leaving a class early or allowing him a hall pass to see the counselor or other designated "safe" adult

- File a report with the school resources officer and/or local police department if the behavior is criminal

- Provide clear next steps

- Schedule a follow-up meeting

## Taking Things to the Next Level

If administrators are dismissive, minimize the problem, or otherwise fail to adequately address the bullying and your concerns, you have options.

If your district has a bullying advocate, you should contact this person. You should also send the superintendent's office a report from the meeting and all your backup documentation. You can also send a copy of that information to the members of your local school board. If the bullying is discrimination based or ongoing, you can file a report with the Office for Civil Rights, as we discuss in Chapter 10.

## Engaging the Bully's Parents or Guardian

In addition to approaching your school, you may also try directly engaging the parents of the bullying child. Know that the instinctual response from parents confronted with their child's bullying behavior may well be to go on the defensive, so it's important you approach the conversation with an open and kind attitude. Instead of having an accusatory tone ("your child did X to my child") ask them by phone or email if they would be willing to sit down with you to talk about concerns regarding how your children are interacting. This may be the first time that the parents are being made aware of their child's behavior, so try to maintain a spirit of working together to solve a problem.

Here are some tips when approaching a bullying child's parents:

- Begin positively. Point out some of their child's good attributes or shared experiences between your kids.

- Describe your concerns using "I" statements. Describe what your child is experiencing using "my child" statements.

- Come equipped with some ideas for how the situation might be remedied.

- Give them the opportunity to express their perspective, and keep an open mind if you discover the situation is more complicated than what it seemed.

- Ask them how you might work together to make things better.

## When Your Child Is the Bully

No parents want to get a phone call from another parent or their school's principal informing them that their child has been bullying other students. As parents, we take great pride in our children's accomplishments, and when they fail or get in trouble, the inverse is true. If our child is bullying others, we may feel it's our fault or that it reflects badly on us. It can be disappointing and disheartening, and if he's rebelling, it may increase our sense that he's "lost" and may make us incredibly angry or defensive.

parent pointer

If you know or suspect your child is bullying, it can have serious consequences for the whole family. In almost half of U.S. states, if a child is accused of assault, causing harm to others, personal injury, or "malicious acts," the parents can be found guilty of negligence if they were aware of the child's behavior.

Although you have every right to ask for evidence that your child is, in fact, bullying, and to be given the full range of circumstances and background of the situation, you need to take the allegations seriously. Try to respond with an open mind, and know that although your instinct may be to stick up for your child, find fault elsewhere, or minimize the behavior, you're not doing your child any favors in the long run by enabling his behavior.

If you child is bullying, your school may …

- Suspend or otherwise penalize your child at school.

- Remove your child from areas of the school campus, and take away bussing, computer, and other school privileges.

- Recommend that you participate in a dialogue with the parents of the target.

- Recommend that your child participate in a problem-solving skills program.

- Have him make restitution to the student he bullied.

- Recommend that he be evaluated to determine whether his behavior is related to faulty thinking or underdeveloped coping skills. He may have inadequate social-emotional-behavioral skills, or other deficiencies of executive functioning.

- Refer him to a mental health professional to determine whether he poses a threat to others and whether he is appropriate to attend school. He may also be referred for counseling.

- Report the offense to the police or file charges.

Try to work with the school on actions that will result in positive long-term change. As the consequences of your child's behavior increase, so can the ways it affects the entire family.

**Bully Buster**

If your child is bullying others and is not respecting his peers, school staff, or you, you may ask that staff help you identify a mentor who can provide some "tough love." This might be an art teacher, a coach, or someone else your child looks up to because of his own aspirations.

## Essential Takeaways

- Most kids don't report bullying to an adult, including parents. Find ways to connect with your child about bullying, or ask questions that might lead to a conversation about it.

- If your child tells you he's being bullied, try to listen before you act, and come up with a plan of action together.

- When it's time to intervene, make a written report to the school, followed by a request for a meeting. Prepare for the meeting by bringing documents, questions, and assembling key staff, and expect to develop an intervention plan before the meeting ends.

- If you receive a phone call from school administrators that your child is bullying others, try to have an open mind and work with staff and other parents to resolve the issue.

# chapter 12

# Helping the Target

- Helping targets develop their potential
- Identifying who can help a target and how
- Giving targets the tools to thrive

We may forget the names of our elementary school teachers or high school crushes, the address of our childhood home or our first phone number, but the names and faces of the children who bullied us, the things they said or did, and where the bullying took place remain emblazoned on our memories for life. Bullying is so universal and touches us in so many ways, because the experience of being targeted defines patterns that can last a lifetime: how we feel about ourselves, the careers we choose, and the roles we play in our families and communities.

While no one should ever have to go through the pain and trauma of being targeted, the outcomes of these experiences don't necessarily have to have long-term negative impacts. In fact, being bullied can open doors for kids to develop skills, maturity, relationships, and independence that can turn a painful encounter into an opportunity for growth. As evidenced by the number of Olympic athletes, such as diver Tom Daley, or people in creative fields, such as Lady Gaga and Demi Lovato, who were bullied as teens, it can also foster the ability to be independent thinkers who don't go with the crowd and who use their creativity to build bridges.

With support from family, friends, educators, and people in their community, kids who are targeted can turn these experiences into opportunities; however, it requires a huge amount of help, reassurance, and commitment, without which targets face a tough road. In this chapter, we look at some of the ways we can support targets, lifting them up to become some of the most important members of our communities and society as a whole.

## The Long-Lasting Scars of Bullying

It doesn't take an impending high school reunion to throw us back to the feelings we had as adolescents. As evidenced by the many successful adults who've recently given voice to the ways bullying has shaped their lives, the emotional trauma can take decades to overcome and leave scars that last a lifetime.

**It Will Get Better**

In October 2010, Fort Worth City Councilman Joel Burns addressed the city council with his own painful account of bullying. In a heartfelt speech, he described the slurs and physical attacks he experienced, breaking down as he attempted to express the impact this bullying had on him. He advised kids, "You will get out of that high school and you never have to deal with those jerks again if you don't want to. You will find and you will make new friends who will understand you and life will get so, so, so much better." A video of his speech quickly went viral and has been viewed by over 2.5 million people. You can view the entire speech at www.youtube.com/watch?v=ax96cghOnY4.

However, many adults who were bullied as kids and who muster up the strength to attend those dreaded reunions often discover their bullies have become losers, while the former target has gone on to have a successful career and supportive family. Extrapolating from the social fabric of adolescence, while kids who bully often do so as a way to increase social status and gain recognition from their peers, kids who are targeted are often ostracized and find themselves out of the competition for status. For some kids, this can open up a certain kind of freedom and new opportunities: if they aren't caught up in the time- and energy-consuming race to be cool or win acceptance, they may seek out other activities to which they commit their energy.

Many people who become successful artists, writers, athletes, filmmakers, scientists, and innovators were bullied as kids, and found their experience of being targeted ultimately led them to think outside of the box, to pour themselves into their passions, to foster kind relationships, and to use their capacity for empathy as an asset in the choices they make later in life. That said, in order for targets to heal from the experience of being bullied, and to transform those experiences into insight and positive motivation, they need a lot of patience, reassurance, understanding, and guidance. They'll also need reinforcement, care, and ongoing commitment from those around them.

# Who Can Help

If your daughter is a target, there are many people who can help, in a variety of ways. One of the things adults who were targeted share is that when they graduated from high school and made their own way in the world, their horizons widened and those comments on the school bus held a lot less weight.

One of the ways we can help targets is to offer them many opportunities to be successful and to further define themselves. So while help may come from people within their school walls, like teachers, counselors, the school nurse, the bus driver, or administrators, it may also come from people outside of school, all of whom are vital in helping our children develop a complete picture of themselves.

## Family Is Vital

As parents, we are our children's greatest source of support. It's up to us to establish an environment in our home where our children understand that abuse—whether it is from a peer, a family member, or a stranger—is unacceptable. Often, kids who are targeted feel like they somehow deserve to be bullied, that it's their fault for in some way being different, for not being cool enough, for not being able to navigate their social spheres smoothly. Or maybe they even blame us. If it weren't for our move to a new place, our daughter wouldn't be the new kid; if it weren't for our financial stress, maybe we could buy her cool clothes; if it weren't for our genes, maybe she wouldn't always be the tallest kid in her class.

Even though it can be painful for us to hear these things, the underlying sentiment is that there's some inherent quality in the target that's attracting the abuse. Changing that perspective, and helping our kids understand that they are who they are and that they don't deserve to be tormented for any reason, is part of helping them grow.

## Coaches and Mentors

In the process of making the movie *Bully,* Cynthia encountered a boy who was terribly bullied within the walls of his school, though outside of school, he was a world-champion Irish step dancer. Although he was beloved by his instructors and peers in the dance world, his dancing was one of the main things he was teased about in school. The bullying eventually became so bad that he switched to a different school, where he resolved to never tell anyone about his dancing. Within a few months he discovered the climate of this new school to be accepting, and with the confidence of competing successfully at the world championship level, he told his peers about his secret "other" life. To his surprise, he found them to be supportive, and by the end of his first year there he was thriving both inside and outside of school.

Giving children who are targeted the opportunity to shine and to partici-pate in activities that allow them to dive into the things that complement their personalities can be a vital asset for them. Your child may lack the gymnastics to be a star cheerleader, but if she gravitates to chess or opera or creative writing, she'll find like-minded peers—and adults—who support her talents. These instructors and peers can be vital in helping a child shed the target identity and the feelings of insecurity, low self-esteem, and depression that often come with it. These experiences can also change a child's expectation of how others treat and perceive her.

**parent pointer**

Many parents whose kids are bullied have found enrolling them in martial arts to be a great way to foster assertion, control, strength, and calmness; they discover the opportunity to be part of a community where respect is the *key* ingredient. Your child's martial arts teacher can be a great ally in helping him gain the self-confidence to appropriately deal with bullying in the moment, and to get help when it's needed.

## Faith Communities

Whether you're Christian, Muslim, Hindu, Jewish, or Buddhist, one value all of these faith communities share is treating others with kindness.

Being a member of a faith community can be a great source of support to a child who is bullied. Although your daughter's school may not have the resources, training, or awareness to take on character education, this is something that's of the utmost importance for leaders of faith communities. If your faith community has opportunities for youth involvement or leadership, this can be a great way for your child to take part in activities she may shy away from at school. Members of your faith community can be great mentors for kids, and can give them someone else to go to besides you for advice on how to deal with a bullying situation. As a parent, talking with members of your faith community about your daughter's bullying might be a great way to get others to rally around creating a positive place for her. And if your child is being bullied for her association with that faith group, it can also be an opportunity to gain solidarity with other families and kids who may also be struggling with bullying for that same reason, and to take action in the larger community.

community watch

Following the 9/11 terrorist attacks, many Muslim and Sikh children were the targets of racial discrimination and bias-based bullying. In New York City, the Sikh Coalition and other advocacy organizations joined together to present a white paper and report card on bullying in New York City schools at a public event. They called on the mayor and the school's chancellor to provide greater protection from bullying, and spoke out to raise awareness about discrimination and bullying of Sikh youth.

## Special-Needs Communities

If your daughter has learning disabilities, special needs, or is on the autism spectrum and is being bullied, know that there are other parents at your school who are very likely in the same position. Often kids with special needs share the same teachers, homerooms, or aides, and you'll meet their parents when you go in for back-to-school or orientation night. Be sure to bring a pen and paper and get their email addresses or contact information if your school doesn't provide it, and plan to keep in touch.

Other parents of special-needs kids can be a great source for getting help with bullying and keeping an ear to the ground, especially if your child has trouble communicating with you about being bullied. Find out from your child's IEP team which other children your daughter gravitates toward, and make a connection with those parents. Sometimes, kids with autism or special needs that affect their communication skills can have a hard time reaching out to socialize; if you can connect with other parents, you can also set up times to hang out outside of school and develop friendships.

As we discussed in Chapter 4, kids with special needs and learning disabilities are disproportionately likely to be bullied, so having a community of parents who are all in touch and keeping track of who was bullied last week, what was done about it, who was the target this week, and so on can help parents collectively assess the climate for special-needs youth at the school and put pressure on administrators if they aren't being protected.

## Other Parents and Peers

Other parents can be vital in helping a target heal and grow. As the saying goes, it takes a village to raise a child, and the more we connect with other adults in our community, the more collective responsibility everyone feels to make sure every child is safe. Often, as our kids grow older and mature, they want to talk less to us but open up to other adults they admire. If your child spends a lot of time at a particular friend's house, that child's parents can be vital in helping build her up if she's being bullied, especially if the child doing the bullying is a member of their group of friends.

The more a community of parents is aware of the behaviors among the kids, the more involved they can be in providing support and looking out for each others' kids.

**parent pointer**

If kids hang out at your house, and you notice one member of the group is conspicuously absent, ask why. Especially among girls, exclusion can be a major bullying weapon, and it may be taking place in your home. Talk to your child and her friends about how they would feel if one of them was home alone while everyone else was here together. You may also want to reach out to the excluded child's parents, to let them know what's going on and find solutions. Although you can't control what happens in others' homes, you can tell your child she may not invite a particular group over if they're excluding a member of it.

# How to Help

As we discussed in Chapter 6, which looked at ways to target proof our kids, there are lots of tools we can give our children to prevent them from being bullied, including:

- Developing self-confidence and the ability to assert themselves
- Working on conflict resolution and problem-solving skills
- Building relationships

However, even with the best prevention efforts, we can't control all of the challenges our children will encounter, especially given the endless reasons young people are bullied—for their weight, for the way they talk, or for the color of their hair or skin.

Helping our children recover from being targeted by bullies is very different than prevention: once a child has been bullied, you have to take into account the emotional trauma and vulnerability they're likely to be feeling. Anyone who's ever fallen off a horse knows it was much easier getting on the first time, when all you were thinking about was how exciting it was going to be, than it is the second time, when you're covered with bruises.

The strategies and suggestions we've discussed throughout this book are useful for working with a child who has been targeted; however, the victim of targeting may need reinforcement of those skills and strategies, along with additional kinds of assistance for varying lengths of time, depending upon their own unique set of circumstances and interpretation of what has happened.

## Recognizing and Addressing Stress Signals

If your child is being targeted at school or elsewhere, she may be sending out signals that she is distressed, such as:

- **Physical symptoms:** Headaches, stomachaches, diarrhea, vomiting, dizziness, bedwetting, changes in sleep patterns, energy level, weight gain/loss

- **Emotional/behavioral symptoms:** Fear, worry, irritability, crying, obsessive behaviors, tics, tantrums, withdrawal, extreme shyness, changes in eating habits, school avoidance, loss of interest in preferred activities or changes in friendships, low self-esteem, running away, cutting, suicidal ideation or attempt.

Parents need to be open to recognizing the signs that something is going on and be willing to intervene on their child's behalf.

Check in with her teachers, school nurse, and school counselor to share your concerns and gain their perspectives. Family members or others who know your child may also have important information or perspectives to share, too.

Talk with your child about your concerns. Be aware that she may be initially reluctant, and likely quite afraid, to discuss what's been happening. She may deny it altogether, or try to minimize it by calling it drama. Don't become discouraged; she really needs your help—immediately!

Talk with her about what you know about bullying and learn what she knows about it, too. Try to find out what's been going on at school, online, or wherever she's being targeted. Let her know that you're there to help her, that it's not her fault, and that she's not alone anymore. Reassure her that you and your family will be working together with her school to protect her and help turn things around.

## Putting Your Child's Safety First

If your child is being bullied, contact your child's school and request a meeting with the principal, her teachers, or other appropriate personnel to discuss your concerns and address safety issues. (Refer to Chapter 11 to review how to get help from your child's school.)

Some protective measures the school can take may include:

- Increased supervision and safety strategies while she's in the identified areas of targeting (the school bus, hallways, locker rooms, and so on)

- Accommodations to support her safety, such as permitting her to leave the classroom early in order to navigate the hallway safely, change clothes for physical education, and/or or utilize an alternative restroom as needed.

- A safe place for her to go during lunch or recess

These should be carefully considered, identified, and addressed.

## Enhancing Friendship Skills

As we mentioned earlier, children are by nature altruistic, assuming the best of those around them. Given this innocence, it can be a real shock to discover a peer is trying to hurt them. While they approach their first friendships with a clean slate and an undiscerning, open attitude, the experience of being bullied can help them make better choices when it comes to the friendships they seek out in the future.

If your child has been bullied by a friend or by a group of friends, it's time to explore what drew them to that group to begin with. Were they the "popular" kids? Were they intimidating? Where did they stand in the social strata in comparison to your child and the school community? What does your child share in common with them and what was the basis for the friendship? What does the child who was doing the bullying think she was getting out of it?

Being bullied can offer some hard-learned insights into human behavior. Whether repairing old friendships or beginning new ones, parents can help their child to …

- Seek out friendships where the power in the relationship is balanced.

- Set clear expectations of how a child wants to be treated.

- Identify when a peer is being abusive or using manipulative or blatant bullying behavior.

- Develop friendships based on solid foundations, such as mutual interests and values, rather than on popularity or cliques.

**parent pointer** Often, your child's best-friend-to-be may be right under her nose; she just hasn't noticed him yet. Although the instinct may be to shut down and withdraw after being bullied, we can help our children reach out and cultivate new friendships by identifying kids she may never have thought of, or by expanding her social circle by offering new activities and opportunities to meet people.

## Teaching Stress Management

Although bullying may leave lifelong scars, the sooner we can help our children cope with the emotional impacts of being targeted, the easier time they will have forming positive relationships and breaking the association between peers and abuse. The tools to manage stress may include …

- Giving them the opportunity to express their feelings.

- Encouraging them to take part in vigorous physical activities and hobbies.

- Eating healthy meals.

- Developing mental exercises, such as picturing a favorite peaceful place, breathing exercises, and progressive-relaxation exercises.

- Handling your own stress calmly; your habits and behaviors will rub off on them.

## Fostering Resilience

Children are incredibly resilient. The more they feel supported, hopeful, and capable, the better they can recover from stressful situations. Here are some ways you can help your child bounce back:

- Foster her sense of effectiveness by giving her tasks she can successfully accomplish.

- Give her opportunities to problem solve and take charge of making certain things better herself, which will allow her to feel a sense of autonomy.

■ Underscore her sense of worth and lovability: give her affection or take time to spend an afternoon doing something special that she enjoys together; if you have a Bring Your Daughter to Work day, participate and highlight her accomplishments.

The more your children feel that they're able to manage difficult situations effectively, and that they can be their own agents of change, the more they'll be able to use their experiences to fulfill their goals.

## Practicing Situations

We've all had the experience of rehearsing in our heads the things we *wished* we had said during a conflict, if only we hadn't been caught off-guard. The more prepared our children are to face potentially stressful situations, the better they can effectively handle them. One way to practice is to role-play. Join her in generating sample scenarios your child has contended with or she might be worried about—at school, outside school, or online. Some things to take into account when role-playing are:

■ Maintaining direct but nonthreatening eye contact.

■ Displaying an assertive, confident posture: head up, shoulders back, arms and hands relaxed at her side.

■ Speaking directly, deliberately, and clearly.

■ Clearly defining the unwanted behavior and expressing that it needs to stop.

> **parent pointer** You may want to help her practice these assertiveness skills in less-threatening situations first, such as sending a dish back in a restaurant, asking for a refund or exchange at a supermarket, or asking for assistance in finding a size, color, or style of shirt from a salesperson in a clothing store.

Keep in mind that everyone has their own personal style, and that it takes lots of practice and patience. It's important to encourage her to be patient with herself as she develops these new skills.

Knowing how to avoid or minimize a stressful situation is helpful to practice, too. For example:

- Practice "fogging," which minimizes the impact of what a bully says by having the target neutralize the meaning of it. For instance, if someone tells your child, "You're fat, ugly, stupid ..." a good response might be "Whatever," or "So I've heard," or "So you think." Such responses take the wind out of the bully's hurtful comments while also being nonconfrontational.

- Avoid potential bullying situations altogether. For example, help her figure out the best time to eat lunch to minimize discomfort, and discuss where and with whom she can sit when she does eat. If she's not ready to eat in the lunchroom yet, help her generate some alternatives.

**Parent pointer**

Look for library books that have stories similar to the stresses your child is facing as a way to spark a conversation about problem solving, or share your own anecdotes of things you dealt with when you were her age and how you got through and grew beyond the situation successfully. For example, Dr. Seuss' *Oh, the Places You'll Go* follows its hero through life's high points, as well as the lows, from mix-ups, loneliness, and fear, to tackling challenges and moving mountains.

## More Ways That Schools Can Help Targets

In this section, we cover additional ways that schools can cultivate a positive climate and help targets recover.

Some schools have programs that connect faculty members to students; they require every single staff member to choose a new incoming middle or high school student to mentor. While administrators are often overwhelmed with the number of things that come their way every day, every single adult at school can be part of looking out for targets. The more connections made between kids and adults in the building, the more everyone will own the culture.

School buses are notorious places for bullying behaviors. Administrators should take special care to address behavior on buses by giving drivers the opportunity to sit down with the kids on their bus at the beginning of the school year to establish ground rules, perhaps even assigning seating. The same is true for the cafeteria. Many schools now have seating assignments in the lunchroom that can be organized with an eye toward preventing cliques and giving targets the opportunity to sit with kids who may be of a similar personality.

Here are some other things administrators can do to help targets:

- Develop peer mentor programs where upperclassmen are paired with younger students to instill positive school values.

- Encourage staff to develop relationships with kids who are vulnerable.

- Educate all students about learning disabilities, special needs, and autism, and promote empathy and understanding.

- Encourage targeted kids to participate in extracurricular activities or school clubs, and encourage coaches and staff to be inclusive and supportive of kids who have been targeted.

## Counseling

Often, kids who have been targeted by bullies need support beyond what family, peers, and schools can offer, especially if they're suffering from depression, anxiety, and self-harming thoughts and behavior. Some schools, by law, now offer counseling to both targets and kids involved in bullying. Your school's counselor can be a great resource in getting help and keeping an eye out for your child while at school. They can also help direct you to a professional therapist outside of school who specializes in working with children and adolescents and can help repair your child's self-esteem and give her additional tools to handle stress and anxiety.

## Essential Takeaways

- Bullying can scar a target for life, but if children are given the proper support to heal, these experiences can offer opportunities for growth and insight, and inform decisions later in life.

- There are lots of people who can support a target: family, coaches, extracurricular instructors, faith communities, other parents, and peers.

- Parents can help children move on from being targeted by offering them opportunities for new friendships and experiences that give them tools to problem solve and gain confidence.

- Schools can help targets by fostering connections between all staff and students, creating mentorship opportunities, and giving targets the chance to meaningfully participate.

# chapter 13

# Helping the Bully

Setting zero-tolerance policies at school and at home

Providing parental support

Helping kids learn new behaviors

Getting schools involved

The idea that a bully is the most despised and feared of all students, and that he is perceived by his peers as unpopular, is simply not true. If that were the case, bullies would be ostracized by their peers, and wouldn't get gratification from their bullying behaviors. In other words, if nobody liked bullies, bullying wouldn't be such a big problem. But the fact of the matter is that bullies come in many different forms and misuse their power in a variety of ways. Bullies are not always obvious, they may be liked by teachers, and they may have quite a bit of status among their peers. The idea that they can just be dismissed as "bad" children is a myth and doesn't do justice to the problem.

To understand bullies requires an understanding of the nuances of adolescent social hierarchies, the impacts of learned behaviors, and the ways in which those with power abuse it and still remain in high esteem by their peers. Bullies often continue to use bullying behaviors because they have found that they work. Unless we create systems in which these behaviors aren't rewarded, and where they don't give the bully what he's seeking from his peer group, we won't be able to change either the bully's behaviors or the expectations of the peer group as a whole.

No matter what the impetus behind a child's bullying behaviors, if we don't help the bully develop appropriate ways to satisfy his desires and to get his needs met, not only are we doing a tremendous disservice to him, but we're also letting other kids in his community down. In the bully triangle, the roles of bully, target, and bystander are interchangeable. If your child were to become the next bully, wouldn't you want someone to step up to help him and your family, too?

# Zero-Tolerance and Tough Love Policies

Many schools have zero-tolerance policies for bullying behavior. Such policies mandate a specific consequence for specific crimes, without any consideration for extenuating circumstances. Everyone gets the same punishment; no questions asked.

Zero tolerance is a powerful stance to take—but difficult to enforce, both in school and at home. The goal behind zero tolerance is to reduce an undesirable behavior. The challenge, however, is that it often makes sense to consider extenuating circumstances, such as the developmental age of the student, their history of problem behaviors, the severity of the crime, or their understanding or intent. We can all agree that bullying cannot be permitted, must be taken seriously, and needs to be addressed immediately. The challenge is intervening in a way that leads to long-term systemic change and prevention, rather than solely by imposing an arbitrary punishment.

Zero-tolerance bullying policies are only as effective as the other prevention, leadership, mentorship, and awareness-building work taking place in the school. Some of the challenges to the effectiveness of zero-tolerance policies include that they lead to under-reporting because targets fear retaliation from bullies receiving harsh penalties. These kinds of policies may also violate IEPs or discriminate against students with special needs. Or they may punish kids who are trying to help—for example, a teenager who jumps into a fight to break it up might get accused of fighting himself.

This is not to say that serious consequences for bullying shouldn't be imposed—they absolutely should. However, kids can be provided with a graduated set of consequences that fit the infraction, along with remedial measures to help kids make positive behavioral changes.

If schools and communities really want to help make a difference, they need to do more than just impose a one-size-fits-all intervention. It's a good idea to dig a little deeper to gain a better understanding of what a child's negative behavior is all about. That will enable us to develop a good set of strategies to help the bully make lasting and meaningful positive changes; knee-jerk reactions can sometimes backfire.

Tough love, with its roots in helping parents deal with out-of-control teens, doesn't mean you treat a child with disrespect, disregard, or insensitivity, despite what you may have heard. It does mean having a clear set of rules and expectations and being willing and able to allow *natural outcomes* and follow through with reasonable and appropriate consequences.

**Definition**

**Natural outcomes** (or consequences) refer to what is likely to happen as a result of a child's behavior, without any intervention from an adult. For example, a child who is mean or cruel is likely to naturally experience a loss of friendships; kids will tend to stay away from him, even more so as they get older. Let your child know that if he isn't nice to other kids, he's likely to lose friends, because most kids really don't like mean people.

## At School

Schools can provide a wide variety of effective consequences for bullying behaviors that are meaningful to kids at various age levels. The earlier behaviors are identified and handled, the better chance they will be prevented in the future. For example, if an elementary school student is seen bullying another during recess, the school might consider the following sanctions:

- Require the student to stay in during recess.

- Involve the student in remedial interventions, such as meeting with the principal or counselor to discuss his feelings, behavior, and what he can do differently to get his needs and desires met next time.

- Have the student telephone his parents to tell them what he did (in the presence of an adult).

- Require the student to apologize to the other student.

- Assign the student a job to do during recess, such as bringing the play supplies out to the playground, which creates responsibility and keeps him out of trouble.

- Provide increased supervision during free playtime until he can demonstrate his ability to play appropriately on the playground.

### Zero-Tolerance Policies Gone Awry

You may have heard of situations in which kids allegedly were suspended from school for questionable reasons: an elementary-school student who brought in a birthday cake and a knife to cut it with, or two elementary school children who were playing a game with finger guns, for example. It's important for schools to develop clear rules and responsible discipline policies, keeping in mind typical behaviors and interests that relate to the age, cultural mores, and abilities of their students.

In the case of an older child who threatens another student's life at school or over the Internet, the school needs to enforce a strict discipline policy. The student will most likely be suspended for a period of time and likely require psychiatric clearance in order to determine whether it's safe for him to return to school, based on a concern that he may pose a danger to himself or others. He is likely to be referred for counseling, and it is frequently suggested that parents deny the student access to Internet, phone, or other privileges, especially in the case of cyberbullying. Police should be notified, and the target's parents or the police may decide to press criminal charges against the student in accordance with district policies or civil law. Parents must always be notified if there is a real or perceived threat, or action taken, to hurt, harass, or intimidate others, or to harm himself.

Schools may have an easier time than parents when it comes to taking a tough love stance with students. That's because schools and classroom teachers generally have a set of rules, expectations, and consequences in place, making it relatively easy to connect a behavior with a consequence. Furthermore, the relationships and dynamics between teachers, administrators, counselors, and students are very different than those within a family.

Most students won't try to negotiate with their teachers to get out of an after-school detention or a suspension as the consequence of a serious infraction in the same way they might try to manipulate their parents into giving them back their cell phones when they're being punished. Kids generally know who enforces rules and who doesn't.

**Bully Buster**    Kids who are aggressive and learn that they can get away with it don't stop their aggression. In fact, it gives them unspoken permission to escalate it.

## At Home

It can be easy for parents to overuse or inconsistently enforce zero-tolerance policies. Overreacting and instituting harsh punishments for relatively minor infractions can send kids the wrong message. Anger, rejection, criticism, shaming, excessive denial of privileges, hitting, and all sorts of punishments often leave a child feeling angry, frustrated, scared, sad, misunderstood, and confused. A parent's reactions can seem especially unreasonable when the punishment doesn't fit the crime or when a child doesn't understand what he did wrong.

Parents can successfully employ tough love strategies to help their kids who bully other kids, treat others—including their parents—with disrespect, or disregard family or school rules. The key is to be clear about what the family expectations are and to have an established set of natural, reasonable, and logical consequences in place that your child understands. The purpose of consequences is to help your child recognize and learn from his mistakes and to make things right, as well as to inspire positive changes in his thinking and in his behavior.

Here are two examples:

**Your son's school calls to tell you that your son got into a fight (again) at lunch.**

- Ask him what happened at lunchtime and let him know what you've been told about it.

- Give him the opportunity to walk through the specific events of the occurrence (what each of the kids said and did), unless he already told you about it when you first inquired.

- Ask why he thinks it happened and how he felt about his behavior.

- Talk about how the other kid might have felt.

- Ask him (or help him if he needs it) to come up with some better choices he could make in the future to deal with this kind of situation.

- Remind him of the rules about fighting and what your family consequences are (no going out this weekend, no computer time, a written apology to the other child, a meeting you'll both be attending at school).

- If he denies it took place, ask the school if they have surveillance cameras in that particular area of the school that you may view, so you can be equipped with the facts.

- If he becomes angry with you or protests the punishment, don't raise your voice back or speak disrespectfully; that only inflames the situation. Calmly repeat the consequence and walk away.

- Enforce the consequence, whatever it is, without giving in.

**Your child speaks disrespectfully to you.**

- Tell him what you saw and heard (I came into your room, I saw you playing video games instead of doing your homework. I asked you to stop playing and to get your homework done, and you told me to leave you alone and to get out of your room.

- Offer him the opportunity to share his perspective of what happened.

- Ask him why he thinks it happened and how he felt about his behavior.

- Ask him how he thinks you might have felt; you can clarify your feelings with an "I" message (see Chapter 6).

- Ask him what he could do differently in the future; help him brainstorm appropriate options if he needs help.

- Remind him of the rules for speaking to you disrespectfully, such as no video games or computer or cell phone use until he speaks to you respectfully for 24 hours.

- Don't get upset if he gets angry, and don't speak to him disrespectfully either; he needs to learn what appropriate behavior is and that you will hold him accountable to the rules.

# Family Involvement and Support

Parents need to take action to help their children if they have trouble managing their emotions, make poor choices, or act aggressively or disrespectfully toward others. If you have a child who is aggressive, either verbally or physically, he really needs your help. The longer you delay, the more difficult it will become to alter his attitudes and change his behavior.

Bully Buster

There are many levels of intervention for bullying behavior, beginning first at home, next at school, and then followed by mental health services, medical intervention, and law enforcement. Don't ignore or enable your child's inappropriate behavior or wait until law enforcement gets involved.

## My Child Would Never …

These can be some of the most embarrassing and regrettable words a parent can say. It can be really hard to acknowledge that your child is aggressive or that he has an attitude problem. It's not uncommon for parents to be shocked to learn that they don't know their children as well as they think they do. Parents can be ignorant of the true nature of their child for any number of reasons, including the first and most obvious one: love is blind (otherwise known as being in denial).

Here are some other possible reasons:

- He's being bullied himself and displacing that aggression onto someone else at school.

- His parents are in denial and don't want to acknowledge it.

- At home his parents give in to whatever he asks for, so the child has no reason to act out around his family.

- His parents are aggressive themselves and don't see anything wrong with his behavior.

- He may have a personality difference with another child or with a teacher.

- He may be having some difficulty in solving problems or managing his emotions at school.

- He may be experiencing stress because of the demands placed on him in the school environment that don't come into play at home—academic frustration or difficulties with transitions from one activity to the next, for example.

- He may be seeking attention or trying to develop or enhance his reputation.

Whatever the case may be, where there's smoke there's usually fire. The matter needs to be thoroughly explored, hopefully with a spirit of open-mindedness and the intention to help everyone involved.

**parent pointer**

Don't shoot the messenger! If someone voices a concern about your child, take responsibility for looking into it and acting upon what needs to be done. Try, as best you can, not to take it as an indictment of your child or of your parenting skills. And certainly don't take out your surprise, anger, or frustration on the person who is reaching out to you—they may be offering you one of the most important wake-up calls you'll ever receive.

## Breaking Through Denial

If you're getting calls from your child's school or from other parents about your child's behavior, it's important for you to break through any resistance you might have. If your child is bullying, or acting aggressively or inappropriately, it doesn't mean you're a bad parent, nor does it mean he's a bad kid. What it does mean is that he has developed a set of inappropriate coping strategies to get what he wants, deal with his feelings, or solve some of his problems.

In addition to some of the signs and symptoms that may indicate a child is displaying bullying behaviors, here are some additional questions you might want to ask yourself:

Does your child …

- Blame other people for his aggressive behavior, make excuses, or get angry when you don't seem to understand or agree with his point of view?

- Disrespect other people's rights and privacy, yet demand that his rights and privacy be respected?

- Try to negotiate his way out of being held accountable, act as if the rules shouldn't apply to him, or debate the fairness of consequences?

- Try to manipulate or intimidate you or others into complying with his demands?

- Idolize, respect, or emulate negative, aggressive, and abusive role models?

- Interpret the actions of others as being aggressive even when they aren't?

- Vie for power and dominance, perhaps even with adults?

If so, it's to his benefit that you recognize these behaviors in him. If you're willing to address these issues, your response speaks volumes about you as a parent. While many people turn away from facing challenges, take no responsibility, and blame everybody else for his problems (especially his school), your child is fortunate to have a parent who doesn't run away from trouble, who models responsibility and accountability, and loves and respects him enough to help him turn things around. If you're this kind of parent, the odds are in favor of your child becoming happy, well adjusted, and successful in life.

**parent pointer**   Most parents would give their son medicine if he had a raging fever. You're not protecting your child by ignoring his aggressiveness or bullying behaviors; in fact, you're actually causing him more harm than good by sending him the wrong message. It's far wiser to be proactive about your child's behavior early on than it is to be filled with regret later.

## Raise and Discuss Your Concerns

You need to be clear with your child about how your family feels about aggression and bullying. Regardless of his motives and whether he's a first-time aggressor or a severe and repeat offender, he needs to understand your expectations and to be held accountable for his attitudes and actions.

Let your child know how much you love him, and then explain what you've been told, heard, or witnessed yourself and that the aggressive behavior you believe he's been engaging in is unacceptable. Tell him that you'll support him in learning to make better choices, and that you'll work on that with him. (Take a look at Chapter 9, which discusses ways you can help him to build social-emotional skills and encourage positive character traits.)

Doing the right thing will make his life, and the lives of others, better. Tell him that he'll feel proud of himself and make his parents proud, too, for taking responsibility for his negative behavior and attitudes, and for working to turn things around. Making positive changes will help him discover his many wonderful talents and the gifts he has to offer to the world. He'll also learn that intimidating or bullying others isn't necessary to feel happy, powerful, and in control of his life.

Let him know that you'll be working closely with his school, maintaining contact on a regular basis to monitor his progress and to support him in his positive growth.

## Setting Expectations and Increasing Accountability

Determine and clearly state your family's position on aggression and bullying. For example, you might say something like this: "In our family we don't disrespect other people; we don't hurt, humiliate, or embarrass anyone. We don't make anyone feel bad or afraid on purpose, and we don't join in with anyone else who's causing harm to other people."

Kids need to be held accountable for their behavior. A child who has a negative attitude toward others and is allowed to engage in disrespectful, aggressive, bullying behaviors has an unhealthy sense of entitlement. Logical and natural consequences help kids learn, so let him know you'll be implementing them.

Here are the steps you can take to help hold your children accountable to the rules and expectations of your family:

1. Describe the behavior that has been reported to you.

2. Let him respond, sharing his sequence of events. Validate his feelings.

3. Remind him that such behavior is unacceptable and that he broke the rule, despite how he felt.

4. Help him problem solve what he could do differently next time.

5. Remind the child of the consequences for breaking the rule about behavior and enforce it.

**parent pointer**

Remember to keep your tone neutral and stay calm when you have this conversation. Getting emotional minimizes your authority and credibility.

Here's an example:

1. Mrs. Jones (school principal) called me today and told me that she saw you push Tommy off the swing at recess.

2. Your child may tell you that he was on the swing first, that Tommy is always annoying and tried to push him off. Validate his feelings by telling him that you understand that he might have felt angry, or frustrated.

3. Remind him that even though he was (frustrated, angry), it is never acceptable to push people off swings.

4. Ask him what he could do differently if he becomes angry or frustrated in the future; help him problem solve if he needs help. For example, he could tell the lunch aide; play a different game; use his words to say how he felt and what he wants. ("I was playing on the swing first, I want you to wait your turn.")

5. Restate the rule and enforce it: You know the rule, and because you pushed Tommy off the swing, you will have to sit out recess tomorrow.

Similarly, if your daughter writes mean comments on another girl's Facebook page, you need to talk to her about her behavior. Remind her that your family doesn't support any acts of bullying or aggression, including on the Internet. Additionally, your daughter will need to publicly confess and apologize to the other girl and to everyone who read the Facebook page. (You need to make sure that you witness it being done.) Because your daughter has demonstrated that she isn't able to handle electronic communications responsibly, she'll lose all such devices for a minimum of a month. Remind your child that social communication is a privilege, not a right.

> **parent pointer**
>
> Aggressive kids like to argue. Don't negotiate a settlement with your child; he needs to be held to the rules. He won't like it, but he'll get used to it if you continue to be calm and consistent. It's what he needs.

Make sure that when you do impose a consequence for an infraction of family rules, it isn't done with shame or degradation. Overly harsh or corporal punishment sends the wrong message: that bullying is fine at home as long as it's the parent doing it. That will only result in negative feelings—and your child may wind up mimicking this behavior with other kids.

Children aren't the only ones who need to be responsible and accountable. Parents need to stop making excuses for their children's bad behavior. It makes no sense to try to justify bad and unacceptable behavior by blaming the school, the other child, or the fact that your child was cranky because he didn't get enough sleep last night. Administrators, other parents, and his peers know the truth, and so does he.

**Take a good, hard look at your family**, evaluating the attitudes and behaviors that are being played out at home and what you're modeling for your child.

**Don't be an enabler.** Love and respect begin at home, and there's no excuse for abuse. Consider joining a parent support group, taking a parent education class, or seeking family counseling.

**Provide increased supervision.** It's important that you know where your son is, who he's hanging out with, and what activities he's engaging in. If he's part of a disrespectful group of friends, do your best to disengage him from them. If he's been using his cell phone or the Internet inappropriately, take them away.

**Think carefully about the kind of media he enjoys.** As we discussed in Chapter 2, violent video games and other media can have a negative impact on kids. A child who's already aggressive doesn't need additional stimulation, suggestion, or reinforcement for aggressive activity and negative and disrespectful attitudes.

**Establish your expectations about what he's to do if he knows someone is being bullied or mistreated.** For example, "We expect that you'll help anyone who's in trouble or is being victimized, and discuss ways you can help."

**Suggest that your child sign an antibullying pledge.** See examples in Appendix A of this book.

# Replacement Behaviors

If you've ever tried to quit smoking, you know that you need to replace that bad habit with a more appropriate one, like chewing gum, knitting, or incorporating a step-down process such as a gum or a patch that reduces the level of nicotine in your system.

The same is true for aggressive and bullying behaviors; when you're trying to change a set of behaviors, it's important to have a replacement set. First, help your child to understand that those negative behaviors are unacceptable and need to be extinguished immediately. Once that's been established, you can work with him to develop a list of more appropriate activities and attitudes that offer healthy ways to release frustration, energy, or aggression, while working toward a positive goal.

**Sign him up for swimming, track, or a martial arts program that embraces respect and humility.** Or take him hiking, dirt biking, snow-boarding, or camping. Scouting, volunteering, helping out at home, or raising a seeing-eye dog are also wonderful and positive activities that will offer your child the opportunity to develop new, healthy hobbies and a way to meet new people.

**Share your feelings about what it means to be a powerful person to your family.** Perhaps it means being able to do great things or helping others or being able to make tough decisions or to persist in challenging tasks. Whatever your family defines as "being powerful," you'll want to make sure it doesn't have anything to do with hurting, humiliating, or abusing other people.

**Help your child learn to identify his feelings and what kind of things he finds upsetting.** Getting to know himself better will help him begin to problem solve more appropriately and to understand how others may feel.

**parent pointer** Empathy is the cornerstone of social success and the key to helping kids who engage in bullying behaviors change their ways. Try to help your child understand his own feelings and how the recipient of violence and abuse may feel.

**Help your child connect with positive role models.** Teachers, coaches, counselors, extended family members, scout leaders, and older kids who are engaging in positive activities all can be mentors who can make a positive difference in your child's life.

**Encourage your child to stop to examine his thoughts before taking action.** It's common for aggressive people to misinterpret the meaning of the actions of others. Teach him to think clearly about what happened, how he felt and thought, and then what he did. Did it work out? Discuss what he could do differently next time.

Take a look at Chapter 9 for numerous suggestions for helping kids develop positive character traits and social and emotional skills. You may also want to refer to Chapter 6 for information on conflict resolution, problem solving, and using "I" messages.

# Interventions at School

School-based interventions can include a wide range of services to help students who are having difficulty managing their emotions and getting along with others, as well as those who are acting aggressively or bullying. The optimal situation is for the student, the family, and the school to establish a good rapport so everyone is on the same page and working together. Take a look at Chapters 7, 9, and 17 for more ideas.

Numerous interventions at school can turn aggressive kids around; here's a short list:

- Set clear expectations, instituted with neutrality and consistency.

- Encourage responsibility by assigning classroom jobs such as making sure the bird feeders are always stocked, reading to a younger child, or taking attendance.

- Enter into a behavior contract to increase positive behaviors and decrease negative ones.

- Offer alternative ways for the child to feel powerful and competent, including engaging in school activities and events, learning to play an instrument, and greeting parents and handing out pamphlets at open-house night.

- Pair students with positive role models.

- Teach them how to recognize their triggers, solve problems, and manage emotions.

- Provide frequent, positive, and honest feedback.

- Provide sensitivity training, including turning the tables to have them be on the receiving end of bullying.

- Work closely with the family.

School counselors and specialists are there to help and can offer school-based counseling services. These specialists, along with your child's teachers, may offer social-emotional and character education, too. As we discussed in Chapter 7, counselors and specialists are also responsible for responding to crisis situations and all aspects of student distress.

**Bully Buster**

Social skills groups can help students develop the necessary skills to manage feelings, develop friendships, and increase effective communication skills. They're particularly helpful in assisting aggressive students to examine their faulty thinking and misperceptions of the behaviors and intentions of others, learn to recognize the feelings of other group members (and themselves), and talk about topics of concern.

These staff members may also be instrumental in creating and implementing behavior-modification plans designed to identify target behaviors of concern, recommend strategies to decrease their frequency and severity, and help students formulate contingency plans for rewards and consequences in connection with appropriate behavior. They monitor progress at school and keep parents in the loop.

The assistant principal is often the administrator who is in charge of discipline and may be the bullying specialist in your child's school. Many have excellent relationships with kids and are great role models.

The bullying specialist and school administrators are responsible for responding to incidents of bullying, following district policies, and implementing procedures to address and rectify these issues.

You may be surprised to learn that bullies, targets, and bystanders alike all have issues they struggle with. In order to reduce bullying and create a safe and positive school climate, everyone's needs have to be understood and fulfilled.

## Essential Takeaways

- It can be hard for parents to recognize or accept that a child has a problem. Breaking through denial is the first step toward positive change.
- Kids may, at first, resist being held accountable for their behavior. They need the strength and persistence of caring parents and professionals who won't be afraid of their protests or enable aggression, disrespect, and bullying.
- When punishing bullying behavior, keep consequences age appropriate and meaningful.
- When families and schools work together to address aggressive behavior, they can achieve positive results.

# chapter 14

# Turning Bystanders Into Upstanders

Helping peers, parents, and school staff take a stand against bullying

Creating upstander climates at home and school

Reinforcing upstander behavior

If you've ever taken part in a protest, rally, or local politics, you've probably felt a rush from adding your voice to others and knowing you're working to make a difference. Standing up to injustice can be an extremely powerful experience, even if yours is the first voice that others join. History is filled with examples of individuals, like Susan B. Anthony and Nelson Mandela, who were catalysts for change and inspired thousands, or even millions, to stand along with them, transforming society.

As parents, we raise our children to believe that they can be anything they want to be. We encourage them to dream big and follow those dreams. Being empowered to stand up to bullying can give our children the confidence to overcome the obstacles they'll encounter later in life. Big goals start with small steps, and showing our kids that they have the capacity to make a difference and be change makers in the lives of those around them is part of helping them grow. That said, standing up to bullying can take a lot of courage, independence, and risk taking. In this chapter, we explore how you can help transform bystanders into upstanders.

# Who Can Stand Up, and How?

Often, bystanders don't realize how the target perceives their passive participation in her suffering. They also underestimate the power they have, by virtue of their numbers, to change the culture of an online group, a school, or their community—and perhaps even save a life.

Anyone who witnesses bullying has the potential to be an upstander. As with the spectrum of bystander behaviors, from silent witness to active instigator, there's a range of ways a bystander can be an upstander, from refusing to laugh when someone is being teased to physically intervening. The more active the intervention, the more courage it may involve, but the more a bystander becomes comfortable with speaking up and protecting a target, the more it will become part of her values and, hopefully, easier to do.

## Upstanders on the Front Lines

Bullying often occurs beyond adults' eyes and ears, so it's up to kids to develop the tools and self-confidence to intervene and stand up. However, as we discussed in Chapter 5, there are lots of reasons why bystanders don't intervene: they're afraid or uncomfortable, they don't want to seem uncool, they're friends with the child doing the bullying, or they're entertained by the bullying and actively participate.

**Bully Buster**
Kids reaching adolescence are looking to their peers to establish the norms and behaviors that lead to status. When popular kids use their power to stand up to bullying rather than using it to bully, this behavior can be contagious. These kids also often have the confidence that can make standing up easier. If your daughter is popular in her school, talk to her about how she can be a leader in making kindness cool and creating a positive climate for all.

It can be incredibly hard to stand up to bullying, especially if no one else is challenging the behavior, or if it's taking place in an environment where bullying is normalized. In these situations, it can require an extra measure of independent thinking by your child to recognize that what she's witnessing is wrong, and confidence in her own values to step in and do something about it. However, when given the tools to stand up rather than participate, kids have a huge amount of power to make the behavior stop. Here are some actions kids can take to be upstanders:

**Be a friend to someone who is being bullied.** Even if you don't intervene during the bullying, there are lots of ways you can offer support: Walk with a target in the hall, sit with her at lunch, welcome her into your group, or "friend" her on Facebook.

**Help the target talk to an adult.** Walk with her to the counselor's office or to a teacher, support her in making a report, or make a witness report if you were there when the bullying occurred.

**Don't participate** in spreading rumors, contributing to online bullying, laughing at mean remarks, videotaping a bullying event, or actively adding to the bullying in any way.

**Tell the bully to stop.** If you see bullying taking place, either at school, online, or anywhere else, assertively tell the bully that you don't like what she's doing, that it's bullying, and it needs to stop. And always speak to an adult when you witness bullying.

**Tell bystanders to stop.** If you see others participating in bullying or laughing along, tell them they're making the problem worse and are also bullying. If you hear someone spreading rumors, let them know that it isn't true.

**Reach out to newcomers.** If you notice a new person at your school, reach out to her; introduce her to your friends and make her feel welcome.

**Don't be afraid to think independently or to be the only one voicing what others are probably thinking.** The people most celebrated in our culture are those who took the risk to speak out and stand up to injustice, even when many others were too afraid to join in.

**Start an upstander club at your school.** Let others know that you're an upstander and someone who others can go to if they're being bullied.

**Talk to parents, teachers, principals, and staff about bullying at school.** Tell them where it's happening, where kids need greater protection, and so on.

**Starting an Upstander Club**

Encourage your child to start an upstander club at his or her school. The Upstander Alliance from the National School Climate Center offers toolkits and support to young people and connects alliances at schools nationwide. Check it out at www.schoolclimate.org/bullybust/upstander.

## Targets as Upstanders

If your daughter has been bullied, her experience can provide a powerful opportunity to empathize with others who are being targeted. Talking to her about how she felt when she was being teased or excluded can help her make decisions about how to react when she sees it happening to someone else. A bystander who has been bullied can identify with the target and may struggle even more than other bystanders when witnessing incidents of bullying.

As we discussed in Chapter 12, part of helping a target recover from being bullied is giving her the confidence and tools to feel empowered to make her own situation better. The empathetic response she feels when witnessing others being bullied may be a powerful motivator for getting help from an adult or reporting the incident. If parents have given their child good tools to handle the bullying she's experienced—confiding in a trusted adult or talking to the school counselor—she can use them to help others.

It would be a huge step for that child to stand up and say something to stop the bullying, but it might take some time for her to feel comfortable doing it. Meanwhile, another powerful step she could take would be to reach out to the person she saw being targeted later, perhaps sit with her during lunch or walk down the hall with her. It would probably be easy for her to think of the things she wished someone had said to her when she was being bullied; now it's her opportunity to say those things to someone else, and perhaps make a new and lasting friend.

# How Parents Can Stand Up

When our kids are in elementary school, intervening in bullying situations is often a matter of instinct. If you see your daughter pulling another girl's hair, taking things from a friend, or calling her friend a bad name, you'll immediately step in. This is the time in life when you're teaching your child values and appropriate behavior, and it's a parent's job to correct and address actions that are inappropriate or hurtful. At this age, you may also find other parents more open to cooperating and helping you resolve a bullying situation; they also want to positively mold their children's behavior.

When kids hit adolescence, however, things get more complicated. At that age, bullying is often harder to detect. Just as teachers have an easier time identifying bullying in elementary school–age kids, so do parents, primarily because it's overt. As our kids get older, bullying usually takes place out of our sight: online, at school, at the mall, at sports events, or other places parents are less likely to be.

That said, parents usually have a pretty good sense of what's going on among their kids. If they're carpool drivers or have a group of kids over after school, they most likely get an earful of who said what or did what that day. If you hear a group of kids speaking badly of a peer or spreading gossip, speak up; ask them how they would feel if someone was spreading rumors about them. You might want to talk to them about your own experiences with being bullied or standing up to bullying when you were their age. Although it can be tricky stepping into the dynamic when you want to allow your children to be independent with their friends, there are several ways you can be an upstander as a parent:

**Make your home a safe, supportive place for your child and her friends.** Speak up if they're spreading gossip or rumors, and keep an eye on what they're doing online. If it's bullying, let them know it and that it isn't permitted at your house.

**Let your child and her friends know that you're someone they can talk to.** Discuss the social fabric and cliques in their school, and encourage them to bring new friends into their group.

**If you know one of your child's peers is being bullied, reach out to her parents.** You may know more about what's happening than they do, especially if their child isn't telling.

**If your child is on a sports team, encourage her to reach out to the weaker players.** Even kids who may not be the fastest or strongest have special skills to contribute to their team and the potential to make the winning play. Sportsmanship on the field is contagious, making it a great place to tackle bullying.

**Set a good example.** If you speak up when you see bullying in your community or in your home, your child will see how it's done. And if there are bullying dynamics in your own relationships, address them.

**If you witness bullying when you pick your child up from school or at a school event, intervene.** Report the incident to school authorities.

**If one of your child's friends is bullying, address the behavior with that child and with your child.** If you suspect the friendship is unhealthy, help your child determine whether it should be continued.

**Talk to other parents about your school bullying policies and prevention programs.** Encourage the school to implement model policies, have strong prevention programs, and develop upstander clubs.

## School Staff Are Upstanders, Too

Unless kids feel they'll be supported by teachers, staff, administrators, and other adults at school, there's little chance they'll intervene when they see bullying. And if kids do intervene and don't see any further action taken, they're not likely to do it again. Standing up to bullying takes a lot of courage and can be a huge risk for kids. If they do it, they have to know that they aren't going to be left on their own and possibly become targets or ostracized themselves.

School staff members who witness upstander behavior should be sure to support that person, letting her know she's done the right thing and that they admire her courage. They should report the bullying to an administrator and make sure that both the target and the upstander are safe, checking back with the upstander to be certain she isn't being retaliated against.

Bully
Buster

In filming *Bully*, Cynthia met with a group of high school football coaches from Iowa who had made it their mission to instill in their teams a sense of family. It makes sense: in many cases players were spending more time with coaches and team members than they were with their parents. There was a boy who was new to the school who had come there to escape the severe bullying he was experiencing at a nearby high school. Within a few weeks, he'd been brought onto the football team and, with the other players rallying around him, the coaches and teachers saw him transforming from a devastated, vulnerable kid to one who was regaining his confidence and thriving.

School staff can also reinforce and commend upstander behavior by giving kids who stand up other opportunities to use their confidence and voice.

While many kids bully to increase their social status and prestige, schools can create merit systems that reward and give status to upstanders instead. For these systems to work, the rewards must be things that are meaningful to each age group. In elementary schools, perhaps upstanders could be made the teacher's helper for the day. In middle school, it might mean getting computer time during study hall; for high school, this might be parking lot privileges, off-campus lunches, or time in the student lounge.

Here are some other actions schools can take to promote upstander behavior:

- Create opportunities for kids to start a community of upstanders.

- Have students produce school plays or musicals that touch on themes of empathy and upstander behavior.

- Foster a gay-straight alliance or other programs that foster understanding and kindness, and that engage the entire student body in actions like participating in the Day of Silence to raise awareness about LGBT bullying. Create peer mentor programs where leaders at the upper level help younger kids deal with bullying.

- Create an atmosphere at school where everyone feels they're a part of creating a positive school climate. Ask students to help contribute ideas on how bullying behaviors should be handled by staff; include bus drivers, lunch and playground aides, and paraeducators in the school's policy development.

- Identify staff members who are on the school safety committee, including the antibullying specialist and those who are instrumental in spearheading antibullying prevention efforts, policies, and programs.

- Provide antibullying pledges for both staff members and students to take.

- Take part in national bullying prevention month in October, getting students involved in meaningful schoolwide projects that encourage kids to take action all year.

- Provide easy, accessible ways for kids to file witness reports, both at school and online.

**Screening Antibullying Films**

MISC.

One way to promote upstander behavior is to incorporate messages in school curricula. Encourage teachers to think about how upstander behavior could be reinforced through social studies lessons, the activities chosen in PE, or even the school play. Several curriculum and teaching guides, including the ones that accompany antibullying films like *Bully* and *Not in Our Town,* focus on creating inclusive communities and are available for teachers to download for free.

## School Climate Surveys

Often kids don't stand up to bullying because they don't feel supported by school staff. Studies report that students often feel school staff and administrators are either not entirely aware of much of the bullying that takes place, or that they don't take action when they see it. However, when kids feel adults are in tune with the things they're going through, and that there are adults at school they trust and who they can go to, the more likely they'll take a risk and speak up, knowing they have someone behind them who will protect them.

Surveys such as the National School Climate Center's Comprehensive School Climate Inventory can be administered to kids at the elementary, middle, and high school levels, as well as to school personnel and parents. Some key components of these surveys include measuring ...

- Students' perceptions of how both kids and adults in the building treat each other.

- Students' level of respect for differences.

- Students' personal experiences of being bullied.

- Staff and students' awareness of bullying behaviors and confidence in their problem-solving skills.

- Students' sense that there's an adult they can trust in the building.

- Which areas of the school staff or students feel unsafe.

- Whether teachers encourage independent thinking.

- Whether staff members feel supported by administrators and encouraged to collaborate.

Many surveys can be very effective in bridging the gap between students' and staff members' perceptions of how serious bullying is in a school and whether or not staff members are dealing with it effectively. Survey results can help administrators identify areas of the school that are bullying hot spots, and which need a lot more supervision or should be made off limits completely.

In a school where staff members don't feel supported, school climate surveys can be very intimidating, especially if the results reveal that students don't feel safe or that kids and parents think teachers and administrators aren't doing enough. While climate surveys are a great first step to addressing where a school stands in its efforts, most administrators will discover they have work to do.

## The Importance of Buy-In

Research has found that unless 75 percent of faculty "buy in" to the goals of upstander education and bullying prevention, the efforts won't succeed. Principals may find they need to really work to enroll all staff members and include them in defining the kind of learning environment they'd like to see realized. Reaching out to the PTA, school board, and others who are influential in the school community; developing a plan to raise awareness;

and assembling committees to help implement plans can be good ways of creating a critical mass toward change.

Depending on an adult's role in the school community, he or she will have a very different window into the kinds of bullying that take place. Crossing guards, bus drivers, and recess monitors all have crucial perspectives on the times, places, and types of bullying that occur—and how bullying could be prevented—that will be different from the experiences of administrators and teachers. Kids are very attuned to the power structures among adults at school. If they think certain adults lack authority or the ability to discipline, they will be more likely to bully other children around them. Making sure all staff members are respected—by both adults and kids—and are empowered to report and stand up to bullying is a critical element of comprehensive climate change.

Many schools find that after they implement awareness building and bullying prevention programs, they see a sharp rise in the number of bullying incidents reported. Although this can be alarming to administrators, it's actually good news: it means kids are developing the tools to recognize bullying when they see it, and know that the right thing to do is to tell an adult and get help. Reinforcing this behavior by taking action when bullying is reported is a critical step in developing a positive, trusting relationship between students and staff, where everybody is taking ownership of school culture.

### Administrator Action

While many schools have anonymous boxes or online forms to file witness reports of bullying, administrators might also want to consider collecting anonymous reports of upstander behavior. Given that most bullying takes place away from adults, it would follow that so does most upstander behavior. By encouraging kids to report their peers' positive actions and rewarding them for it, you can increase their feeling that peers are looking up to them for standing up, and that it's a good thing to do, even if an adult isn't looking.

# Upstander Behaviors Take Many Forms

Teaching kids how to be upstanders is part of teaching them good citizenship and how to create the community they want to belong to. It's a big goal, and we must recognize that many kids will be upstanders in many ways. The more options we give kids to meaningfully stand up to bullying, the more bullying behaviors will become unacceptable in that culture.

Being an upstander may mean simply refusing to spread gossip or join a hurtful social networking group. Or it may mean physically putting oneself between a bully and her target. Depending on a child's personality, physical size, confidence, and standing in the social strata at her school, she may take very different actions. Developing upstander behavior early can help children make choices in the kinds of fields they pursue, their civic participation, and the kinds of relationships they foster.

## Essential Takeaways

- Standing up to bullying can take many different forms, from refusing to spread gossip to physically intervening.
- Peers, parents, and school staff can all be upstanders in different ways and help foster a culture in which standing up is the norm.
- Being an upstander takes a lot of courage and confidence, especially if the person standing up has been a target in the past. In order to be upstanders, kids must feel that adults will support them.
- Schools can foster upstander behavior in a variety of ways, including creating meaningful incentives and leadership opportunities.

# chapter 15

# When More Help Is Needed

Most people who dream of getting married and raising a family have a vision of what their lives will be like: how many children they'll have, the things they'll do together, and the things they'll do differently than their own parents did. New parents welcome their babies into the world with a sense of excitement, anticipation, and hope.

But sometimes things don't go according to plan. You never can tell what challenges will cross your family's path, and the time may come when you'll find yourself faced with a situation over which you have little control but still feel fully responsible for the outcome.

Many school-aged children and adolescents require additional support in school for a variety of reasons, from temporary situations or stress to significant challenges that require comprehensive interventions and continuous support.

In this chapter, we take a look at some of the kinds of challenges kids and their families face that may require more help. These situations can increase a child's risk for being targeted by bullies or to engage in bullying behaviors themselves. Kids facing these challenges benefit from having caring adults available to lend extra support when needed. Additional sources of intervention and assistance can be provided by school specialists, peers, social services agencies, physical and occupational therapists, speech-language therapists, mental health and medical professionals, self-help groups, and even law enforcement.

# Family Problems

Children and teens in families that are dealing with excessive stress or significant family problems may find themselves in situations that they can neither comprehend, control, nor resolve.

For example, a child who is bullied, neglected, or rejected by one or both of his parents is vulnerable to developing difficulties with attachment, self-esteem, academic success, and social interaction. He can also have difficulties in managing his emotions and behavior. The child in this circumstance may be left to fend for himself in making sense of a world that's hard to predict or understand. He needs extra support, encourage-ment, and understanding, and may need to be connected with social services as well.

Children who live in families where sibling bullying exists are vulnerable to becoming bully-victims or targets themselves, and may have difficulties making friends. Sometimes, however, these kids thrive in social settings, like schools where there is a sense of safety, order, and peace and where they can find nice kids to befriend.

In the following sections, we provide additional examples of family problems.

## Divorce and Separation

Nearly half of all kids live in single-parent households. A divorce may ultimately be a good thing for the emotional or physical well-being of the spouses and the family in general, but the process still takes its toll on family members, and it can be particularly confusing and scary for kids.

We don't mean to suggest that a child whose parents are divorced or separated will become a bully or a target because of what happened between his parents. Rather, the way a child or adolescent deals with his feelings about his family situation may increase his risk for acting aggressively and impulsively toward others or to experience some difficulty asserting himself. The situation is likely to negatively impact his mood, behavior, or self-esteem, at least temporarily, as he adjusts to changes related to his new family constellation.

## The Death of a Parent or Guardian

No words can express the depth of suffering kids and their families experience in response to the loss of a parent or guardian. While adults tend to grieve with deep and profound intensity, kids jump in and out of the grief process for an extended period of time, feeling devastated one minute, focusing on a play date with a friend or asking for some cash to see the latest movie the next. Make no mistake, though: kids who have lost a parent or loved one need adults and friends who are empathic and caring.

Many grieving kids in schools also find themselves on the receiving end of insensitive comments by cruel and aggressive kids, or even thoughtless and ignorant adults. For example, we know of a situation in which a student whose father had just died overheard a school lunch aide sharing a rumor that his dad committed suicide. It wasn't true, but it created quite a stir among the children and provided ammunition to aggressive students, who proceeded to taunt and tease the bereaved student about the circumstances of his parent's passing. This student had been targeted by bullies in the past, which added fuel to the fire.

## Illness in the Family

When a family member is ill, it can be distressing to children, and stressful to everyone in the family. When stress levels rise and emotional, financial, and physical reserves are depleted, it's not uncommon for parents to be more agitated and less patient with their kids. This in turn can create additional confusion and frustration for kids, who may act out those feelings with aggression toward others or by shutting down. Family stressors and challenges, of any sort, can lead to changes (often temporary) in children's moods, behaviors, or self-perceptions.

## Job Loss, Poverty, and Homelessness

It's hard to be the kid whose family can't provide him with the clothes, accessories, experiences, and privileges his peers enjoy. Living in economic hardship can be a serious threat to a family's stability, leaving kids more vulnerable to targeting or mocking. In addition, a child whose family is experiencing financial difficulties may unleash his anger and frustration on others around him. It's important to note, however, that bullying exists within all socio-economic groups, and should absolutely *not* be considered as being a "poor child's problem" any more than it is "any child's problem." Bullying has as much of a chance to exist in a prep-school environment as it does in inner-city schools.

**Kids Can Overcome Challenges**

Misc.

Many resilient children who come from families that have experienced a wide range of challenges go on to become self-reliant, industrious, responsible, and successful adults. They understand the meaning of hard work, integrity, and persistence.

## Substance Abuse or Mental Illness

Kids who are living with parents who abuse drugs or alcohol or are mentally ill are often faced with a barrage of problems, from increased responsibilities to the fear of divulging family secrets outside the home. Kids trying to reconcile love for an irresponsible or neglectful parent have a lot on their plate. They live in an unpredictable and insecure world and often aren't able to participate in social or extracurricular activities. Without adequate adult support and assistance, they may be late to, or absent from, school, and their homework is often not done consistently so they're at risk of falling behind academically as well as socially and emotionally.

Parents who put their substance of choice ahead of the needs of their children, or who are struggling with chemical addiction, may damage their children's sense of self-worth and provide them with a distorted sense of what relationships are supposed to be about. How can they feel safe with others when they aren't safe in their own home?

Research indicates that nearly 18 percent of American adults grew up living with an alcoholic, and that there may be as many as 11 million kids under 18 with an alcoholic parent today. Additionally, there's scientific evidence that alcoholism runs in families. Substance abuse is linked with domestic violence, child abuse, murder, and robberies, and the children of substance abusers are at risk for behavioral problems, aggression, and impulsivity. Children living with mentally ill parents face a number of similar challenges. If the parent is both mentally ill and chemically addicted (MICA), the child may be predisposed to either of these conditions, and also at risk to experience social, emotional, behavioral, or academic problems. A child living with a parent who is a substance abuser, mentally ill, or a combination of both, is depending on an adult who can't meet his own needs, let alone the needs of a child.

## A Violent Life

Kids who live in families where disrespect, aggression, and violence are accepted face a range of problems. These families can be extremely challenging for schools and law enforcement to manage because they don't ascribe to expected societal values or standards of behavior.

Kids from violent and aggressive homes who are witness to, or subjected to, bullying by their family members may develop the persona of a target or a bully-target. Should they adopt the role of a target, they see themselves as powerless and may not take action on their own behalf against mistreatment from others. Kids who learn that it's better to feel powerful than powerless are at risk of becoming aggressive toward others as they try to replace the pain of victimization with the satisfaction of bullying. Either way, they need extra care and support.

**When a Parent Is in Prison**

The incarceration of a parent or family member can be very difficult for a child to understand or emotionally reconcile. Should other kids get wind of this situation, both he and the rest of his family need to find a way to deal with the potential response of both peers and adults at school, along with any teasing, taunting, and humiliation he may experience.

# Learning or Achievement Difficulties

As discussed in Chapter 6, it's important to identify learning differences and academic difficulties as early as possible in a child's life. When children experience difficulties in school, many begin to feel that they're different from their peers and start to lose their self-confidence. They may begin to act differently, too.

Kids who struggle academically and don't get appropriate help at school may fall further and further behind. They may act out their frustrations by lashing out at others or by shutting down. Other kids notice that the child is falling behind, too, which can lead to social exclusion and teasing.

If you begin to see that your child is avoiding doing homework and falling behind, or if you start receiving calls from his teacher or see poor grades coming home, you need to take action immediately to avoid it turning into a bigger problem.

If your child has been receiving extra help and additional services at school and is still having difficulties, he might have a learning difference (or disability). Be proactive; early intervention often yields quick, positive results. Children who struggle in school often experience anxiety, distress, decreased self-esteem, and compromised social relationships. It's not unusual for them to become vulnerable to targeting or rejection by other children or to begin to act out aggressively themselves—all good reasons to deal with any difficulties as soon as possible.

As discussed in Chapter 10, students who have a variety of conditions that impact their learning or development are entitled to a free and appropriate public education in the least restrictive environment under the U.S. Federal Individuals with Disabilities Education Act (IDEA). Early intervention programs for children from birth through the age of 3 are often administered through a state's office of health and human services or office for children. From that point forward, these programs are facilitated through local district boards of education.

**parent pointer**  Resist becoming angry with a child who is experiencing academic difficulties or avoiding doing schoolwork at home, but at the same time don't minimize these issues, either. These are signals that he is having problems he doesn't know how to resolve. Contact his teacher immediately and request a conference. When you meet, try to keep an open mind and elicit assistance in developing a plan to get your child the help he needs; it will make both you and your child feel much better.

# Inattention, Disorganization, and Impulsivity

How often do you have to go to your child's school because he left his book or homework at home? Are his notebook and locker a total mess? Does he have difficulty paying attention in class, miss important details, or forget what you just asked him to do?

Lots of kids are disorganized, forget things, and would rather think about playing video games than pay attention to schoolwork. Teachers realize that, too, but if you're getting calls from school about his inattentiveness, there's a good chance he's displaying these behaviors more than the average child. Try not to get too upset or defensive about it, though; there are lots of things you can do to help.

When a child is having more difficulty than his peers, he may be experiencing symptoms of attention deficit hyperactivity disorder (ADHD). That's not to say he necessarily has it—but whether he does or not, the important thing is for you to come to an understanding of what ADHD is and how you and his teacher can help him thrive. According to the Centers for Disease Control and Prevention (CDC), ADHD is a relatively common neurobehavioral disorder. In fact, reports estimate that somewhere between 3 and 15 percent of school-aged children in the United States have been diagnosed with ADHD.

Some of the symptoms of ADHD include:

- **Inattention:** a short attention span, difficulty persisting in a task, appearing to not be listening or have difficulty concentrating, making careless mistakes when not paying attention to details, difficulty with organization, easily distracted, often forgetful or loses things.

- **Impulsivity:** difficulty waiting, impatience, interrupts others, answers before the question or directions have been completed, acts without thinking.

- **Hyperactivity:** restlessness, difficulty sitting still, overactivity, difficulty physically calming down.

A diagnosis of ADHD without symptoms of hyperactivity is referred to as ADHD—Inattentive Type. A diagnosis of ADHD where the difficulties are predominantly hyperactive and impulsive is referred to as ADHD—Hyperactive-Inattentive Type. And a child who has symptoms that include inattention, hyperactivity, and impulsivity is referred to as having ADHD—Combined Type.

Kids with significant symptoms of ADHD may face social-emotional, academic, and behavioral challenges, including the risk of being targeted or bullying others. Other kids can become annoyed by the impulsive, distracting, or insensitive behaviors and comments of the child with ADHD as well as the time teachers may have to spend redirecting or responding to his needs.

parent pointer

If your child has been diagnosed with ADHD, don't let him fall into the I'm-not-responsible-for-my-behavior-because-I-have-ADHD trap. He needs assistance to help him learn ways to deal with his challenges, just like everybody else. At the same time, he may require modifications to his program, extra assistance, and lots of encouragement.

Here are some tips for helping kids with symptoms of ADHD:

**Impulsive kids** may benefit from reminders of appropriate behavior, rules, and consequences, and increased supervision or limited access to places or situations where they tend to get into trouble. A child who gets into fights during recess may be more successful in an alternate setting during that time of day; a child who makes inappropriate comments to other players on the baseball team might be given the job of scorekeeper, which keeps him otherwise occupied.

**Kids who have difficulty managing their emotions** need to learn how to anticipate situations that may cause them distress and to develop coping mechanisms to handle them. Children who become anxious may benefit from learning relaxation techniques and positive self-talk; those who become easily agitated need to develop the ability to press the "pause button"—that is, to stop, take a step back, calm down, think about what's going on, examine perceptions, consider alternatives, and weigh them all before taking action. These skills are critical to making good decisions and getting along with others.

**Disorganized kids and those who lack time management skills** benefit from using different-colored folders for different subjects, a calendar or agenda book for writing down assignments, schedules, timers, and reminders. Electronic devices can be useful organizers, too, though disorganized kids tend to lose them. Daily routines such as coming home, having a snack, doing homework, etc., are helpful. Having a place for everything helps kids with organization.

**Children with short attention spans and poor planning skills** can be assisted by the use of chunking tasks into smaller pieces with short breaks in between one part and the next; using timers, reminders, and visual and physical cues; helping the child get started; offering opportunities for physical movement and fun activities; getting the child's input about what he thinks would be helpful and about the way he'd like to proceed; and providing supervision, reward systems, support, encouragement, and praise.

Many kids with symptoms of ADHD experience decreased symptoms and positive results from taking medication. That, of course, is a family decision you may wish to discuss with your child's pediatrician or neurologist. Counseling can also help kids and families understand their condition and help them come up with new ways of thinking and developing strategies to deal with their emotions, behaviors, challenges, and their ADHD.

# Limited Social Skills

As discussed throughout this book, children who lack social communication skills are at the greatest risk for being rejected and targeted by aggressive kids. Professionals such as special education teachers, speech-language specialists, behaviorists, counselors, IEP teams, and psychotherapists have specialized training to assist children with social communication deficits.

Studies have found kids on the autism spectrum are particularly vulnerable to bullying, which affects their social communication skills. Although kids with autism can be helped to better recognize social cues or ways to interpret peers, we must remember that autism is a disability, and the onus can't rest on the child to change his behaviors: if he could, he probably would have done so already. Children with ASD require a range of comprehensive services and supports.

One of the best things we can do to help kids with ADS is to educate all students about the symptoms of autism and the many ways it might make kids with this disability easy targets, including the following:

- Difficulty with motor skills and coordination
- Problems maintaining eye contact or interpreting body language or nonverbal signs
- Repetitive body movements
- Preoccupation with parts of objects
- Adherence to particular routines or rituals and an unwillingness to alter them
- Difficulty starting or maintaining a conversation
- A tendency to take things literally, even when they're not intended as such

Most kids know that it's unacceptable to bully a peer who's in a wheelchair or has a physical disability they can easily see. When the disability is invisible, however, kids often bully with impunity. All students should be educated about autism, learning disabilities, and special needs so they can better understand their peer's behavior, treat him with respect, regard him with empathy, and respond appropriately.

According to the U.S. Centers for Disease Control and Prevention (CDC), approximately 1 in every 88 children is diagnosed as being on the autism spectrum. ASD is significantly more prevalent among boys than girls, affecting 1 in 54 boys out of those 88 children.

parent pointer

If your child is 2 years old and has a significant delay or loss of language, doesn't respond to affection, or exhibits limited social interaction skills, or becomes stressed by even small changes in his environment, talk to your pediatrician to determine if there is a problem. Intervening at an early age can make a huge difference in a child's development.

## Anxiety

Anxiety is a normal and expected emotional response to stress. It's the feeling of being worried, nervous, fearful, or apprehensive in the face of challenge or uncertainty—the pit in your stomach or sweat on your palms when starting a new school or going away from home for the first time. It's the fear that your face will turn red and you'll forget your lines in the school play.

What about kids who are bullied? It would stand to reason that they would be nervous, worried, fearful, apprehensive, and anxious—and in their shoes, who wouldn't be?

Kids who have been bullied can develop many symptoms of anxiety disorders. In addition to the typical interventions for treating anxiety disorders (discussed later in this chapter), these kids require additional school, home, and community protections and interventions. Furthermore, psychotherapy with a mental health professional who is knowledgeable about working with kids and the families of those who are bullies and/or targets, as well as how to work with schools, may be warranted. Psychiatric intervention, including medication, may be appropriate as well. Some kids may require an alternative school placement.

In addition, kids who struggle with anxiety disorders can be vulnerable to targeting because they frequently lack self-confidence, have low self-esteem, and have difficulty asserting themselves. They experience significant anxiety that can interfere with their ability to function successfully in their day-to-day activities.

Aggressive kids can also suffer from anxiety. People who deal with their uncomfortable feelings through aggression and bullying briefly release their inner tensions and relieve their low tolerance for frustration outwardly, resulting in them feeling more powerful and in control.

community watch Approximately 13 million American children are bullied at school every year. As many as 3 million kids miss school every month because they are fearful for their safety at school. Kids who are targeted at school are prone to anxiety and depression. They are hyper-vigilant and suffer undue emotional stress.

Anxiety disorders are among the most common mental health disorders. The good news is that, with treatment, they can usually be successfully overcome. Several subsets fall under the anxiety disorders umbrella, including the following:

**Separation anxiety disorder** is the experience of excessive worry or fear about being separated from home or from a parent or other person a child is attached to. It's developmentally appropriate, for example, for an 8-month-old to demonstrate symptoms of separation or stranger anxiety when separated from a parent, but not for an 8-year-old. It's not uncommon for kids to be a little anxious when they start a new school or go to sleepaway camp for the first time. The difference between a natural and an unnatural state of anxiety is in whether it interferes with the child's ability to function in age-appropriate situations. Separation anxiety disorder is typically treated with gradual exposure to being separated from the parent and providing opportunities for the child to develop self-confidence in the parent's absence.

**Specific phobia** is an excessive fear of a particular object or situation. Treatment of specific phobia is often conducted by altering behavior through gradual desensitization. School Phobia is an excessive fear of coming to school. In the case of kids who are being bullied and are afraid of coming to school for that reason, they need more than gradual desensitization; they need protection, skills, and strategies, as we stated previously.

**Generalized anxiety disorder (GAD)** refers to excessive worry experienced in a variety of settings that's difficult to manage. GAD is often treated with varying forms of psychotherapy, sometimes assisted by medication.

**Social anxiety disorder** relates to excessive worry and discomfort in social or performance situations, generally related to fear of embarrassment. For example, a child might not want to participate in a play or perform in a recital, or he might even find it difficult to take part in social conversations. Children who have social anxiety find the use of technology helpful, but it's important for them to develop the skills to cope so they're able to function in the classroom, on a play date, and so on. Treatment is often through cognitive-behavioral psychotherapy and teaching social skills.

**Obsessive-compulsive disorder (OCD)** is characterized by recurring thoughts and impulses that create excessive worry and compulsive behaviors such as putting things in a certain order, repeating words, or counting. OCD is often treated with a combination of medication and/or psychotherapy, particularly in the form of gradual exposure to facing the fear situation and not being permitted to respond in the typical manner. Kids with OCD are prone to targeting if their behaviors are perceived as being different or weird by their peers.

**Post-traumatic stress disorder** is characterized by repetitive and excessive anxiety following a traumatic event; in recent years, we've come to associate this disorder with combat soldiers, but it can also follow some other shocking or terrifying experience in which a person felt threatened or helpless. He may attempt to avoid people, places, things, and thoughts that trigger flashbacks or memories of the traumatic event. Posttraumatic stress disorder is typically treated with psychotherapy and desensitization. Kids who have been severely bullied may share some of the symptoms of one who is suffering from PTSD.

**Panic attacks** are characterized by sudden and unexpected bursts of intense and excessive anxiety, fear, or worry that's very often hard to trace back to its roots. When someone has a panic attack, he may experience dizziness, sweating, shaking, heart palpitations, shortness of breath, or other symptoms. Panic attacks can usually be treated successfully through psychotherapy, sometimes with the assistance of medication. It is not uncommon for kids who are being bullied to experience panic or anxiety attacks.

## Tourette Syndrome

Tourette Syndrome (TS) is a neurological disorder. Kids who have TS exhibit repeated involuntary vocal or physical tics such as shoulder shrugging, eye blinking, facial grimaces, throat clearing, or involuntary sounds. People often think of TS in connection with instances when a person shouts obscenities or blurts out inappropriate things. Most kids with TS don't exhibit those symptoms, though it's easy to understand why they may be vulnerable to bullying or social rejection. Obsessive-Compulsive Disorder, Attention Deficit/Hyperactivity Disorder and Learning Disabilities may be associated with TS.

TS is more common in males than females and usually presents in childhood or early adolescence. For many people, the symptoms come and go in frequency, duration, and severity. They generally decrease in adolescence and adulthood. TS is typically treated with medication for physical symptoms, as well as psychotherapy to address emotional issues and other strategies to deal with the challenges of the disorder. Kids who have TS may also have features of OCD, ADHD, or mood disorders.

Kids with TS are particularly vulnerable to targeting because their unusual vocal and motor tics make them stand out, which they can have real difficulty trying to control. School faculty should be knowledgeable about TS and students should learn about TS, too. A caring school community can help increase understanding and support and decrease incidents of bullying.

## Depression

We all feel down in the dumps some days—some of us especially on Mondays! We know what it's like to be sad, disappointed, and lonely. However, intense and unrelenting feelings of hopelessness, helplessness, and worthlessness that persist over time and significantly interfere with normal functioning are more than the blues; they may be signs of a depressive disorder.

When it comes to bullying, how can anyone who experiences being a target or who witnesses bullying behaviors not be depressed by it? These children may feel angry, anxious, violated, confused, guilty, powerless, frustrated, or distressed. While it hasn't been determined that bullying *causes* depression, it has been acknowledged that it's linked to psychological distress and may be one of many risk factors that increase the likelihood of developing depression in some individuals. Research indicates that there's a higher incidence of depression in children who have been bullied, have witnessed bullying, or have bullied others (including cyberbullying) than in those who haven't been so exposed. Studies also indicate being depressed can raise a child's chances of being bullied. The primary treatments for symptoms of depression include psychotherapy and medication.

Kids who have been bullied may develop many symptoms of depression, such as:

- Depressed mood

- Decreased, or lack of, interest in most activities

- Changes in eating

- Changes in sleep patterns

- Low self-esteem

- Fatigue/low energy

- Feelings of hopelessness

- Self-loathing and negative self-talk

- Inability to concentrate, or indecisiveness

- Impairment in functioning in day-to-day activities

- Irritability

- Cutting

- Suicidal ideation or attempt

Targets or bullies who experience symptoms of depression also need extra support. In addition to the typical interventions for treating depression,

these kids require additional school, home, and community protections
and interventions. Furthermore, psychotherapy with a mental health
professional knowledgeable about working with kids who are bullies and/or
targets may be warranted. Psychiatric intervention, including medication,
may be appropriate, as well. Some kids may require an alternative school
placement.

# Handling Risks

Children today face many risks, from academic failure to substance
abuse, gangs, sexual abuse, and poverty and homelessness. Kids who have
vulnerable family situations need additional support, such as counseling
and psychotherapy services, early intervention, and links to social service
agencies that can provide appropriate financial, housing, education,
health, parenting, family support, and other assistance. A child's teacher
or pediatrician can often identify risk factors for kids and teens through
physical examination and family consultation. Schools are an excellent
resource in the identification and prevention of risk behaviors and
addressing social, emotional, and academic needs.

When these problems go unchecked, the child will either consciously or
unconsciously try to resolve his own problems. Sometimes his solutions
work out great; at other times, they can create more problems, like
aggression, targeting, and problematic social relationships. If you have
concerns about your child or teen, don't hesitate to seek assistance from his
school, his pediatrician, or your local mental health center or child welfare
agency.

## Suicide

According to a 2007 report by the Centers for Disease Control and
Prevention, suicide is the third-leading cause of death in children ages 12
through 18.

Children who are depressed are at greater risk for attempting suicide,
and the kids who are bullied are at greater risk for depression than their
nonbullied peers. LGBT kids report greater incidents of bullying and
violence than their heterosexual peers. Kids don't usually want to die; what

they want is for the pain to stop. When they've run out of tools to solve their problems, some see suicide as the only way out.

Many schools have adopted suicide prevention as well as antibullying programs. They often have social workers, school psychologists, or other counselors on staff who are trained in identifying and assessing students who are at risk for suicide and in making referrals to additional mental health services. They also provide training in suicide prevention to administration, faculty, and other staff. Some schools are beginning to provide more comprehensive mental health services in their districts, as well.

Current trends indicate that reports of student suicidal ideation and attempts at suicide by elementary school students are on the rise. Should a member of the school community become aware that a student is considering suicide, they're required to act immediately, contacting the appropriate specialist in their school, meeting with the student, and notifying his parents. Your child's pediatrician is trained in recognizing symptoms of stress, distress, and depression and can be very helpful to your child and your whole family; he or she can also be a good person to talk to about bullying issues.

Psychiatrists, psychologists, and psychotherapists skilled in identifying symptoms of depression and risk of suicide are adept at helping children resolve their social, emotional, and environmental challenges and concerns.

Other parents, clergy, scout leaders, extended family members, coaches, and other adults who care about your child can help him develop self-confidence, self-esteem, and engagement with positive people and healthy age-appropriate activities, reducing the likelihood of his becoming distressed and increasing his feelings of self-confidence and self-worth. Television programming that models healthy kids, teens, and adults is just one example of an influential source to help your kids develop a positive outlook on life.

Don't be afraid to talk to your child about his emotions; ask him about incidents of bullying in your neighborhood, on his sports team, and in school, and how these problems are being addressed. Ask him about his ideas and feelings, and what he thinks would help, too. Take any concerns he has seriously. If there's anything that's making you suspicious or frightened, don't hesitate to take action.

## Threatening Others

It is not uncommon for kids who have been bullied to imagine being able to make it stop, become victorious, and turn the tables on their bullies. That's commonly regarded as being a "wish fulfillment" fantasy. The vast majority of these kids don't act aggressively or pose any kind of threat to anyone else. However, there are some kids who just can't reconcile or resolve their feelings of victimization and rage. They harbor fantasies of revenge through violence, oftentimes not only against their bully, but against faculty or bystanders who did not step in to help. Sometimes they don't care who they punish; these kids lack empathy and self-control; they are psychologically disturbed and extremely dangerous. These are the kids we hear about in the news—the kids who were bullied in school and who commit school shootings.

If a member of the school community becomes aware that a student has threatened another child, either in school or online, they must take immediate action by contacting the appropriate specialist in school. The school official must then meet with the student, notify his parents, and contact law enforcement if deemed appropriate.

## Essential Takeaways

- It's important to recognize that a child's behavior may reflect serious challenges he's facing at home.
- Learning differences or disabilities can create multiple challenges for kids, leaving them vulnerable to targeting, social rejection, and decreased self-esteem.
- Symptoms of ADHD are often misunderstood and can lead to significant behavioral, social-emotional, and academic problems.
- Anyone who experiences bullying, or who witnesses it, may become anxious or depressed.
- Families and schools need to be proactive in identifying and intervening on behalf of kids who may be contemplating suicide or be a threat to others.

# Part 4

# Moving Beyond the Triangle

Bullying is finally beginning to get the attention it deserves. Many people have spoken out against it, and a wide variety of organizations have initiated antibullying campaigns. In this final part of the book, we talk about what parents, kids, teachers, and counselors have to say about bullying. We further explore ways in which communities are coming together to turn the tide on bullying. We discuss the many projects and initiatives that are raising consciousness, fostering empathy, cultivating new models of education, and making strides in encouraging bystanders to speak up.

# chapter 16

# Rethinking Bullying and Prevention

Reaching a bullying tipping point

Civil rights and our perceptions of bullying

Listening to what parents and kids have to say

Taking a whole-community approach to bullying prevention

In April 2009, following the suicides of Carl Walker Hoover and Jaheem Herrera, two 11-year-olds who were chronically bullied, bullying quickly became one of the top concerns for parents and kids across the United States. In the same way that the tragedy of Columbine sparked the first bullying prevention statutes, these suicides created a national outcry against the long-held attitude that bullying is just a natural part of growing up.

In the weeks that followed, the mothers of the two boys appeared on television programs, including *Ellen* and *Oprah,* to speak about the bullying their children endured. After each appearance, thousands upon thousands of kids, parents, grandparents, and teachers filled the show's online community boards with their own stories and asked for help.

In a very short time, bullying has become an issue that's motivated us to rethink education, parenting, online and offline behaviors, and the fundamental values of our culture. People often ask if bullying has gotten worse over the years. Of course, with the Internet and cell phones, there are more ways to bully, but it's nothing new in our society. What *is* new is our growing awareness of how deeply entrenched it is in our culture, and the changing perception that it isn't just a rite of passage or an inevitable part of growing up.

As stories of young people who have tragically taken their own lives continue to fill national headlines, more people with a stake in this issue have been compelled to take a hard look at the problem and commit to improving the climate for youth, inside and outside of school. In this chapter, we explore some of the attitudes kids, families, educators, and others have about the challenges that lay ahead, and some things that have made a difference.

# What Makes Attitudes Change?

For decades, bullying has been widely perceived as "kids being kids," an unavoidable consequence of any social situation in which there are unequal power dynamics. For a long time, bullying was thought to be an intrinsic, and therefore unchangeable, fact of human nature.

So why is it that we're finally starting to reevaluate these assumptions and establish new expectations for behaviors that have previously been deeply ingrained? Many people say peer-on-peer abuse is the last form of violence that has been widely tolerated. As our society strives to protect more people from abuse, we're less willing to permit injustice and more appreciative of individual differences.

## Civil Rights and Bullying

The twentieth century was a watershed in civil rights in the United States. As advances have been made to provide equality to all people, regardless of race, gender, religious affiliation, or disability, more individuals have been empowered to raise awareness about individual differences and get protection from bias-based harassment and discrimination. As a result of the Americans with Disabilities Act, we now see access ramps and elevators and lifts for people with disabilities on most new public buildings and transportation. With the gains in equality women have made in the past several decades, we have seen growing awareness about domestic violence and support for women who leave abusive spouses.

Among those on the front lines of advocating for bullied youth is the LGBT community, many of whom experienced horrific bullying as kids. Yet, homophobia still exists. Today, it's a civil rights violation to bully anyone based on either their sexuality or perceived sexuality, or for not conforming to gender stereotypes. However, according to a 2009 study by the Gay, Lesbian, and Straight Education Network, 9 out of 10 LGBT students experience harassment in school, and at least one third of LGBT students had missed at least one day of school in the past month because they felt unsafe there.

### Support for LGBT Youth

MISC.

Studies have found that having a gay-straight alliance (GSA) at school results in a more supportive school experience for LGBT youth. Kids at schools with GSAs report fewer homophobic slurs, less targeting on the basis of sexual orientation or nonstereotypical gender expression, and greater inclusivity in the school community. If students at your school are interested in starting a gay-straight alliance, you can support them by directing them to www.glsen.org, where they can find resources on how to start and register their GSA and network with existing GSAs.

Just as we still have a lot of work to do in providing equal rights and opportunities to all people, we also have a lot of work to do to provide an equal education to kids who are bullied, some of whom may go on to pass the first federal antibullying law or start a movement that protects kids like them.

## Workplaces Demand New Skills

As we have evolved from an agrarian and industrial society to a technologi-cally advanced and specialized society, workplaces have increased their demand for different and varied skill sets. Many of today's business leaders and icons of entrepreneurship were formerly known as the geeks and nerds in school. Because of their success, we are beginning to recognize the value of academic success and intellectual curiosity. As we prepare our kids with the tools to succeed, we want them to be able to compete in a world where innovation and curiosity is the key.

 **parent pointer** Some kids are bullied for getting high grades or academic awards by their less successful peers, or because school culture dictates getting good grades isn't cool. If you sense that your child isn't working to her potential or if you see a sudden drop in her grades on material she's confident with, talk to her about what might be going on. She might be dumbing herself down for her peers. Give her challenges and exposure to role models she'll want to impress.

As American schools grapple with a global achievement gap and outdated schools and learning models, educational philosophies are moving away from one-size-fits-all standardized tests and rote memorization to skills that require ingenuity and creativity. Here are some higher-order skills that increasingly are being seen as critical to children's education:

- **Critical thinking skills** that encourage kids to be comfortable with complex problems

- **Leadership skills** and the ability to work with, and present ideas to, a group

- **Flexibility,** the ability to think on your feet, and the capacity to develop more than one right answer

- **Initiative,** which is the ability to take action without being directed

- **Effective oral and written communication skills**

- **Good judgment,** or the ability to assess information and distinguish between what's trustworthy and what isn't

- **Creativity and the ability to come up with innovative solutions**

People who possess these attributes are far less likely to put up with bullying in our culture. As children are taught to value creative thinking and ingenuity, they'll begin to respect differences and appreciate different skill sets. The more young people are taught that a key part of leadership is working with a group, the better social skills they'll exhibit. And the more their communication and problem-solving skills are developed, the more likely kids will be to stand up to bullying and work to find solutions in their school.

# Bullying and Public Health Concerns

Bullying is not just a critical issue for kids, families, and educators; it's also a concern for health-care professionals. The Centers for Disease Control recently declared bullying a major public health problem and launched several studies on rates of victimization, risk factors associated with bullying behaviors, and the effectiveness of various preventions.

The Children's National Medical Center, recognizing bullying can lead to headaches, stomachaches, sleeplessness, depression, anxiety, irritability, injury, and suicidal behavior, has a specific clinic for health problems related to bullying. This clinic offers evaluation and treatment for both youth who are targeted and who are bullying, and each child's team provides advocacy about prevention involving parents, educators, and the whole community. The American Academy of Pediatrics has also published information on bullying prevention, while the World Health Organization has called on health-care organizations, families, and educators to work together to develop bullying prevention strategies, highlighting the need for the public health sector to take a leading role in dealing with the issue.

# What Kids and Families Are Facing

Bullying affects people from all walks of life, cutting across geography, socioeconomic background, gender, weight, religion, and race. People living thousands of miles apart and from widely different backgrounds appear to echo one another when they talk about how bullying has touched their lives.

## What Kids Are Saying

One thing we heard kids say time and time again in schools where bullying isn't effectively addressed and kids don't feel safe is that administrators, school staff, bus drivers, teachers, and cafeteria aides frequently witness bullying but don't do anything about it. Kids everywhere share that they think adults don't do enough to respond to bullying and become frustrated when they report bullying and nothing changes. Many kids also expressed a sense of resignation after having told a faculty member about bullying and feeling nothing had been done because it continued.

Here are some other experiences and perspectives by middle and high school kids who attend schools where they've been bullied, and the school either couldn't or didn't try to put a stop to it:

- "Most kids think they can get away with bullying. Kids aren't thinking about what's going to happen, they think about what's happening now."

- "It starts from about fourth grade till you're out of school. It gets worse as you get older. Once you get older they come up with rumors and fights."

- "It mainly happens to the kids who nobody likes. Most of the time if you're not popular, it's because you're not rich or you're really smart and you're not tough."

- "If you're gay, everybody turns against you. All of a sudden you're not cool, nobody likes you and people wish you would just disappear, and the teachers don't care."

- "Sometimes you don't have anybody to go to when bullying is happening. Even if you do have somebody, you're afraid to tell them, because when you're being bullied your friends leave you. They'll leave you because you're not cool anymore, nobody likes you, and they don't want it to happen to them."

- "If you stick up for somebody and nobody knows you and you're not strong, the other people will fight and hurt you just like they were hurting your friend. Kids are more likely to just stand there and watch it than go to an adult."

- "People don't tell their parents because if you do they go to your school and then everybody knows. The principal will call in the bullies and when they hear your parents came in, they go after you and hurt you more than they already did. We don't tell teachers for the same reason."

However, in kid-friendly, caring schools that have a positive school climate and where bullying is taken seriously and addressed proactively, kids share feedback like this:

- "I used to get bullied in my old school. I used to get my head slammed into lockers. But in this school, things are different. They take it seriously."

- "Jillian told me that other girls are calling her a slut and slamming her online. I told her to come down to guidance because I know that you'll help her, just like you helped me last year when I didn't want to go to class because kids were saying bad things about me."

- "It's surprising to see how many kids in my high school are members of our gay-straight alliance group."

- "Me and my friends don't think it's right to make fun of people, and we're not afraid to say something about it."

- "We told our teacher that our friend said she wanted to kill herself. It was really scary. She didn't want us to tell anyone, but we knew the school would get involved, and they did. She's getting help and she's doing a lot better now."

## Parents' Concerns

Many parents of chronically bullied kids feel like they get labeled as "problem parents," when the problem really is that the situation hasn't been adequately resolved. Although it can be incredibly difficult for administrators to tackle a pernicious bullying situation, unresolved bullying of their children can leave parents feeling targeted as well.

Here are some other things parents of bullied kids in schools where they weren't getting help or support had to say:

- "I felt like I was told it was my child's fault for being bullied because he's different."

- "When you're powerful and popular your kids can get away with it. When you're not, and your kid is being bullied, nobody wants to help."

- "There are great teachers at [my daughter's] school, but if the principal doesn't care, there's nothing they can do. If they start making a fuss about bullying it makes the school look bad."

- "We tried our best to help. But when it didn't make a difference [our daughter] just stopped telling us."

- "When I tried to get protection from bullying included in my child's IEP, the school said they couldn't provide that, even though it's required by state law."

- "We tried to go to the other parents, but they just said their kids would never do those things, and so we had no other choice than to press charges."

In more caring, proactive, and supportive schools, you're likely to hear comments like these:

- "I want to thank everybody who worked so closely with my son this year. He had a lot of trouble being bullied, and now, for the first time in years, he likes going to school."

- "My daughter was terrified for me to call the school; she was afraid it would make things worse. And I knew that she might be right. But I had a really good feeling about the people at her school so I took a chance. I spoke to the vice principal and she invited me to come in to talk about what was going on. She took me seriously and addressed the matter immediately. Things didn't get worse for my daughter, they got much, much better."

- "Thank you for helping my daughter break away from the kids she was hanging out with and find new friends who are much nicer and who care about her."

## What Works, What Doesn't Work

Clearly, there are lots of ways in which kids and parents are still struggling to get protection from bullying and to work with school staff to find solutions. But many schools are getting the job done, and they are able to do so because they provide professional development for educators, teaching them how to effectively handle bullying at school. Successful schools also provide parents with tools to address the issue at school, at home, and in the community.

> **parent pointer**
>
> Many states now issue model bullying policies that schools are encouraged or mandated to adopt. Visit www.olweus.org, the website of the Olweus Bullying Prevention Program, and click the "State Information" link to find your state's policy and a link to the model policy, if applicable. You can download it and compare it to the bullying policy in your school's handbook. If your school doesn't have a proactive antibullying policy, you may want to contact the administrator, board, or superintendents' office, or speak with other parents about encouraging your district to adopt an effective program.

Policies, research, and best practices regarding bullying are quickly evolving. Researchers are finding that several techniques and practices work, including the following:

- Build positive connections between school staff members and between staff and students to provide alternative ways for adults and kids to relate to one another. For example, have a staff versus students ultimate Frisbee tournament or a student-staff chorus.

- Develop clear and consistent rules and interventions, giving students the opportunity to help develop and enforce discipline actions.

- Follow up to make sure there hasn't been fallout as a result of discipline. Have things gotten better, has anyone retaliated, or have things gotten worse?

- Tackle low-level bullying before it escalates by teaching staff to recognize exclusion, teasing, or social manipulation.

- Make upstanding the norm, and encourage peer mentorship to make other students feel more comfortable and supported in standing up.

And then there are practices that haven't proven effective:

- Tell young people it'll just blow over, or discourage them from asking for help.

- Advise targets to "just ignore it" or "just walk away." Targets will be left with the knowledge of what has happened and feel powerless to do anything about it.

- Put up "No Bullying Zone" signs where bullying openly exists but isn't addressed.

- Establish zero-tolerance regulations that aren't enforced.

- Host visiting speakers or hold assemblies on the topic of bullying without following up with in-depth bullying prevention and intervention work throughout the year.

- Provide simplistic assertiveness training for targets or empathy training for kids who bully, or make them sit together and "work it out."

- Remove the target from the environment or provide individual counseling with no efforts at climate change.

- Try to shame bullies, or suggest they're bullying because they're in some way emotionally vulnerable or insecure.

## The Whole-School Approach

Many schools work to create and maintain a positive school climate. In those schools, community members work diligently to foster a sense of safety and a caring learning environment for all students. They take a proactive stance against bullying, and their school culture reflects that position. They embrace the rights, needs, and concerns of all the members of their school community.

That's not to say that bullying doesn't occur in these schools. Unfortunately, even in the best schools bullying does happen, and it's likely to continue to occur. What it does mean is that these schools don't ignore bullying, and when it occurs they take action. We discussed some of the things good schools do in Chapters 7 and 9.

Unfortunately, there are multiple reasons why bullying is so pervasive and can be so hard to change in some schools, beginning with denial and the lack of motivation to make changes.

**MISC.**

### Administrator Action

It requires bravery for a principal or superintendent to acknowledge that bullying is a problem in her school or district. She may fear a backlash from the community or losing her job, and she may not feel supported by her staff. Many administrators feel ill equipped to address the problem with any consistency, either because they lack funding for programs and training or their school culture has a history of negativity, violence, or disrespect that makes any change seem like an overwhelming undertaking. However, the more administrators reach out to members of their community, the more support they'll have in confronting the problem.

Despite systematic problems and challenges, schools aren't excused from taking responsible action to turn things around. Children's lives depend upon it.

Many programs offer tools to help improve a school's climate and to prevent and intervene in incidents of bullying behaviors, and many schools welcome the help. Schools that acknowledge that bullying is a problem and institute proactive, school-wide changes in how they address the needs of their students can greatly reduce bullying in their schools.

Some characteristics of holistic change include the following:

- Start early! It's never too soon to start bullying prevention, social-emotional learning, and character education at home and at school.

- Get involvement from all school staff and administrators, making sure they all have a voice in shaping policies and all receive training in how to intervene.

- Coordinate in-school efforts with out-of-school behaviors. Connect staff with parents and community members, involve the whole community in the efforts, and provide ways for community leaders, parents, educators, and kids to interact.

- Connect upstanding with civic values, and strengthen partnerships between schools and their communities.

## Essential Takeaways

- Bullying is reaching a tipping point moment where there's a growing awareness and shared sentiment that it's time to change how we perceive and deal with the problem.

- Advances in civil rights and the new kinds of skills our kids will need to join the workforce have all played a role in changing attitudes about bullying.

- In schools where bullying isn't adequately addressed, parents of kids who are chronically bullied often feel marginalized and frustrated by the lack of response.

- Cultural shifts require a whole-community approach, connecting educators, kids, parents, and community leaders committed to creating a positive climate.

# chapter 17

# Sharing School Perspectives

Building bridges and expanding communities

Making face-to-face connections

Listening to what teachers and counselors say

Although it's true that bullying behaviors transcend ages and grades, middle school is *the* hotbed for bullying. Some schools have a pretty good handle on bullying behaviors, know what's going on with their students, and take a proactive approach. But even with comprehensive prevention programs and positive approaches, bullying still happens, although with far less frequency, duration, and intensity than in schools that don't share this perspective.

We know that taking a school-wide and whole-community approach, where everybody participates in creating a positive school climate, makes a big difference.

In this chapter, we share information from the perspectives of school administrators, teachers, counselors, and specialists (school social workers, school psychologists, and others), as well as bus drivers, crossing guards, aides, custodians, and cafeteria workers, all the people who work with kids. For efficiency's sake, unless we're speaking about a specific group of these adults, we'll refer to them as "faculty" or "members of the school community."

# Little Things Add Up

In order to transform a school community from an atmosphere of aggression, disconnection, and distrust to one that's friendly, welcoming, safe, and connected, it helps when faculty members know not only their students, but their families as well. School communities that are aware and respectful of cultural differences, family concerns, and individual student interests and issues help kids connect with their school and fellow students. That makes everyone involved members of not only a child's school, but of his larger community as well.

The connections between schools, students, and families are solidified when members of the school community attend athletic games, concerts, and special events—even family events, like memorial services. This isn't to suggest that everyone who works in a school should be expected to attend every event involving their students; that would be impossible. However, when kids feel connected to the adults they spend time with during the day, good things happen.

When faculty reach out to join with kids and their families, help them access services, learn how to problem solve, succeed in school, and get along better with others, students feel understood, respected, and good about themselves. Kids know how much their school cares about them because it shows. When members of the school community show their interest in the things students are interested in and passionate about, kids feel it, and the caring community grows.

**Caring Pays Off**

Working at a school isn't just about teaching; it's so much more. Most people who work in schools know that if they can show interest, respect, and caring by their good intentions and actions, they'll be much more successful with their students. When you respect and care, it's usually reciprocated, both at school and at home.

Just smiling and saying hello to kids and to fellow faculty, and encouraging kids to do the same with each other as they pass in the halls, can transform an environment. You might be surprised to see how such a little thing as greeting someone can break down barriers and bring down the walls that separate kids from each other and from faculty.

Even older kids like it when adult members of the school community have lunch with them, or give them a high five or a pat on the back. It makes them feel special, valued, and connected. When kids feel like their faculty care about them, they begin to care, too. They start to do things to please these caring adults: doing their homework, speaking respectfully, treating each other with kindness, following school rules, acting like upstanders, and making responsible decisions.

## Face Time Matters

There's no replacement for quality face-to-face interaction. Teachers, counselors, and specialists who work with kids know that human connection—time spent together, a hug from Mom or Dad, and a face-to-face conversation with a good friend—works wonders for kids and everyone else.

Members of the school community can provide a positive and safe presence as they see kids move through their school day, during after-school activities, and as they board the school bus home. But they can't watch over them while they're in one place where kids spend a lot of their free time these days: on the Internet. And when families are under pressure or working late, media and technology continue to fill the time, just as television did for baby boomer parents and their children.

## Dealing with Mixed Messages

Today's kids are bombarded with messages from peers, adults, celebrities, the news, and other media sources that can give them the impression that violence and bullying, disrespect, and casual sex are totally fine, or that drugs, alcohol, or cutting can be solutions to problems.

Members of the school community and parents at home have many opportunities to be good role models for kids, to challenge and to replace the role models they have on TV and elsewhere who exhibit negative attitudes and destructive, self-serving behaviors. We need to model appropriate behavior, good values, and the importance of acceptance of others and respect for all.

Manners matter to everyone in the school and home community. Just because good manners isn't a specific subject taught in school doesn't mean we shouldn't be taking opportunities to teach and use them there, as well as at home. "Please," "thank you," and "excuse me" show regard for others. Requests, rather than demands, are appreciated and respectful ways of asking for something we want.

It's been said that you only get one chance to make a first impression, but homes and schools are places of learning where it's understood that making mistakes is a part of the learning process. We don't have to be perfect, but we do have to be held accountable. We all learn as we go; it's how we address and correct our mistakes that matters most.

## The Pleasure Principle

The pleasure principle says that people will naturally do things that make them feel good and will try to avoid doing things that don't feel so good, even if it's just for a few moments at a time.

It's quite common for a kid who's having trouble with math to avoid doing it. In school, he might get up from his chair repeatedly, play with the items on his desk, or talk to his neighbor. Parents see it at home, too. It can take forever to get homework done due to stalling, pleading, arguing, and assorted avoidance techniques. Despite the fact that the entire episode may seem futile, for the moments that he's avoiding the pain of the dreaded task, he's enjoying the pleasure of not having to do something difficult.

The pleasure principle applies to bullying, too. If a child enjoys being aggressive toward another and is successful in getting his way, it makes him feel good. And he's likely to keep doing it until someone makes him stop or, for whatever reason, it doesn't make him feel good anymore.

**Bully Buster**

Some kids (and adults, too) are of the opinion that being bad and acting aggressively is how people gain respect. This is a great time to do away with that misconception. Most people neither respect nor like people who behave badly. They try to avoid them, and they may fear them, as well. Fear doesn't equal respect.

Kids usually love doing things for the people they care about. Many schools these days offer opportunities for kids to volunteer, even at young ages: peer tutoring, reading to a younger child, being a buddy to kids who have autism or other difficulties, taking care of school pets or plants, helping teachers, participating in student government, raising funds for worthy causes, and taking active roles in the community.

Most kids want to do the right thing. They feel proud when they work hard and achieve good grades or score a goal for their football team. Most kids feel good about themselves when they help a friend who's having a hard time and when they make good choices. It's everyone's job to do what we can to help kids derive more pleasure from doing good things than engaging in behaviors that cause pain or suffering to others. We all need to work together to change the culture and make it uncool and socially undesirable to be a bully.

## Changing Bad Habits

Most people know that eating healthy and exercising will help them lose weight, and that quitting smoking is one of the best things they can do for themselves. So, if they know what to do, why don't they just do it? Because they don't feel like it; or they like what they're doing better; or their behaviors are entrenched. It's very difficult to change old behaviors and habits, even when you know you'll feel better once you do.

Bad habits can be hard to break, especially if you're not totally sure you want to change. Don't let your child wait until he feels like acting better; that day may never come. Most of us know that you can't *feel* your way to better behavior, but you can *act* your way to it.

**Bully Buster**

Teachers, counselors, and specialists can't put things off when it comes to addressing issues and helping your child make positive changes. Even though he doesn't feel like changing his aggressive or inappropriate behavior and may resist at first, people who work with kids know he'll feel better about himself when his grades rise, his parents are proud of him, and he stops getting into trouble. Most kids will like him more when he stops bullying other kids, so there's a good chance he'll end up having more friends, too.

You might be surprised to learn that you can help significantly decrease incidents of aggression and frustration just by supporting a child in making small changes:

- If Johnny always gets into trouble when he takes the three o'clock bus, maybe he can take the one that leaves at 3:30, carpool with a friend, or ride his bike home from school.

- If he has trouble navigating the rules of the basketball court at recess, he can be assisted in finding an alternate activity.

- If he has difficulty managing his emotions and behavior, his teacher, counselor, or specialist can talk with him about that and work with his family, too, to help him develop more appropriate coping skills.

You may want to review Chapter 6 for some suggestions on helping your child develop assertiveness skills, resolve conflicts, and increase self-confidence; take another look at Chapter 9 for information on social-emotional skills and character development; and check out Chapter 13 for ways both you and your child's school can help a more aggressive or impulsive youngster make positive changes in his behavior and his relationships at home and at school.

## Educators Taking the Lead

In global educational rankings, the United States continues to fall behind nations such as Singapore, Hong Kong, South Korea, and Finland. As we rethink how we invest in education, we need to close the link between student safety and academic achievement. Students who are bullied perform much worse than their counterparts, and the experience of being continually bullied degrades academic performance even further. Bullied students find themselves in a vicious cycle, afraid to participate in class for fear of being called dumb or, lacking confidence, perform even worse, increasingly lowering their status.

In order to raise student achievement, many districts are investing in social-emotional learning (SEL) from preschool through high school. Studies have found students receiving SEL instruction have more positive attitudes about school and improved their scores on standardized tests by 11 percent, compared to their peers without SEL programs.

The Collaborative for Social Emotional Learning, or CASEL, has been developing district-wide SEL programs in large public schools in Anchorage, Austin, Chicago, Cleveland, Reno, Oakland, and Sacramento. These are all large school districts with tens of thousands of students, faced with budget cuts, achievement gaps, truancy, and bullying, but these programs set a precedent for changing perspectives on academics. CASEL also offers educators advice on how to integrate various ongoing efforts into an SEL framework.

MISC.

### SEL in Your State

If you'd like to find out more about your state's educational standards related to social-emotional learning, visit www.casel.org/policy-advocacy/sel-in-your-state to find a national map with state-by-state SEL information. And turn to Chapter 9 for more information about character education and social-emotional learning.

## School Counselors

School counselors and specialists such as social workers, psychologists, and behaviorists work with individual students and groups, and they help families, too.

School counselors and specialists have expertise in helping kids increase their self-awareness and self-control, develop good character, and identify and address problems related to achieving academic, vocational, personal, and social success. They're also involved in crisis management.

Many of today's school specialists are also licensed mental health professionals, and many school counselors—the title that's replaced guidance counselors—are likely to have more advanced training in counseling students regarding a variety of issues and concerns than their counterparts of yesteryear, whose primary responsibility was to provide career guidance.

Today's counselors and specialists can help kids achieve many of the following goals:

- Learn more about themselves, including identifying academic and other needs, strengths, and weaknesses
- Learn to recognize their triggers, the situations that cause them distress, anger, or other negative emotions
- Develop empathy and increase acceptance and tolerance for others' differences and points of view
- Learn the meaning behind their behavior and how to express their emotions appropriately
- Decrease negative attitudes and behaviors and increase optimism and the ability to tolerate frustration
- Develop age-appropriate interests and learn self-assertion skills
- Reduce the need and desire to bully other kids and increase positive social skills, including becoming an upstander
- Help kids reduce their likelihood of being targeted
- Increase self-help and friendship skills
- Increase self-esteem, resilience, and the ability to view situations and problems from multiple perspectives

Behaviorists have particular expertise in analyzing the function of a child's behavior and designing strategies to reduce negative behaviors and increase positive ones, while speech language professionals provide instruction and foster the development of good social-communication skills.

School counselors and specialists love working with kids and helping them make their lives better. It's exactly what they went to school to learn how to do. Unfortunately, the need for counseling/specialist services far outweighs the number of available counselors and specialists. School counselors express frustration at their lack of availability to maintain the kind of ongoing contact and support that would best benefit the children they serve.

In some districts, school psychologists and social workers also manage heavy caseloads of students who have IEPs. Administrators agree that schools need more counselors, social workers, and psychologists, just as more teachers, aides, and support staff are needed.

## Teachers Care About Kids

Teachers know the importance of providing children with a good education and creating a welcoming learning environment. They witness your child's ups and downs and all-arounds, and can be a constant source of reassurance, guidance, genuine caring, and safety.

Most teachers will tell you that they'd like to be able to teach them more about the things they need to know to feel good about themselves, to be able to get along well with others, and to enjoy a happy and successful life. Helping children learn to walk quietly through the halls and wait their turn on the lunch line, standing up for their convictions, reaching out to a new student and participating as part of a group, fostering a positive attitude, rejecting bullying, and becoming an upstander are just a few things your child's teacher does every day—in addition to teaching math, social studies, science, and language arts.

In addition to counselors and specialists, teachers can implement research-based bullying prevention programs, social-emotional learning, and candid classroom and individual discussions about drama, bullying and the bullying triangle, violence, suicide, relationships, problem solving, and self-assertion. Although these critical topics are often covered in health class, they can also be linked to English or social studies, or in such classes as law, psychology, or sociology.

Most teachers welcome training in bullying prevention and intervention, and embrace the tenets of social-emotional learning and character education. They're sensitive to the needs of individual children and welcome input from parents.

Most middle and high school teachers have an excellent understanding of the changes their students go through as they enter adolescence. They're the first ones to notice when a student doesn't seem like himself, appears to be distressed, or is being left out of the social group. It's not uncommon for students to reveal their conflicts, worries, and deep emotional pain in the pages of their journals, which are shared with their teachers. The lives of countless students have been saved by the interventions that are put into place at school when a teacher or other member of the school community becomes aware of a student's despair, and brings that information forth to the appropriate school specialist.

## The Wheels on the Bus

Bus drivers are responsible for safely shuttling children between home and school and back again, as well as transporting kids on class trips. School buses can have upwards of 50 kids, and the bus driver is often the only adult on board, meaning that he or she is not only responsible for driving the kids safely to their destination, but also for maintaining order and attending to any emergencies. As you might imagine, driving a bus can be a challenging, daunting, and thankless task.

All the adults who work with your children, including bus drivers, cafeteria workers, crossing guards, and custodians, deserve respect, appreciation, and support. Should the driver come into the school building to let staff know about an incident on the bus, he needs to be taken seriously and the matter needs to be followed up on the same day. The same is true if a child reports an incident on the bus.

Whether or not there are children who ride the school bus who pose a potential threat, it would seem helpful (and logical) to have the two eyes of the driver facing forward and an additional pair of eyes on the students to ensure everyone's safety and to establish and maintain a positive school bus climate. Unfortunately, not many districts make this a priority or are willing or able to provide the necessary resources to have an additional adult on board the bus.

When bullying violates the protections guaranteed by Title IX amendments to the Civil Rights Act, which prohibits discrimination on the basis of race, color, national origin, sex, disability, and age, it doesn't matter whether the bullying occurs on the school grounds or the school bus.

In addition, a child who has been determined to be eligible for special education services and has an IEP is offered certain protections and rights under the Individuals with Disabilities Act. You may wish to speak with your child's case manager at school, the director of special education for your district, or your Office for State-wide Advocacy to help you determine whether your child is eligible to receive accommodations to ensure his safety while riding the bus.

Here are some suggestions that may be helpful if your child rides the school bus:

- Have him sit up front, near the driver, with a friend or a well-behaving child, if possible.

- If there have already been incidents of bullying or intimidation, make sure the driver knows about it.

- Drop him off at a bus stop where a friend boards the bus, if it's closer to school.

- Role-play bus situations with your child, using assertiveness techniques.

- Start a petition requesting a bus aide or organize rotating parent volunteers to ride the bus; maybe there's a teacher or para-professional who could use a ride to or from work and will be willing to ride the bus.

- Have your child call you or send you a text from the bus to check in. A secret word between the two of you can be a clue that he needs you to meet him at the bus stop or that he's in trouble.

**parent pointer**

Have you thanked your child's bus driver lately? There have been numerous instances in which drivers have saved the lives of kids by evacuating them safely from burning buses, performed the Heimlich maneuver on kids who were choking, helped kids remain calm in the face of accidents or while stuck in traffic jams, protected them from aggressive and unruly students, sat with children whose parents haven't arrived home on time, provided care for special-needs kids, or simply started the children's day with a smile.

# Teachers and Counselors Weigh In

This isn't an easy time to be a young person. In a world where kids are bombarded with mixed messages about what's important and appropriate and excessive demands on parents to keep their families afloat, kids need to connect with caring adults more than ever. Here are some ideas, requests, and suggestions from concerned professionals in today's school districts who care about your kids and families:

**Take time to enjoy your child every day.** It's easy to get caught up in the responsibilities of being a parent, especially if a child isn't doing well in school. It's easy for parent-child relationships to revolve around school problems and to forget about all the good qualities your child has. Try to take the time, even if it's just a couple of minutes, to have a nice conversation, tell a joke, have dinner together, or play a game. These things make your child feel loved and valued, which in turn raises his self-esteem and self-confidence.

**Set up a reward system for the child, and follow through on consequences.** For example, if your child has not been handing in his homework, set up a contract with him (and the school) whereby for every day he hands in his homework, he gets a point, a checkmark, or a sticker in order to give him feedback on how he's doing and to tally his success. When he has accumulated a certain number of points, he receives a reward, such as a sleepover, homework pass, or other reasonable item of his choice. Similarly, if he violates a rule, he should face consistent consequences.

**Keep working at it.** For kids who are stubborn or resist buying into a plan, you may have to keep working at it. It isn't at all uncommon for kids to need to feel understood and cared about by the adults in their lives before they're willing to invest themselves in learning, accept responsibility, and make good choices.

**Ask for help.** Just ask your school professionals for help; they have lots of tools in their toolkit and will also offer referrals to therapists or other helpful professionals when appropriate.

**Model courtesy and good manners** at the ballpark, in the car, at home, and everywhere you go. Your children will pick them up from you.

**Be a role model for self-assertion, self-confidence, and self-respect.** Support and encourage the same in your children.

**Be a good listener, offering your child your undivided attention.** Kids who don't feel listened to or understood often become frustrated, disappointed, or angry. They may seek more information and guidance from the Internet than their families because the Internet is always available.

**Try to look at things from the teacher's perspective.** It can be difficult for a teacher to manage a class of 25 kids, making sure they all get along and that everyone's needs are met. While it's the teacher's responsibility to maintain a disciplined and safe environment, personalities do clash and everyone has a bad day from time to time.

**Make sure your children know that fighting is a very dangerous way to try to deal with an aggressive person and is not a good idea.** This can be a big dilemma, because we can all probably recall an incident where a kid who got picked on decided they'd had enough, hit back, and that was the end of it. We get it. At the same time, we also know that violence often begets violence, and that the older kids get, the higher the stakes get raised, sometimes resulting in group attacks or use of weapons. Social skills, self-confidence, just-right responses, upstanders, and prevention strategies still trump responding with violence in most cases.

**Be an active participant in your child's education.** Read to him, talk about school—his projects, teachers, peers, clubs, the dating scene, the Internet experience, bullying, and so on—every day.

**Treat your children with respect,** and require them to treat their parents, adults, and peers respectfully, too.

**Come to school meetings.** Your attendance lets your child know how much you value education and how important he is to you. Parents who don't attend school meetings or participate in their child's education often regret it later. Schools know how difficult it can be for parents to take off work to make a meeting, and most are more than happy to accommodate a phone conference or make another arrangement with you; lots of parents find email a helpful and effective means of keeping in touch.

**Demonstrate respect for the school faculty.** While you may not like your child's teacher this year, unless she's causing him harm or not addressing his needs, he'll benefit much more from knowing that you support her and his school than from bad-mouthing, disrespecting, and disregarding an adult who is trying to help him as best she can.

**Teach your child acceptance and tolerance.** Show your child that, although he may not like everyone he has to spend time with, working with a variety of people builds character and the ability to accept and appreciate differences.

**Hold members of the school community responsible for behaving responsibly and appropriately.** You and your child have a right to have teachers who are good role models for children, competent in their subject areas, exhibit self-control, and speak with students and parents respectfully. Teachers shouldn't be socializing with kids on Facebook or any other social media. Parents should conduct themselves with dignity and self-control as well, even when frustrated.

**Make sure your child comes to school on time and is ready for learning.** If your family is having financial difficulties or other logistical challenges, make sure the school social worker knows about it; they can often be very helpful in linking you to services to support you and your family.

**Make a conscious decision to do the right thing.** Keep in mind that your child (and your relationship with him) will fare much better if you put his needs ahead of your wants and do what's right for him instead of what's easiest for you.

**Become cyberwise and monitor use of technology, including video games and social networks.** Don't give in when it comes to video addiction; do everything you can to offer your child a variety of positive activities.

**Power struggles between adults and students have no place in school.** Children have the right to feel emotionally, physically, and socially safe at school; the same goes for your neighborhood. Keep an eye out and an ear open to be sure your child is safe on play dates, on camping trips, and in dating relationships, too.

**Learn the lingo of bullying.** Lots of middle school and older kids refer to it as "drama." Talk to them about school drama, whether they've ever been harassed, shut out, etc.

**Remember the old African proverb: "It takes a village to raise a child."** All of the members of his school and greater community are members of your child's village.

P.S. If you can read this, thank a teacher.

## Essential Takeaways

- A whole-school approach is further enhanced when members of the school community connect with students' families and their larger community.

- Bad habits can be hard to break; you can't feel your way to acting better, but you can act your way to feeling better.

- Although school counselors and specialists have expertise in assisting targets, bullies, bystanders, and families, they're often in short supply.

- Teachers are the cheerleaders and champions of children, and they welcome your help. When parents join forces with schools, kids thrive.

# chapter 18

# A World Without Bullying

Using the Internet as a place for positive connections

Instigating community campaigns

Using star power to turn the tide on bullying

Changing perspectives on school safety

Although bullying has been in the spotlight for a relatively short period of time, we've already seen significant changes in how our laws, schools, and the media regard bullying.

Bullying is one of those rare issues that has touched all of us. At some point we've either been a target, a bully, or a bystander. We're affected by bullying in our children's schools, in our relationships at home, in the workplace, and in the dynamics of our communities. Many of us also have a stake in this issue as educators, doctors, policymakers, and community leaders.

The best way to prevent bullying in school is to involve everyone—from recess monitors to principals—in working to find a solution. Preventing bullying in our communities also means a widespread commitment to changing our behaviors and ideas about what's acceptable, from the things we do online to the people we admire as role models.

In this chapter, we look at some of the ways our perspectives on bullying are shifting, both inside and outside of our schools, and how we're getting closer to a culture where bullying is history.

# A Whole New World Online

Although the Internet has been used as a platform for bullies to harm their targets, it's also at the forefront of the battle against bullying. People confronting bullying online can take advantage of the same features that bullies use—such as the Internet's capacity to quickly spread information—to create awareness about bullying and to provide positive connections for bullied youth.

## It Gets Better Project

One of the most influential online antibullying campaigns is the It Gets Better Project. Launched in response to the suicides of several bullied gay youth, the project has posted thousands of videos offering hope and support, particularly for LGBT kids. While many of these messages come from individuals, some have been contributed by businesses, educators, entertainers, athletes, and political and government officials—even President Obama! Here are some notable contributors:

- Celebrities, including Justin Bieber, Lady Gaga, Kathy Griffin, Tom Hanks, Anne Hathaway, Janet Jackson, Kesha, Anna Paquin, and Katy Perry

- Cast members from *Wicked, Jersey Boys, True Blood,* and *Chicago*

- Employees from Apple, Dreamworks Animation, Facebook, the Gap, General Motors, Google, Microsoft, Pixar, Sony Pictures Entertainment, Visa, and Yahoo!

- Sports teams, including the Baltimore Orioles, the Boston Red Sox, the L.A. Dodgers, and the Seattle Seahawks

- Political figures such as Secretary of State Hilary Clinton, Vice President Joe Biden, Senator Nancy Pelosi, Representative Jon Runyan, and President Obama himself.

The range of voices participating in the It Gets Better Project is an indication of the extent to which the bullying of LGBT youth is devastating millions of teens and has become an issue of importance to everyone, regardless of sexual orientation. It also offers hope for real change as awareness is raised in different sectors of our society, many of which are in a position to shape our culture, values, and laws. If you'd like to add your voice to the It Gets Better Project, all you need is a computer with a webcam, a YouTube account, and a message of hope to bullied youth. Go to www.itgetsbetter.org to find out more.

**community watch**

Studies show that a third of all gay youth have attempted suicide versus 13 percent of their straight counterparts. However, antibullying laws that protect LGBT youth have been challenged by groups claiming policies aimed at protecting youth from homophobic slurs and attacks are promoting a "gay agenda." In Minnesota's Anoka-Hennepin school district, where Christian activists forced a measure through the school board forbidding staff from discussing homosexuality, nine kids have committed suicide over a two-year period, four of whom were gay or perceived as gay. The district is currently being sued by two civil rights groups for its failure to address antigay bullying and harassment in its schools as a result of this "neutrality policy."

## Social Networking Sites

Although social networking sites have been used to exclude or antagonize targets, the majority of things taking place on these sites are positive, and it's only getting better with time.

Many Facebook groups are devoted to standing up to bullying, raising awareness, or creating ways for kids who are bullied to talk about their experiences, connect, and get help. Facebook has also launched Causes, which allows users to connect with issues (including several bullying prevention initiatives), and even donate money to these causes.

Schools and organizations are beginning to provide more ways to report bullying online, and social networking sites are taking an active role in fighting cyberbullying by removing negative posts or shutting down inappropriate groups. Also, users are speaking up and intervening when they witness bullying online, whether they know the target or not, to support them and to disparage the bullying.

## Getting Support on YouTube

Many teenagers use YouTube as a place where they can post intimate testimonials of their experiences with bullying, talk about how it's affecting them, and reach out for help. As kids were gearing up to go back to school in August 2010, Jonah Mowry posted a video in which he held up note cards describing how bullying has driven him to cut himself since the second grade and how he has contemplated suicide as a result of being "torn down" every day at school. In the video, Jonah admits to having only one friend at school and being afraid of going back, wondering why everybody hates him and how he can go on.

The video quickly went viral, receiving over nine million views and eliciting an outpouring of support from viewers leaving messages of hope and friendship. Many other viewers posted their own "Dear Jonah" videos, in the same style as his, composed on handwritten note cards, letting him know he's not alone and talking about their own experiences of bullying.

**parent pointer**

In September 2011, 14-year-old Jamey Rodemeyer took his own life a few months after he created a video for It Gets Better that described the homophobic bullying he was experiencing at school and the hate messages he received through his Formspring profile. A week prior, he posted a message online saying, "I always say how bullied I am, but no one listens. What do I have to do so people will listen?"

Talk with your child about notifying you if she ever encounters someone online who needs help or is talking about harming herself, even if she seems okay for the moment. Aside from sending messages of support, you can contact the site administrator and your local police department for help.

# Grass-Roots Campaigns

A multitude of grass-roots campaigns on and offline are bringing together youth, parents, educators, health-care workers, brands, organizations, and media networks to take action to prevent bullying and create positive community climates for all.

**National Bullying Prevention Month.** October is National Bullying Prevention Month. Created by the PACER Center in 2006, during October communities nationwide are encouraged to take action against bullying.

Participating schools and individuals can sign The End of Bullying Begins with Me digital petition, talk to local media about bullying-prevention activities in school, organize events and walks, download toolkits, and find other ways to take an active role. In addition, many of the PACER's National Partners—including BullyBust, GLAAD, and GLSEN—sponsor special events and programs. To learn more, visit www.pacer.org/bullying/nbpm.

community watch

Just because October is National Bullying Prevention Month doesn't mean that you can't raise awareness about bullying throughout the year. For instance, April 20 is the Day of Silence, where participating schools are silent for the day to raise awareness about harassment of LGBT youth. If your community has had a significant bullying-related event on a particular day, commemorate that day and take it as an opportunity to raise awareness and reinforce upstander behaviors throughout the year, every year.

**Bully Bust and *Wicked*.** The National School Climate Center has recently partnered with the Broadway musical *Wicked* to create upstander toolkits and curriculum using the story of Ephelba, the misunderstood witch at the center of the story, as a way for kids to talk about bullying. The campaign also includes essay contests for upstanders, ambassador awards, and a "videos for good" contest. Winners receive grants for their school and even visits from the cast of *Wicked*.

**DoSomething.org.** DoSomething.org offers a range of grants and support to students taking positive social action in their community, such as launching an event to raise awareness about people with disabilities or starting a local DoSomething club. DoSomething.org has lots of ways to get involved in issues related to bullying, including projects on school violence, dating abuse, gang violence, cyberbullying, bullying, and child abuse. For each project area, DoSomething suggests ideas on how to take action, resources, and access to specific antibullying grants. They also sponsor the annual DoSomething awards, honoring young people 25 and under as "the nation's best young world-changers." Five semifinalists win $10,000 in community grants, and one grand prize winner is awarded a $100,000 community grant. DoSomething also works extensively with celebrities in positive causes as role models, publishing an annual top-20 list of Celebs Gone Good.

**The Cartoon Network's Stop Bullying Speak Up.** The Cartoon Network recently launched the Stop Bullying Speak Up campaign, encouraging kids to intervene when they see or experience bullying by telling a teacher, parent, or other trusted adult. The Stop Bullying Speak Up website also offers kids opportunities to make their own Stop Bullying comic, tip sheets for parents, polls about bullying, and videos on how to deal with bullying in the moment.

These are just a few of the many campaigns taking root to raise awareness about bullying and to reinforce upstander behavior. Here are a few more:

- Human Rights Campaign's Welcoming Schools initiative, giving educators tools to create LGBT-inclusive learning environments.

- The National PTA's Connect for Respect program, encouraging members to start dialogues about bullying in their communities.

- StopBullying.gov from the Department of Health and Human Services, Department of Education, and Department of Justice, offering resources about bullying and cyberbullying, information about state laws and policies, and ways to get help, including contact links for the U.S. Departments of Justice and Education.

- The Anti-Defamation League's Bullying Resource Center, which includes great information for advocates on bullying laws and policies, as well as resources for kids, parents, and educators on bullying, cyberbullying, and hate speech.

- BBYO, a Jewish youth organization that's activating teen members to stand up to bullying from a faith perspective, modeling empathy and upstanding through the lens of Jewish values, and launching various youth leadership initiatives around the issue of bullying.

- The Gay & Lesbian Alliance Against Defamation (GLAAD), a vocal defender against uses of media that are homophobic or discriminatory. GLAAD seeks to highlight positive images of LGBT people in film, on TV, in music, and on social media. GLAAD has several action initiatives through petitions, PSA campaigns, and their site also provides a portal to report defamation.

For a list of great resources and ways to get involved in your community, see Appendix B at the end of this book.

## Role Models Taking Action

Celebrities and professional athletes are in a position to influence young people to treat each other with respect and find the courage to speak up to prevent bullying. They're influential because they're popular and confident, and a lot of them are extremely strong, to boot.

Many celebrities and athletes also have a very personal connection to bullying; some were driven to their passion to escape bullying, while others were bullied for being exceptional. As our children's role models, these stars are in a unique position to shape our culture, not only through their talents but through the kind of team players they are, the issues raised by the art they make, or the audiences they seek out with their music.

community watch

In spring 2011, a 13-year-old Philadelphia boy, Nadin Khoury, was kicked, beaten, dragged through snow, stuffed in a tree, and then hung by his coat from a spiked fence. A video of this brutal incident was posted on YouTube by one of the bullies, and Khoury went to the police. The video soon sparked national outrage. When the NFL's Philadelphia Eagles' DeSean Jackson, Jamaal Jackson, and Todd Herremens heard about the incident, they took action. Appearing on *The View* with Nadin and his mother, they commended him for his courage and, following the show, DeSean Jackson has devoted himself to the issue, speaking to schools, prisoners at San Quentin, student councils, and at-risk youth in Los Angeles.

Many celebrities have taken a powerful stand against bullying, including Ellen DeGeneres, Anderson Cooper, Kelly Ripa, and Jane Lynch. Perhaps the most influential celebrity for youth today, Lady Gaga, has spoken out extensively about bullying and about her own sense of being an outcast as an adolescent. Having channeled that feeling into a hugely creative career, this independent personality has given a tremendous boost to bullied youth. In the summer of 2011, she met with President Obama's top advisers at the White House to discuss the dimensions of the bullying crisis and ways to support affected youth. She also launched the Born This Way Foundation, focusing on bullying prevention and promoting acceptance, individuality, and youth empowerment.

Some other notable celebrity campaigns include

- Demi Lovato's Love Is Louder Than the Pressure to be Perfect, about bullying and body image.

- Will.i.am has launched The Peapod Adobe Youth Voices Academies, with the goal of empowering youth to use their talents to realize positive social change.

- Daniel Radcliffe, star of the *Harry Potter* films, has been a vocal supporter of the Trevor Project, offering suicide prevention support to LGBT teens and appearing in their PSAs.

- Taylor Swift has used her big country voice to release an antibullying music video titled "Mean," as well as speaking out about her own experiences of being bullied.

## Professional Organizations and Teachers Unions are Standing Up to Bullying

Teachers are on the front lines when it comes to bullying, and their unions are helping them to be equipped with the tools to effectively respond.

The American Federation of Teachers (AFT), representing 1.5 million members, has launched the See a Bully, Stop a Bully campaign to give educators, school leaders, and advocates resources and tools to effectively respond to and prevent bullying. The AFT has also partnered with GLAAD on a series of public service announcements about LGBT bullying and verbal abuse.

The United Federation of Teachers has also launched several bullying prevention and awareness initiatives, including an antibullying hotline for students and the Be BRAVE Against Bullying campaign offering educators workshops about bullying prevention, and resources and information for teachers.

The National Education Association, the nation's largest professional employee organization, with affiliates in more than 14,000 communities in the United States, has created Bully Free: It Starts With Me. The program includes the Bully-Free pledge, tips on how to introduce a bully-free campaign in your school, resources for bus drivers on preventing bullying on the bus, and additional tools.

The National Association of Elementary School Principals has also taken a stand on bullying, providing resources to members on its site, as well as a help line for principals needing support, professional advice, and guidance.

Educators can refer to Appendix B for more resources, tools, information, learning guides, lesson plans, and other ways to get involved in bullying prevention in your school.

# Education Support Professionals Are Crucial

Education support professionals, or ESPs, are the people who make our schools run: custodians, school chefs, crossing guards, bus drivers, and paraeducators. Paraeducators are particularly instrumental in supporting our kids; they work as classroom aides, library technicians, assistants, and monitors on the playground, in the hall, and on the bus. ESPs often develop close bonds with our children and can be great advocates and allies, especially as they are often present in the areas inside and outside of school where kids are most vulnerable to bullying.

In 2010, the National Education Association released a survey of ESPs with their perspectives on bullying. Ninety-two percent of the 470 bus drivers who participated in the survey indicated they feel it's their job to intervene in bullying; however, only 56 percent had received training on their school's policy and a mere 23 percent had been included in their district's committees on bullying prevention. The survey indicated that bus drivers want to be trained and equipped with the tools to effectively handle bullying and to be part of their district's policy development.

The NEA survey also found that students who have been targeted feel safer when paraprofessionals are nearby, and that paras are more likely than teachers to be in situations where they witness and intervene in bullying situations. However, they also indicated that they receive few opportunities to get training on how to properly handle bullying. Given that many bullying situations occur on playgrounds, in lunchrooms, in hallways, in class before the lesson begins, or other places paras are often present, the need for them to be trained is urgent. Over two thirds of the paras in the survey said they need additional training on how to address bullying across the spectrum, from physical and verbal to relational, cyberbullying, and sexting.

The NEA survey also revealed that students are more likely to talk to paraeducators about bullying than any other adult in the school building; 40 percent of paras surveyed had had a child report an incident of bullying to them in the past month, and over half indicated that they witness a student being bullied several times a month. Paras are also more likely than other ESPs to report bullying. If your child is a target, ask her if there's a paraeducator who makes her feel safe or who she trusts to talk to.

## Essential Takeaways

- Cultural attitudes toward bullying are changing for the better. Examples of positive changes are the many antibullying campaigns that take place on and offline, from the It Gets Better Project to DoSomething.org to Wicked and BullyBust.

- Despite the prevalence of cyberbullying, the Internet is increasingly a place where bullying is not accepted, and many kids are using social networking sites and YouTube as a way to tell their stories and get support.

- Many celebrities and athletes are using their star power to stand up to bullying and encourage kids to prevent it in their communities.

- Superintendents and administrators across the country are implementing innovative district-wide social-emotional learning initiatives aiming to create comprehensive climate change.

- Teachers unions and education support professionals are taking action to make bullying prevention a priority. If your child is being bullied, an ESP could be a great ally.

# Sample Antibullying Pledges and Letters

An anti-bullying pledge is a promise not to bully others. It should include an age-appropriate set of actions each participant agrees to do and refrain from doing in an effort to prevent and intervene in suspected bullying situations. You can create your own pledge or use a copy of the pledge provided in this appendix.

You can administer antibullying pledges in the classroom, at a school-wide kick-off for an antibullying campaign, or as part of any youth organization, such as camps, houses of worship, boy or girl scouts, or athletic teams.

Signing a pledge is one way to affirm and take ownership of a set of rules and expectations. Pledges can build group cohesion and are a very useful tool in addressing behaviors or attitudes that are not in alignment with the components of the pledge. For example, if a child signs a pledge promising, "I will not bully other students," and then does so, the pledge is a frame of reference to help the student reflect on his behavior and make a correction.

# Sample Pledges

Use these antibullying pledges in your child's school or organization.

---

## Antibullying Pledge for Elementary School Children

I will not make anyone feel bad or afraid on purpose.

I will not join in with anyone who is being mean, or hurting or scaring another boy or girl.

I will tell my teacher and my parents or another adult if someone is acting like a bully to me or to anyone else.

I will do my best to be a friend to any child who is being bullied. I will be nice to them and try to help them get away from the bully and help them to be safe.

I will be kind to others who are being left out.

Signed: _____ Date:_____

---

## Antibullying Pledge for Middle School Children

I understand that **"bullying"** is when someone uses his or her power to hurt and control another person by doing or saying things on purpose that physically hurt them or make them feel bad, sad, lonely, unimportant, injured, or afraid. That includes bullying behavior that is physical, verbal, or social, and that takes place anywhere, including the Internet, social networks, or by using any electronic devices.

I promise not to bully other people. I will not try to make anyone else feel bad or afraid on purpose.

I will not try to get other kids to be mean to anybody else or to leave kids out on purpose just to be mean. I will not join in with anybody who is being mean; who is trying to embarrass, humiliate, or threaten others; or in any way is acting like a bully.

I will talk to my parents about bullying.

I understand that a **"bystander"** is a boy or girl who is neither a bully nor a target of bullying behavior. Because there are so many bystanders, they are way more powerful than any bully and can do a lot to help someone else. An **"upstander"** is a bystander who takes action against bullying.

As an upstander, I promise that if I know or think that someone is being bullied, or if I see or hear that someone might be being bullied, I will help in a way that I can feel safe.

I pledge to take **at least one** of these actions:

- I will not leave the target of bullying or aggression alone with the bully.

- I will do my best to help the person who is being bullied or excluded from the group.

- I will inform my parents, a teacher, a guidance counselor, or a school administrator if I think someone is being bullied or if I am having a problem with being bullied myself.

- I will say something to the bully to try to get him or her to stop.

- I will try to distract the bully/aggressor from what he or she is doing and help the target get away and be safe. Telling a joke or starting a conversation with the aggressive person might work.

- I will invite the target of the bully/aggressor to join me or my friends.

Signed: _____

Date: _____

## Antibullying Pledge for High Schoolers

I understand and agree that no one should be allowed to violate the rights of another individual by acts of physical, sexual, verbal, or relational aggression in any form, including through cybermedia.

I promise to respect the rights of others, whether or not we are friends. I will not join in with anyone who is attempting to violate those rights, whether it's by another student or by an adult. I will do my best to help others who are being excluded from the social group on purpose.

I pledge that I will take action, in a way that I can still feel safe, to come to the aid of someone who I believe may be in trouble or who has shared with me that they are frightened, hurt, or being victimized. I will also seek assistance from an adult if my rights are being violated.

Signed: _____

Date: _____

# Sample Letters Reporting Antibullying Incidents

If your child is being bullied at school or online by another student and has been unable to resolve it successfully, he may need additional assistance. When you contact school authorities or other authorities, it's a good idea to submit your queries in writing and provide as much relevant information as possible. This way, your concerns and the sequence of events are clearly expressed and documented. We provide two sample letters for your use.

## Sample Letter to the Principal

Your Name
Your Address
Your Phone Number

Principal's Name
Name of Your Child's School
School Address

Date

Dear Principal _____:

I am the parent of _____, who is in ___ grade.

*Paragraph One: describe the circumstances of the bullying in detail, including date, time, place, names, and witnesses.*

My child has been bullied at school, and I am requesting an investigation and a prompt response from the principal's office to ensure that the bullying will stop. The incident occurred on (date) at approximately (time) on the school bus. Shortly after the bus left the parking lot, my child was assaulted by another ___ grader named _____, who choked (your child's name) by wrapping his hands around his neck and holding him against the seat back. This incident was witnessed by several children, including _____ (grade), _____ (grade), and _____ (grade).

*Paragraph Two: if this is an ongoing situation, inform them of the steps you have already taken to bring the issue to the school's attention.*

This is not the first time this situation has happened this year. (Your child's name) has been repeatedly assaulted both on the bus and in the school building, in the presence of teachers and the bus driver (names of witnesses). Both he/she and I have reported the bullying to his teachers (names); unfortunately, they have been unable to put a stop to it.

*Paragraph Three: remind the school of its responsibility to provide a safe learning environment for your child, and request a time to meet with the principal in person to resolve the situation.*

I would like to schedule a meeting with you to discuss this matter further and agree on how best to intervene so the bullying stops. It is the school's responsibility to protect my child on its grounds and to provide an environment in which he/she can learn. As a result of the bullying (your child's name) has endured this year, he/she has missed school on account of stress-associated stomach illness and has refused to ride the bus out of fear (list consequences or effects).

Should you have any questions, please contact me at (phone number(s) and/or e-mail address).

> Sincerely,
>
> Your Name

Keep a copy of the letter for yourself. To make sure the letter is received, you can hand-deliver it to the principal or send it by certified mail, return receipt requested. It is recommended you also send a copy to your superintendent.

# Sample Department of Education/Office for Civil Rights Complaint

Your Name
Your Address
Your Phone Number

U.S. Department of Education
Office for Civil Rights
Customer Service Team
400 Maryland Ave. SW
Washington, DC 20202-1100

Date: _____

Dear Secretary of Education _____ (name current secretary),

I am writing to file a complaint with the U.S. Department of Education regarding _____ School District's failure to protect my child from bullying at _____ Elementary/Middle/High School located in (city), (state).

My child, _____, has been bullied since the _____ grade. He/she is currently in ____ grade. Within the last 180 days, he/she has been the target of the following acts of bullying and harassment on the basis of his/her _____(race, national origin, sexuality, gender, disability, religion).

Date: _____ (incident and who it was reported to)

Date: _____ (incident and who it was reported to)

Date: _____ (incident and who it was reported to)

These abuses have taken place at school/on school grounds/during school hours and have created a hostile environment at school. Although school staff has been notified of these acts of bullying and harassment, they have failed to adequately address the bullying or prevent it from recurring.

As this bullying and harassment is based upon a characteristic protected by Title IX of the Federal Civil Rights code, I am requesting that the Office for Civil Rights investigate _____ School District's failure to protect my child from bullying that it was aware of, and therein, its failure to uphold Title IX obligations.

Attached, please find records of reports/e-mails/letters and other documents supporting my attempts to involve the school in protecting my child. I would be happy to provide any further information. You can contact me at (phone) or (e-mail) or at the return address listed above.

Thank you for your time.

Sincerely,

# Resources

This appendix provides a variety of valuable resources on bullying prevention and intervention for parents, youth, and educators.

## Resources for Parents

**AbilityPath.org**
Toolkits and resources for parents of special needs youth.
www.abilitypath.org

**ACLU**
Information for LGBT youth and bias-free schools
www.aclu.org/lgbt-rights/lgbt-youth-schools

**ADL**
Resources and advocacy tools for bullying and cyberbullying
www.adl.org/education

**Autismspeaks.org**
The largest organization of it's kind; funds autism research, provides advocacy, and raises awareness about autism.
www.autismspeaks.org

***The Book of Virtues* by William J. Bennett**
A collection of stories that helps kids learn about several moral character traits such as responsibility, courage, compassion, friendship, and more. Also great for educators. (Simon & Schuster)

***The Bully Action Guide: How to Help Your Child and Get Your School to Listen*** **by Edward Dragan, EdD**
School safety expert Edward Dragan argues that parents need to be proactive in looking out for their children's social well-being at school. From his many decades as a Board of Education insider, he argues that schools are self-protective entities and reluctant to address bullying themselves. (Macmillan Publishing)

**Bully Police USA**
State-by-state bullying laws and assessments
www.bullypolice.org

**The Bully Project**
Information, resources, and toolkits for parents, kids, educators, and advocates
www.thebullyproject.com

**Centers for Disease Control and Prevention (CDC)**
Bullying information and resources
www.cdc.gov/violenceprevention/pub/measuring_bullying.html

**Cyberbullying Research Center**
Information and resources on cyberbullying
www.cyberbullying.us

**Education.com**
Great articles and tips for parents, kids, and educators
www.education.com

**The Interactive Autism Network (IAN)**
The largest online autism research effort worldwide, which brings researchers together with people affected by Autism Spectrum Disorders.
www.ianproject.org

***Miss*Representation.org**
The documentary *Miss Representation,* and *Miss*Representation.org expose and challenge media's misrepresentation of the value of girls and women and spearhead a call-to-action social initiative to inspire change and eliminate gender stereotypes. *Miss Representation* is a Jennifer Siebel Newsom and Regina Kulik Scully film.
http://missrepresentation.org

**National Center for Learning Disabilities**
Resources for parents of children who have learning disabilities
www.ncld.org

**National Crime Prevention Council**
Resources on bullying and cyberbullying
www.ncpc.org/topics/bullying

**National PTA**
Information about the Connect for Respect initiative
www.pta.org/bullying.asp

**Office for Civil Rights**
How to file a Title IX discrimination complaint
www2.ed.gov/about/offices/list/ocr/index.html

**Olweus**
Bullying resources and information, and an up-to-date state-by-state bullying law map
www.olweus.org

**PACER'S National Bullying Prevention Center**
Bullying information, resources, and toolkits
www.pacer.org/bullying/resources/

**PBS Parents**
Offers a variety of information for parents on child development, early learning, and children's television programs.
www.pbs.org/parents

**Rosalind Wiseman's Blog**
Author of *Queen Bees & Wannabes* on creating cultures of kindness
http://rosalindwiseman.com/

**StopBullying.gov**
Information and resources for parents, kids, and educators
www.stopbullying.gov

**The School for Parents**
Parent education, consultation, support, and psychotherapy services.
www.theschoolforparents.com

**StopBullying.gov**
Information and resources for parents, kids, and educators
www.stopbullying.gov

**The Total Transformation Program**
A step-by-step, comprehensive program to help parents understand,
manage, and transform difficult, defiant, aggressive, and disrespectful kids.
www.thetotaltransformation.com

**The Verbally Abusive Relationship; The Verbally Abusive Man, Can He
Change?; and Controlling People by Patricia Evans**
These books offer tips to help recognize and to respond to controlling and
verbally abusive people.
www.verbalabuse.com

## Resources for Children and Adolescents

**121 Help.Me**
A project of the North American Alliance of Child Helplines connecting
youth to immediate bullying crisis support counselors online and on the
phone.
www.121Help.Me

**Beyond Bullies**
Help and resources for teens to stand up to bullying
http://beyondbullies.org

**BullyBust**
Promoting upstanders
www.schoolclimate.org/bullybust

**Cartoon Network**
Stop Bullying/Speak Up Campaign
www.cartoonnetwork.com/promos/stopbullying/index.htm

**Cesar Millan, It Gets Better Video**
The Dog Whisperer himself has created an inspiring video (under four-
minutes, English and Spanish versions) for children and teens about his own
bullying experience as a child.
www.cesarsway.com/newsandevents/cesarsblog/Cesar-Millan-It-Gets-Better

*Don't Look at Me* **by Doris Sanford**
A book about feeling different and the importance of having a friend.
(Multnomah Press)

**DoSomething.org**
Grants for young people to take action on bullying in their schools
www.dosomething.org/whatsyourthing/Violence+And+Bullying

**Facebook Safety Center**
Information, tools, and resources for online safety and reporting Facebook
bullying
www.facebook.com/safety

**GLSEN: Gay, Lesbian & Straight Education Network**
Resources for LBGT youth and bullying
www.glsen.org

**Hey Ugly.org—Unique, Gifted, Lovable You**
Self-esteem and teen tips, newsletter, and school assembly presentations.
www.heyugly.org

**It Gets Better Project**
Inspiring videos offering hope and support to bullied youth
www.itgetsbetter.org

**MTV—A Thin Line Campaign**
A campaign educating youth about cyberbullying and digital abuse; The
MTV Digital Rights Project
www.athinline.org

*My Secret Bully* **by Trudy Ludwig**
When a child is bullied by a friend at school, but not outside of school,
she learns about relational aggression and what friendship really means
(Tricycle Press)

*One* **by Kathryn Otoshi**
A beautifully written and illustrated book for young children that speaks to
the difference just one person (or color, in the case of this story) can make
in standing up to bullies. Encourages bystanders and targets to become
assertive upstanders. Great for educators, parents, and mental health
professionals, too. (KO Kids Books)

**Seventeen: Delete Digital Drama**
*Seventeen* magazine's information and resources on cyberbullying
www.seventeen.com/entertainment/features/delete-digital-drama

**STOMP Out Bullying**
Information, celebrity PSAs, and access to help for teens
www.stompoutbullying.org

**The Trevor Project**
Crisis intervention and suicide prevention for LGBT youth
www.thetrevorproject.org

## Resources for Educators

**Allan L. Beane, PhD,** *The Bully Free Classroom: Tips and Strategies for Teachers K-8* (Free Spirit Publishing)

**The Bully Proof Classroom Graduate Course**
Professional Development for Educators
www.bullyproofclassroom.com

**Caring School Community Initiative**
Providing professional development and leadership support to create caring learning environments
www.devstu.org/caring-school-community

**CASEL (Collaborative for Academic, Social and Emotional Learning)**
Resources and Information about Social and Emotional Learning
http://casel.org

**Character Education Partnership (CEP)**
Tools for developing and assessing school culture
www.character.org/uploads/PDFs/White_Papers/
DevelopingandAssessingSchoolCulture.pdf

**Dr. Jean M. Alberti Center for the Prevention of Bullying Abuse and School Violence at the University at Buffalo**
Research and dissemination of resources on bullying
http://gse.buffalo.edu/alberticenter

*The Social Skills Picture Book* **series and other books by Dr. Jed Baker**
A clinical psychologist and the Director of the Social Skills Training
Project, Baker has written several books on supporting and enhancing
social-emotional communication skills for children and adolescents who
are on the Autism Spectrum (Future Horizons)

**Challenge Day**
Inspiring and powerful school programs to promote connection and
celebrate diversity. More than one million students have participated in the
program.
www.challengeday.org

**Educators for Social Responsibility (ESR): Professional Services**
Professional development and resources for educators
http://esrnational.org/professional-services

**Edutopia**
Grade-by-grade resources and information on innovative teaching
www.edutopia.org

**Facing History and Ourselves**
Guides for teaching tolerance and justice
www.facing.org

**John P. Halligan, Ryan's Story**
Student assembly presentations for grades 6–12; a unique perspective
from inside the family of a child who was the victim of bullying and
cyberbullying
www.ryansstory.org

**The Hamilton Fish Institute on School and Community Violence**
Resources, information, and support for creating safe schools
www.hamfish.org

**Human Rights Campaign's Welcoming Schools**
Lesson plans toward creating bully-free school climates
www.welcomingschools.org/lesson-plans

**School Climate Assessment for K–5 educators and administrators**
www.welcomingschools.org/2012/03school-climate-assessment/

**Mentors in Violence Prevention (MVP)**
Gender-based violence prevention and education training
www.jacksonkatz.com/mvp.html

**NASSP (National Association of Secondary School Principals): Bullying Prevention**
Resources for administrators, parents, and students
www.nassp.org/KnowledgeCenter/TopicsofInterest/BullyingPrevention.aspx

**National School Climate Center**

Activities for promoting upstander behavior:
www.schoolclimate.org/bullybust/educators/activities

Breaking the BullyVictimBystander Cycle Tool Kit:
www.schoolclimate.org/climate/documents/toolkit_info.pdf

Educator Bullying Prevention Guidelines:
www.schoolclimate.org/bullybust/_documents/educators/
bullyPreventionGuidelines.pdf

Measuring School Climate
www.schoolclimate.org/programs/csci.php

Partner Schools Program
www.schoolclimate.org/bullybust/educators/partner_schools

**NEA's Bully Free: It Starts with Me**
The National Education Association's bully free campaign connects educators and students to resources to prevent bullying, research-based briefs about bullying, pledges, tools, and ways to take action in various campaigns.
www.nea.org/home/NEABullyFreeSchools.html

**No Bully**
Resources and workshops for teachers and administrators
http://nobully.com/admin.htm

**Perfect Targets: Asperger Syndrome and Bullying, Practical Solutions for Surviving the Social World**
Written by Rebekha Heinrichs, this book offers practical solutions, prevention and intervention guidelines and strategies to educators to help address bullying and create a safe environment for kids with Asperger's Syndrome and High Functioning Autism, a group particularly vulnerable to bullying. Published by Autism Asperger Publishing

**Safe and Supportive Schools**
Programs, information, and support for a better school climate
http://safesupportiveschools.ed.gov

**Southern Poverty Law Center: Teaching Tolerance**
A program to foster inclusive, nurturing school climates
www.splcenter.org/what-we-do/teaching-tolerance

**StopBullying.gov**
Federal government website providing information about bullying, including policies and laws.
www.stopbullying.gov

*Sticks & Stones*
A powerful and riviting film about the dangers and devastating consequences of cyber-bullying. Has been featured on PBS, NBC, and multiple news programs.
www.chasewilson.com/sticksandstones

**University of Northern Iowa Center for Violence Prevention**
Professional development and training in bullying prevention
www.uni.edu/cvp

# Index